# THE GIFT OF A GARDEN
## or Some Flowers Remembered

BEVERLEY NICHOLS

# The Gift of a Garden

## or

## Some Flowers Remembered

*Edited by John E. Cross*

With Decorations by Rex Whistler

DODD, MEAD & COMPANY
NEW YORK

First published in the United States 1972

ISBN 0 396 06575 9
Library of Congress Catalog Card Number: 78-39240

Printed in Great Britain

# CONTENTS

# FORTY YEARS ON

*In Which the Author excuses Himself*
*For accepting an Encore*

Mr Cyril Connolly once observed that he would be happy if any of his books had a life of ten years. His modesty, though unassumed, was unnecessary. Some of Mr Connolly's books have lasted, and will last, a great deal longer.

Dipping my pen into the same modest ink-pot, I may be allowed to record that this book, or 'digest' of books, has lasted for nearly forty years. *Down the Garden Path*, the story of my first garden, was first published in 1932, and its reception was so gratifying that the youthful author immediately proceeded to write an account of the cottage which nestled—it really did 'nestle'—in the garden. This was called *A Thatched Roof*—an apposite title, for the roof in question was sorely in need of re-thatching, which is an expensive business, and the royalties from the first book enabled me to write the second in comparative comfort. Again, to the author's surprise, and a great many other people's, the public responded, and the book was a best-seller. Whereupon the author looked out of his study window, observed other peoples' thatched roofs in the distance, studied the comings and goings of their eccentric occupants, took pen to paper, and produced *A Village in a Valley* in the space of rather less than six weeks. This was published in 1934 and once again it hit the jackpot.

At my time of life, the thought of all this literary outpouring provokes a feeling of profound fatigue. How did one keep it up? It wasn't as though one were doing nothing else; one wasn't a secluded littérateur, working to a regular schedule, attended by adoring slaves. One was a hard-working reporter, a conscientious critic, a dramatist manqué and frustrated composer, and one also had a private life which was not without its complications. Most important of all, one was a gardener, and gardens, like mistresses, cannot be neglected. They demand unremitting attention, endless flattery, and a constant outflow of cash.

Maybe that was the reason, that was the impelling, inescapable motive for it all. The short foreword to *Down the Garden Path* ends with the words . . . '*A Garden is the only mistress who never fails, who never fades.*' This phrase may not deserve inclusion in an anthology of immortal prose, but it was at least sincere. The garden was my mistress, and these books were written under the spell of her enchantment. In spite of their lapses into 'whimsy', the unforgiveable sin of the modern era, they were written with dirty fingers, with mud under the nails. Next to the ink-pot there always lay a trowel. Mixed up with the manuscript there were fragments from seedsmens' catalogues, and the pages were usually tied up with tarred string, which evoked disapproving sniffs from my typist, who preferred more delicate aromas.

The value of this foreword, if it has any, must be practical rather than sentimental, though I am obviously a very sentimental gardener. I am, indeed, an anthropomorphological gardener, who really does worry about the personal feelings of the flowers, shrubs and trees which it is his privilege to tend, who even speaks to them, sometimes kindly, sometimes severely, when there is no danger of any-body overhearing. As a matter of hard, horticultural practice this is not such a bad idea, though I should have to write another book to prove it, for it would take us into the realm of E.S.P., which is outside our present province. So let us keep our feet firmly on the soil—the basis of it all, where it all begins and where, inevitably, it ends.

The interesting *practical* lesson to be gained from *Down the Garden Path* is that if I had learned even the rudiments of the gardener's art I should never have bought the place at all. The briefest inspection of the small tangled plot out-side the sitting-room, the most cursory glance at the barren fields beyond, would have informed me that here was a terrain that could only be knocked into shape by Herculean efforts. The main drawback was the soil, a heavy sullen clay, plentifully impregnated with lime. This would have been ideal for growing brussels sprouts, or admirably suited for a botanist who was spending his declining years preparing an authoritative treatise on the more virulent members of the nettle family. But for a young man of exotic tastes, dreaming of the day when he would wander through groves of eucalyptus in order to gather wreaths of the white camellias which, he fondly believed, would shortly be glistening at the end of the avenue . . . no. In a sheltered Cornish valley, during an exceptionally mild winter, it might have been possible, after the passage of forty years and the expenditure of a considerable fortune. But in the bleak, wind-swept wastes of the East Midlands . . . no.

And yet, this is precisely what I set out to do. The nurserymens' catalogues accumulated on the rickety desk of my smoke-filled study. (The logs were damp and the chimneys had not been swept for years.) Night after night I studied these alluring documents, gloating over their

highly-coloured photographs of shrubs laden with blossom, transplanting them in imagination to the fields
which shivered beyond the garden hedge. Having gloated,
dreamed, and ecstasized I would then reach for the order-
forms, take out a cheque-book, and dispatch my com-
mands to all the corners of the country, adding a postscript
to the effect that since the matter was of great urgency,
everything must be sent with the minimum of delay, and
the larger the shrubs, the better. After all, my expectancy of
life in those days was only fifty years. This was no time for
dilly-dallying.

It was all, of course, sheer madness. It was also sheer
delight, and I do not regret a moment of it. Nor, perhaps,
need the readers of these books regret it, for looking back on
these early chronicles I realize that they record, in considerable detail, a classic treatise on How Not To Do It, which
is the first step towards technical perfection in each and
every art. G. K. Chesterton once observed that if a thing is
worth doing at all, it is worth doing badly; we might go
even further, and suggest that before a thing can be done at
all, it *must* be done badly. At the keyboard, the young
composer learns more from his own mistakes than from the
most exhaustive instruction in harmony and counterpoint;
indeed, by making some of these very 'mistakes' he may
strike chords, almost by accident, that stimulate the
creative processes.

So it was, as I made my painful progress down the garden
path. And whatever else may be said about these mistakes,
nobody could deny that they were on the grandest scale,
conceived in the darkest ignorance.

For example. One of my first and most lavish orders was

for a group of mimosa trees . . . *Acacia dealbata* . . . a Latin name that I am never likely to forget. In Australia, when the hounds of spring were on winter's traces, I had wandered through the woods, watching the wind take their branches and toss them to the sky in drifts of golden spray. So, I decided, it should be in my own pleasance. Result, disaster. The trees arrived when the ground was hard with frost, they were planted bang in the middle of a field, completely exposed, improperly staked, in hastily dug holes that would have taxed the survival powers of the toughest laurel. Needless to say, they promptly died.

This sort of thing happened again and again. But though the episode of the mimosas was a particularly spectacular folly, as an effort to transplant the tropics to the Home Counties, my most costly and painful mistakes had another cause; they all stemmed from the same fatal root—my ignorance of the soil I had to work upon, its nature, its potentialities, its likes, and even more important, its dislikes. Thus, simply because I loved the glorious company of rhododendrons, I ordered them by the dozen, expecting to duplicate the vistas of scarlet and purple which glowed in the background of so many stately homes. Out they were bundled into the open fields, which were beginning to resemble an area reserved for an exercise in trench warfare. Into the hostile soil they were thrust, while I hovered round them, prodding their roots, arranging their branches, fondling their buds, imploring them, *sotto voce*, to start growing as quickly as possible, as time was so short. Whereupon they proceeded, without exception, to die. Not quickly—that would have been bad enough—but slowly, week by week, and in obvious agony. Their leaves turned yellow, their buds fell off, their branches became sere and brittle, and finally they gave up the ghost, and were carried off in a melancholy cortège to the rubbish heap.

All because nobody had told me that rhododendrons will not tolerate lime. Nobody had pointed a warning finger at those sinister little specks of white in the soil. Or if anybody had told me, I had not listened. I was a young lover with a mistress by whom he was besotted; my garden was my mistress and no word must be spoken against her. Maybe this was why my few more knowledgeable friends refrained from intervening. After all, if you have a young friend who is enamoured, you hesitate before telling him that his mistress is unfortunately riddled with lime, and that any form of dalliance with her will probably be fatal. Such strictures would be ill-received.


'How not to do it.'

A study of these juvenile excursions, I suggested, may give useful instruction to the young gardener of today, or of any age, if only to warn him of the pitfalls that he will encounter in the fairest fields. But this foreword would fail in its purpose if it were to be confined to a catalogue of 'don'ts'. What about the 'do's'? After all, one has learned something about gardening during all these years; indeed, one has learned quite a lot. And since some of the lessons I have learned are of importance, and since, perhaps, they are not always given the priority they deserve, I would like to put them on record. What does the Beverley Nichols of 1971, looking through his autobiographical telescope, say to the Beverley Nichols of 1931? How does he speak from a purely practical point of view, as an old gardener who has been through it all, to a young gardener whose back is still unbent? I would say . . .

'*Begin with the soil.*' You came from the soil, by various

devious routes, and you will certainly return to the soil, as Shakespeare, among others, has reminded us. Sometimes I am inclined to think that you *are* the soil—you and all the rest of us. I have a profound and maybe mystical belief in the relationship between a man and the soil he treads upon. In gardening terms it is a question of an 'acid' soil, an 'alkaline' soil, a 'neutral' soil, with all the variations on that theme, a clay soil, a sandy soil—even, in these days, a soil which is polluted with all the impedimenta of an industrial society, rubble, broken bottles, and old tin cans.

Whatever variations you may choose to compose upon that theme, the key word is soil. The nature of the soil should be uppermost in the thoughts of every young couple who are buying a house where they hope to create a garden, and in the thoughts of every old couple who have saved up for a country cottage where they hope to spend their last years pruning the roses. Needless to say, they will not always be able to choose their ideal terrain; if a young man is starting a business within sight of the white cliffs of Dover, he must realize his horticultural limitations, and so must his wife. Once he has realized those limitations, he can begin to make a garden. But first, if he is to be a true gardener, if his life is to be widened and enriched and en- nobled by this most rewarding of all the arts, he *must* establish his personal relationship with the soil. As I suggested before, this is to some extent a psychic question, and, as such, is seldom if ever examined in horticultural literature. But it is so vital that I will risk being a bore about it.

What sort of 'soil-person' are you? An acid person or an alkaline person or a clay person or a sandy person? These questions are not as foolish as they may sound, though it may take you many years to realize it. Coming from the general to the particular, an acid person is somebody who loves heathers and azaleas, whose heart beats more swiftly when he comes into country thick with bracken, shining with silver birches and alight with wild rhododendrons. The most 'acid person' in literature, I suspect, was Emily Brontë. On chalk she would have died, and there would have been no *Wuthering Heights*.

I repeat, these questions are not as foolish as they may sound, for until you have answered them you will never be a serious gardener; indeed, you will never even be able to read a seedsman's catalogue with proper understanding. The briefest walk through any garden-suburb is enough to prove that the vast majority of the British public have never asked themselves what sort of soil-persons they are. All the wrong shrubs planted in all the wrong places in all the wrong soil, sporting their pathetic little nurserymens' labels —labels which should be flags fluttering to a brilliant, blossoming future, but which will, alas, prove to be certificates of death. On my occasional excursions through such districts I find difficulty in refraining from pushing open the gate, ringing the bell, and telling the house-holders how mad they are being. Once I did this very thing, but the outcome was unhappy. For the lady of the house was quite evidently chalk, and the gentleman was solid clay, and between the three of us, there was little sympathy.

My next vital instruction concerns Time, on which I can certainly speak with authority, having had an all too large experience of it. This lesson can be summed up in four words. Plant for the Future. Not for any moral reasons; Posterity, as far as most of us are concerned, can look after itself, though there is small evidence that it is preparing to do so. No—planting for the future means realizing, at the age of twenty-five, that shrubs and trees have a habit of growing, sometimes quite fast. It means that the dainty little conifer you place under your study window in the year 1971 will develop, sooner than you think, into a dark, encroaching monster whom you will be obliged to destroy, unless you are prepared to live permanently by artificial light. But planting for the future means more than that—it means saving yourself a lot of money and many heartaches. Supposing a young married couple are planting a tree; in ninety-nine cases out of a hundred they make the same cardinal error as I did, in the beginning; they buy as large a tree as they can afford. Even if the tree survives, which is by no means certain, even if it is properly planted, soundly staked, and regularly watered, for at least two years it will be recovering from the shock of its uprooting, which is akin to a serious surgical operation. Whereas, if they had bought a young specimen of a quarter the height, within those same two years it might well have outstripped its unfortunate elder, at a quarter the price.

But we are getting too practical, which is as tiresome as getting too sentimental. And so, having stressed two of the most important lessons which I have learned in the past forty years, let us widen our horizons.


From time to time, as these books have come into the world, a few kindly critics—(Constance Spry and Virginia Sackville-West are the names I value most)—have suggested that in some aspects of practical gardening I may have been a 'pioneer'. This is a flattering accolade, bestowed by gardeners of such knowledge and such grace, but has it been deserved? I am hardly the one to answer that question, but perhaps it would not be too much to suggest that there are a few gardens—very beautiful gardens too—in which some of my ideas have taken root.

Consider the question of winter flowers. From the beginning, long before I planted my first shrub or sowed my first sweet pea, I had this extraordinary passion for winter flowers. Even to myself, in whose heart the passion still beats strong, it is somewhat inexplicable. If I were ever to consult a psychoanalyst my problems would not be concerned with sex, nor should I ask him to interpret my burning desire to murder my aunt. I should ask him why my blood-pressure mounts so rapidly at the sight of the first snowdrop; why a few mud-splattered winter aconites gleam more brightly for me than a whole field of buttercups, why a Christmas rose—*Helleborus niger*—is still more precious than the most pampered beauty of July. Why?

The urgency with which I asked myself these questions is conveyed in the chapter called 'Midwinter Madness', which is my favourite of the innumerable chapters I have written, in fact or in fiction. It may not be too much to claim that this chapter, and the many variations in it which I have composed over the years, has had its effect. Forty years ago very few people realized that they could have drifts of heather on Christmas Day, thicker and whiter than the snow on their roofs. They had little knowledge of the honeysuckle that could scent their drawing-rooms on New Year's Eve (*Lonicera fragrantissima*). Their lives were not brightened, in the darkest months, by the orchidaceous glitter of winter irises. Etc, etc and again etc. To suggest that I actually discovered these treasures, and their many brave companions, would be presumptuous; but my need for them, my search for them, and when I had found them, my fanatical championship of them, did get through to the gardening world. One of the most amusing letters in my files, dated September 9th, 1933, is from one of our largest bulb merchants, imploring me to stop writing about winter aconites. Since the appearance of *Down the Garden Path*, they complained, they had been sold out, and still the orders were pouring in, and I was causing them a lot of trouble. My reply, suggesting that a ten per cent commission might not perhaps be excessive, was unanswered. But the commission has been earned in other ways through many winters, in glints of gold, in gardens large and small, in the chance phrase . . . 'We first read about them in your book.'

To revert to the word 'pioneer'—we are nearing the end of the trumpet-blowing—I believe that some of these books may have helped some people to bring colour into their gardens, or rather, to think about colour in a new way. I have asked them to remember that the foliage is at least as important as the flower, and to turn away from the garish hues of the herbaceous border in order to appreciate the exquisite beauty of the greys, the greens, and most of all, the whites, for there are, of course, an infinite variety of whites. If I had my time over again I should like to create a garden in which there were no flowers at all—a garden with a tapestried background of conifers, ranging from palest grey to darkest green with solid blocks of vivid gold. (A quite practical proposition, as it happens.) At the foot of this tapestry there would be a *mélange*—a positive whirl-pool—of pearl and platinum and ivory, from the hosts of silver-leaved plants which . . . No, Nichols. Stop. You should not go on like this, at your time of life. Tapestries of conifers, whirlpools of silver . . . it is altogether too much. In the present climate of political opinion, it would probably bring you into collision with the police.

So be it. All the same, it is worth recording that this horticultural vision could be translated into growing, glorious fact by anybody who happened to be a millionaire, with a conviction that he is immortal, firmly established on an acid soil, and resolutely determined to bring heaven down to earth. Which, in my dreams, is what I have always been.

Literary footnote, in case these books last for yet another forty years.

The village of 'Allways', where these chronicles are set, is in fact the village of Glatton, in Huntingdonshire. It lies about a mile off the old Great North Road, three miles to the south of Stilton. (Which has nothing to do with the cheese.) The cottage stands alone at the entrance to the village, in the shadow of a cluster of giant elms, as it has stood since the days of the Tudors.

As for the characters who flit through the pages, although some readers have been kind enough to respond to them as though they were drawn from life, they are part fact and part fiction, which is about as much as one can say of any author's characters. 'Miss Hazlitt' was a portrait of my old governess, and though I contrived some of her adventures, I did not contrive either her nature or her spirit, for she was nearer to sanctity than anybody I have yet met in this world. 'The Professor' was based on an eccentric genius called Professor A. M. Low, who was much in the public eye before the war. 'Undine' was a *mélange* of a great many tiresome poseuses who had come my way. She is still to be frequently encountered, *mutatis mutandis*, in modern society.

'Mrs Wrench', my formidable housekeeper, was very real indeed, and—I would like to think—still is, though my efforts to contact her have been fruitless. The same goes for all the others, with, oddly enough, the single exception of the lady to whom I gave the name of 'Mrs M.' There never was a Mrs M., and the reason I call this 'odd' is because, of all the people in the books who have established themselves in the readers' imaginations, Mrs M. seems to have aroused the most lively curiosity. Even to this day I get letters about her. Was she really as infuriating as all that? Was she so pleased with herself, so ineffably superior? And—this is the most frequent question of all—why had she never sued me for libel? These letters are difficult to answer, because some/times I have an uneasy suspicion that the reason Mrs M. stands out so clearly is because she may be a projection of one of the less pleasing sides of my own personality, which it would be wiser to forget.

And what about the cottage today—and the garden and the wood? Here I must draw a veil, swiftly and finally. Only once did I return to the scene of this young love affair, and that was enough, more than enough. Long before I arrived I began to realize that Time had marched on, with a very cruel tread. The little villages where I had been wont to pause for a glass of beer had vanished, to be re/placed by gaunt sattelite towns of stucco and concrete; instead of driving through narrow rose/wreathed lanes, one sped over arterial thoroughfares designed to conduct the traveller, with the utmost dispatch, to hell. And when, at last, I turned into the little by/way that had been the prelude to so much enchantment, I saw, in the distance, a sinister army of pylons, coming closer and closer.

The cottage was still there—yes. Through a gap in the hedge I could detect the ghost of a garden, and the rough

outline of a strange, neglected forest that had once been my
wood. But the glory had departed, the magic had flown
over the hills and far away, and even as I stood there, the
pylons seemed to be moving closer. Within three minutes,
I was gone.

One should never go back.

The foreword to *A Thatched Roof* begins with an imaginary dialogue between a traveller who returns to a garden he
had loved and finds a sundial waiting there—a broken
monument of stone which had once recorded his hours of
greatest happiness. He pauses, and the sundial speaks.
What it says—or rather, what I made it say—is so un-
cannily prescient that perhaps it is worth recording, if only
as an example of one of those curious psychic moments in
which a man's future sometimes intrudes upon his present
and his past.

This is what I made the sundial say.

'You were happy in this garden once, and you are
therefore a fool to return to it. All the men who come
to ask me the time are fools . . . because they are all
looking for something they left behind, and they can
never find it. Why—there was a man and a girl only
yesterday. They had been in this garden before—a
year ago. They had sat under that big yew tree, over
there, and her face was as white as the moon, with
love, as he kissed it. A year ago! They could tell the
time by me then, because the moon was so very bright.
It turned my dial to silver and my hour to gold . . .
a very tiny hour it was, before they went. But yesterday
there was no moon—only a cold wind, which bore
the sound of their angry voices to me. They did not
come to ask the time, because they stayed only a little

while, as they could not find the happiness which they had left behind. It is a pity, because they might have struck a match and read the motto which is engraved on me . . . can you read it yourself?

> Time as he passes us has a dove's wing,
> Unsoiled and swift and of a silken sound.

'You have read it? You understand? Well, you would be surprised at the number of men who don't. They all try to call the dove back. They call and call, but nearly always the skies remain blank and empty, and the men go away with heavy hearts. It is best that they should go away, for sometimes the dove comes back. It flies haltingly . . . it is tired and wounded . . . and it falls at their feet with crippled wings. That is what happens when men try to recapture some happiness which they have known . . .'

The light fails . . . 'Without the shadow, Nothing.' And the voice of the sundial fades into a whisper. But I have learnt its lesson.

These words, remember, were written nearly forty years ago, when my world was young, and when the garden path stretched to an infinite, glimmering horizon of delight. What made me write them? Who guided the pen? I wouldn't know. All I know is that they expressed a moment of ecstasy and of truth.

With the exception of the last line. I have *not* 'learned the lesson', and I never shall, as long as I can get down on my knees, and take comfort from the soil, and receive its blessing. 'A garden is the only mistress who never fails, who never fades.' Not immortal prose, as I said before. But as near to truth as we are likely to get, in these uncertain times.

## Chapter 1

## THE GARDEN GATE

I bought my cottage by sending a wireless to Timbuctoo
from the *Mauretania*, at midnight, with a fierce storm lashing
the decks.

It sounds rather vulgar, but it is true. The cottage used
to belong to a charming American, whom I knew very
slightly. I read of his death in a paper which I picked up in
the stuffy, pitching library of the aforesaid vessel. It told me
that Mr So-and-So had died, and that he had left all his
property to his sister . . . who was one of my best friends.

The liner dipped and tossed. I studied the paper. I saw
that Wall Street, the night before, had been giving one of its
celebrated impersonations of the fall of Jericho. People had
been leaping from the tops of skyscrapers with monotonous
regularity. Nothing seemed stable in this world. And then,
looking again at the little obituary notice of this man whom
I had scarcely known, I remembered that among his pos-
sessions had been an exquisite thatched cottage, where I
had once spent a week-end. The garden had been a blaze
of roses, and there was a row of Madonna lilies on either
side of the porch. The scent of those lilies assailed me. I
reached for a piece of paper, scribbled the name of the
American's sister and the word Timbuctoo, whither she
had ventured on a wild excursion. I rang the bell and wrote
an offer. As the page boy took my cablegram I scratched
two hundred pounds from the sum I had proposed. He had

hardly left the lounge before I tried to call him back, for I regretted the whole idea. But he was gone, and the night was very stormy indeed, and the decks were dark and slippery. Before I could reach the wireless operator's head-quarters, the message was sent.

Thank God for that storm at sea. My offer was accepted. Within a week I was driving through the quiet lanes to-wards my inheritance.

§ 2

I usually skip topographical details in novels. The more elaborate the description of the locality, the more confused does my mental impression become. You know the sort of thing:

'*Jill stood looking out of the door of her cottage. To the North rose the vast peak of Snowdon. To the South swept the valley, dotted with fir trees. Beyond the main ridge of mountains a pleasant wooded country extended itself, but the nearer slopes were scarred and desolate. Miles below a thin ribbon of river wound towards the sea, which shone, like a distant shield, beyond the, etc etc.*'

By the time I have read a little of this sort of thing I feel dizzy. Is Snowdon in front or behind? Are the woods to the right or to the left? The mind makes frenzied efforts to carry it all, without success. It would be very much better if the novelist said '*Jill stood on the top of a hill, and looked down into the valley below.*' And left it at that.

But in a book of this class you really must get topo-graphical details in your head. You will be walking through my garden from the first pale mists of spring to the urgent, stormy nights of November. You will be shading your eyes from the sun under arches that reel with the intoxicating scent of syringa, and hurrying through the little french

SPRING

windows to escape the menace of the blue-black clouds of April. It is vital, therefore, that you know where you are going, or you will trip up. You will forget the step that comes before the lupin bed, and crack your head on the branch of the damson tree.

Therefore, soon we will draw a plan. But, first of all, we must take a wider view.

If you look at the map you will find, somewhere in the east of England, a county called Huntingdonshire. There is no smaller county in the land, except Rutlandshire, which is really so small that it is no longer funny. There is no county more essentially English than Huntingdonshire. If you go into its sleepy little capital and drink a bitter at one of the little inns, you will find farmers who speak with a dialect which would have sounded familiar to Pepys, who had a cottage in the neighbourhood. The poor devils are mostly bankrupt now. They stand at the doors of their inns, looking out with puzzled eyes at the great charabancs that sweep by from Newcastle . . . down the same Great North Road which once echoed to the hoofs of Dick Turpin's horse, on clear frosty nights.

The village in which my cottage is situated is called . . . well, Allways is as good a name as any other. It is not unlike its real name. And it is not inappropriate . . . All Ways. For, though it lies a mile from the Great North Road, there is a tangle of white, winding country roads that meet and lace and part again, at its village green, running from haven to haven, over hills and valleys that seem to have been forsaken by the rest of the world.

On the wall over one of the staircases (I have three staircases, and no man can decide which is the smallest) there is a map, dated A.D. 1576. It is a very beautiful map. Two cherubs, in the last stages of elephantiasis, spread gilt and bloated limbs over its pale parchment. A crown, a turtle, a stork, a dragon, a bunch of pears, and many exquisite scrolls and devices, touched with blue and scarlet, are scattered over the widely painted acres. In the right-hand bottom corner there is a lion, rampant—oh, most exceedingly rampant, with a scroll that comes from his mouth, on which are written the words Pestis Patria Pigricies. If you have the faintest idea what that means, you are to be congratulated. There is a sound of the plague about it, and, for all I know, the sound may have an echo of sense, for the land round the cottage is low lying, and the fields, in November, are the scene of many strange sarabands, as the mists drift over the willows, pause, curve, drift nearer. . . . But I would not have it changed.

Often, as I have carried my lonely candle to bed, I have paused and studied this enchanting document. The candle-light gleams and flickers on the dragon and the tortoise and the stork; many pale points of gilt glitter through the glass —as perhaps they glittered, three hundred and fifty years ago, for other natives of this dear stretch of earth. I explore, in a fine sweep, the flat lands from Cambridge to Stamford— which in those days was spelt with an N, and I see the grey marshes which have long been filled in . . . the faded, formal bunches of trees which have long been cut down. . . . I see the proud flourishes over Huntingdon, whose head, then, was so highly lifted. And finally, with a catch of the breath, I put the candle closer, and read, with a quite unjustified sense of proprietorship . . . the word All-ways. There is a little green mill sign above it, and a cross for a church. There is also a tiny speck which I try to persuade myself is my cottage. But it is to be feared that it is only the mark of a very old-fashioned beetle.

We are hurrying towards the garden gate, and in a

moment we shall be able to lift the latch. But there is one final introduction to be made, to the cottage itself.

It stands on the road . . . a very quiet road. It is thatched with reed, and heavily timbered, with beams that have been twisted, by Time, into lovely shapes. It is really three cottages knocked into one, which explains the phenomenon of the three staircases. There is a little patch of grass outside which is filled to the brim with crocuses, white and yellow for spring, and mauve for autumn. People say that the sight of the crocuses, blazing away in March and September, is one of the prettiest things a man could see. They are right.

My cottage is much bigger than you would think, from the outside. This is as it should be. For you alight at the tiny front door and look up at this charming old box of a place, and then, on entering, you find an unsuspected wing, hidden from the road by a thick bank of may and lilac, and when you get into this wing you step out into a secret garden, and behind the secret garden. . . . But here we are, with the latch not only lifted, but the garden gate swing- ing wide, and the whole thread of the narrative lost. I must get back quickly, to the beginning, to that evening in early April when I jostled along the country road in the village Ford, prepared for Paradise.

*Chapter 2*

## SALVAGE

A narrow lane, that twists and turns, directs you from the Great North Road to the village of Allways. It is seldom that one meets any traffic on it. A startled child, pressing back into the hedge with exaggerated caution as you pass by, a woman on a bicycle, with a floppy, old-fashioned hat and a curved back . . . an occasional farm cart, which can only be passed with great ingenuity and many amiable sallies. For the rest, the only other occupants of the road are the rabbits, which are legion. In the spring there are many young ones, so pathetically innocent and silly that sometimes it is necessary to stop the car, dismount, and speak quite rudely to them before they are so obliging as to run away. At night their eyes glow with phosphorescent fire, and sometimes they are hypnotized by the lights of the car, so that one must pull up and turn out the lights in order that they may recover their self-possession. Very pleasant are those little halts, in the dark, with the wind playing in the high trees above, and the rain dripping monotonously on the windscreen.

There were rabbits in plenty on the day that the car rattled down the lanes towards my inheritance, but I was too excited to be overanxious about their welfare. Though I had only spent a single week-end in this place that was now my own, I remembered the countryside as clearly as if I had lived in it for many seasons. The flat, quiet fields with

28

their ancient willows that would so soon be feathered with green . . . the wide, meandering stream by the side of the road . . . the coppice of beech and chestnut with catkins swinging in the breeze.

And now, the familiar bend in the road, the glimpse of a thatched roof, the sudden view of the white walls sturdily timbered. And it was mine!

I jumped out of the Ford. The car turned, shunted, and drove away. For a minute I stayed there in the road, staring at this beloved thing. It was difficult to realize that it was mine, from the top brick on the chimney to the grass at the foot of the walls. No . . . right down to the centre of the earth and up to the heavens above, it was mine. But one cannot grasp these things as quickly as all that.

§ 2

I stepped through the window. Stopped dead. Blinked and looked again . . . and the spirit seemed to die within me.

It was a scene of utter desolation. True, it was a cold evening in late March, and the shadows were falling. No garden can be expected to look its best in such circumstances. But this garden did not look like a garden at all. There was not even a sense of order about it. All design was lacking. Even in the grimmest winter days a garden can give an appearance of discipline, and a certain amount of life and colour, no matter how wild the winds or dark the skies. But this garden was like a rubbish heap.

In my mind's eye there had glowed a brilliant bouquet of flowers. I cherished the memory of beds that had glowed like the drunken canvas of an impressionist painter. I recalled arches weighed down with their weight of burning blossom. Through my mind there still drifted the languid essences of July, a summer halo encircled me and . . .

And now? Nothing. Earth. Sodden grass. Rank bushes. A wind that cut one to the marrow. I shivered.

Then I pulled myself together. It was unreasonable, I told myself, to be shocked by this prospect. One could not expect summer glory in the middle of winter.

But this mood did not last for long. For it was *not* the middle of winter. It was the beginning of spring. One knew enough poetical tags to be aware that daffodils took the winds of March, that snowdrops had been nicknamed the 'fair maids of February', that more than one poet had chronicled the advent of the primrose. But here was no daffodil, no snowdrop, no primrose.

I pulled the collar of my coat up and strode into the garden. As I walked round I saw, everywhere, the evidence of appalling neglect. Ignorant as I was of all the technicalities, I knew, at least, that good gardeners did not leave the old shoots of pruned roses lying on the ground. I knew that good gardeners did not allow hedges to grow apace, nor let ivy trail up the stems of young trees, nor permit the paths and borders to be swallowed up by ugly weeds. Why— there were even old newspapers lying sodden in the orchard!


§ 3


And now the work of salvage began. There were tools to be ordered, a wheelbarrow to be bought, beds to be filled with roses, hedges to be clipped, bushes to be uprooted. The greenhouse had to be patched up, the toolshed needed a new roof. We had to decide on a place for a

rubbish heap, to fix the limits of the kitchen garden. We
had to rush about with quantities of manure, pushing it
into the ground with a feeling of supreme benefaction.
We had to get weed killer (the non-poisonous sort), and
sprinkle it on the overgrown paths. We had to leap with
heavy hatred upon ants' nests and squash the brutes, which
were overrunning the whole garden. We had to burn and
destroy and ravage before we could really create. And the
extraordinary thing about it was that gradually my impatient desire for immediate results, which is the besetting
sin of all beginners, died down. I began to take a joy in the
work for its own sake.

Until you actually *own* a garden, you cannot know this
joy. You may say, 'Oh, yes, I love a garden.' But what do
you really mean by that? You mean that you like to wander
through rows of hollyhocks, swathed in tulle (you, not the
hollyhocks), and that you like to drink lemonade under a
tree with a nice young man who will shortly pick you a
large bunch of roses. You hope he will take the thorns off,
and that there will not be any earwigs in them, because if
you found an earwig on the rug in the car you would die
with horror. (So should I.)

You like walking out on to a terrace and looking up at a
wall that is covered with the pale, tipsy plumes of wisteria
. . . to walk under arches of orange blossom, thinking the
prettiest thoughts. You might even stoop down to pick a
bunch of pansies, if they match your frock. You like these
things, yes.

But you do not like grovelling on the earth in search of a
peculiarly nauseating slug that has been eating those pansies.
You do not like putting a trowel under the slug, hoping
that it will not suddenly burst or produce fearful slime, and
tipping the slug with gratified horror into a basket. You do

not like bending down for hours to pull up hateful little weeds that break off above the root . . . not groundsel, because groundsel is a lovely weed to pull up, but small docks and wretched things like that. You do not like these things, for one reason and only one reason because you do not *own* the garden.

All gardeners will know what I mean. Ownership makes all the difference in the world. I suppose it is like the difference between one's own baby and somebody else's. If it is your own baby you probably quite enjoy wiping its nose. If it is somebody else's you would have to use a long pole with a handkerchief on the end.

That was why I loved all this early work, because the garden was the first thing I had ever really owned. It took ages to realize it . . . to this day the realization is not complete. I would stand before a hedge with a pair of shears in my hand, saying, 'I can clip this hedge exactly as I please. I can make it round or square or like a castle. If I choose, I can clip it away altogether, and nobody can arrest me.'

To dig one's own spade into one's own earth; Has life anything better to offer than this?

§ 4

Topography in a garden book corresponds to genealogy in a novel. The best genealogist in fiction was Anthony Trollope. He had a gift of making his readers take a deep breath, swallow, and then glue themselves to his early pages until they knew everybody's aunts, uncles, and cousins much better than they knew their own.

Would that I had this gift in such a book as I am

writing! For I want you so much to know the way the paths run, to be aware that you must bend your head under this bough to avoid the sparkling raindrops, and step high, on a dark evening, as you enter the little box garden, so that you may not trip up. I fear that the gift is not mine, so that in a moment we shall have to show you a plan of it all . . . and I think that a plan is as tiresome as a family tree. Yet, it is necessary. How, otherwise, can we Make the Tour?

Let me explain. Whenever I arrive in my garden, I Make the Tour. Is this a personal idiosyncrasy, or do all good gardeners do it? It would be interesting to know. By Making the Tour, I mean only that I step from the front window, turn to the right, and make an infinitely detailed examination of every foot of ground, every shrub and tree, walking always over an appointed course.

There are certain very definite rules to be observed when you are Making the Tour. The chief rule is that you must never take anything out of its order. You may be longing to see if a crocus has come out in the orchard, but it is strictly forbidden to look before you have inspected all the various beds, bushes, and trees that lead up to the orchard.

You must not look at the bed ahead before you have finished with the bed immediately in front of you. You may see, out of the corner of your eye, a gleam of strange and unsuspected scarlet in the next bed but one, but you must steel yourself against rushing to this exciting blaze, and you must stare with cool eyes at the earth in front, which is apparently blank, until you have made certain that it is not hiding anything. Otherwise, you will find that you rush wildly round the garden, discover one or two sensational events, and then decide that nothing else has happened. Which means that you miss all the thrill of tiny shoots, the first lifting of the lids of the wallflowers, the first precious gold of the witch-hazel, the early spear of the snowdrop. Which recalls one of the loveliest conceits in English poetry, Coventry Patmore's line about the snowdrop:

*And hails far summer with a lifted spear!*

It would require at least sixteen thick volumes bound in half calf, with bevelled edges, to contain a full account of a typical tour round any garden. There is so much history in every foot of soil. So one can only hurry through it very briefly, to get the main outlines, and then draw a plan.

You step through some french windows into a small square garden, bordered with hedges of clipped black-thorn. Through the arch at the end is another garden, con-sisting of two big herbaceous borders and a little circular lawn beyond. This gives straight on to some quiet fields, dotted with elms and oaks.

To the right, through another arch, is an orchard, across which I have cut a path edged with deep herbaceous borders. Beyond the orchard there is a coppice of poplars and sweetbriar which hides the kitchen garden.

That is really all, except that there is a little Secret Garden on the other side of the house. It is only the size of a large room, and it is cut up into six box-edged beds filled with roses, and one large flower border, against a white wooden wall.

All of which leaves you, no doubt, in the same state of confusion as you were before. However, it had to be done. And at least, after this excursion, we shall have some justification for christening the various portions of the garden.

First comes the Front Garden. This is a very obvious title. In fact, its obviousness is its only claim to respect. It sounds prim and solid, like the front parlour. Which is what I try to make it. I like the flowers in it to be very well behaved, very formal, like glistening china ornaments on the mantelpiece of a house-proud woman.

The part beyond the Front Garden, through the afore- said arch, we will call Antinous' Garden. For I forgot to mention that there stands, in the centre of the little circular lawn, a statue of Antinous. I don't like garden ornaments, as a rule, especially in a humble garden like mine. I have a horror of those leaden cupids who illustrate, so gruesomely, the ultimate horrors of Bright's disease in many suburban pleasaunces. I cannot bear those grim terracotta pelicans that peer sharply from thickets of bamboos in the grounds of tasteless Midland persons. I am depressed unutterably by those horrible little German mannikins which some people scatter over their properties—grouping them, oh! so archly —popping out of the rhododendrons, or lifting their horrid heads from a lavender thicket.

My Antinous, I feel, is of a different class. He is very beautiful, in himself. He once stood in the garden of an old house in Bedford Square. He was covered with grime, and his limbs seemed stained eternally. I saw him first after lunch on a grey day of February. After shameless hinting and ogling I persuaded my host that he was unhappy in London; that it was no rain that trickled from his pale eyes, but tears; that his feet were weary for the green grass. My host agreed. He really could do nothing else. It was ordained.

Antinous arrived in a crate and was set in the centre of the little lawn. And gradually the sweet country rain washed his limbs, and the wind played about him. From his tired, worn fingers the grime departed, and his perfect, lyrical shoulders began to glisten in the sunlight. Now he shines and sparkles. He is spotless. To see him when the snow is on the ground, when the snowdrops are pushing humbly at his feet, when the winter sky is silver, white, and blue . . . ah; that is to see Man as a flower, yes, as a strange white flower.

There remains only the Orchard and the Secret Garden, which need no christening.

Here, therefore, we can draw the plan.

## § 5

At this point the book begins. And it begins with mushrooms.

It is the very last thing that it should begin with, but we cannot help that. For I could not really tackle the flower garden till April, and then it was too late to do much more than get the soil in order, tidy the hedges, and discourage the more loathsome weeds. All these things took time. For the summer display I had to content myself with seedling stocks and antirrhinums, bought in boxes and pushed straight into the ground. (A degrading practice, this.) The first real experiment was with mushrooms, and, like all first experiments in gardening, it was a mistake.

One day I was walking in my large field looking for things. I was not looking for any particular thing—just things in the grass to pick or eat or play with. Then, over the fence, in a field that was not mine, I saw a mushroom. And I remembered glorious mushroom mornings in my boyhood, mornings when the long fingers of the sunlight were stretched flat on the fields. One had picked mushrooms then and had eaten them for breakfast. Why not again?

Why not indeed? I had a field, and I could do what I

liked with it. Bears could be kept in it. Holes could be dug in it. It could be covered with sand, while one pretended to be at the seaside. I did not want to do any of these things. I wanted to grow mushrooms. I went indoors and looked them up in the Encyclopaedia.

The Encyclopaedia said '*see* Agaricus'. I saw Agaricus, and was rather pained by the squalid atmosphere in which mushrooms appeared to flourish. There were all sorts of references to fresh horse droppings, stained straw, and decayed top⁄spit loam. Moreover, when one came to the mushrooms themselves, there was no reference to seeds or cuttings, but only to 'spawn'.

Spawn? Spawn sounded very obscene. If one started throwing spawn about, anything might happen. Perhaps the Encyclopaedia was wrong. I turned to Sutton's catalogue. Here again was the hated word, and underneath it a picture of a mushroom bed so prolific that it looked like a crowd scene in one of Rex Ingram's mammoth pictures. There was also a pretty little illustration of Amateur's Mushroom spawn, in which the mushrooms looked a little smaller, modester, and generally less aggressive. So I ordered a lot of Amateur's spawn. I also ordered a cartload of manure, and quantities of nitrate of soda and sulphate of ammonia (those were recommended as tonics).

The Encyclopaedia said you had to plant them—or rather 'it'—in the middle of June. I did the planting on June 15th, all over the field. It was a stormy day, and the wind was in the north—if that interests anybody.

On June 16th I made a thorough examination of the places where we had planted 'it'. Nothing had happened. Feeling slightly hysterical at the delay, like an anxious father, I sped into Peterborough and bought a lot of little flags at Woolworth's. I chose flags of all the nations and

tore back home again. There was still no sign of any mushroom. With a heavy heart I made the tour of the field,
sticking in the flags. The vicar asked me, that evening, if I
was going to have a fête. I gave him a mirthless smile, and
said, 'I hope so.'

That was on June 16th. By August 16th all the flags
had blown down, or had been eaten by rabbits, or stolen by
the village boys. But not a mushroom had appeared. The
field of my neighbour, who had done nothing to deserve it,
was white with mushrooms. They sprang up overnight and
stared at me with mocking faces.

I tried to console myself with the thought that they might
be only toadstools, but even this illusion was taken from me,
for my housekeeper began to pick them and give them to
me for breakfast. They were disgustingly good.

Then, one day, an astonishing thing happened. I was
walking through the kitchen garden when I saw a white
spot on the vegetable marrow bed. It was a mushroom!
Closer inspection revealed that it was surrounded by
literally hundreds of mushrooms. I rushed to the house and
breathlessly spread the news. S.—my gardener—came, with
maddening slowness and deliberation, to the scene of
action. 'Oh, yes,' he said. 'When you were putting 'em in
the field, I just crumbled up a brick of spawn and shoved
it in here for luck.'

'You did *what*?'

He repeated the information. I could not disguise my
fury. Here he was, talking about 'just crumbling up' one
brick and 'shoving' it in. Whereas I had not 'just crumbled
up' my spawn: with infinite reverence I had divided the
particles, not of one brick, but of hundreds. Encyclopaedia
in hand, I had covered myself with manure and rushed
about with cans of water. I had sprinkled powerful tonics

on my spawn, breathed prayers over it, and decorated it with flags. And not one mushroom had appeared.

The crowning insult came a week later. I had just arrived, and had shunted my car into the makeshift garage, which had a brick floor that is usually covered with oil and petrol. As I stepped out of the car I saw a large white patch in the corner. With a glazed eye, I approached it. Mushrooms! Half a dozen . . . of superb size and quality, pushing up through the bricks, the oil, and the dust.

S. arrived to take my bag. Speechless, I pointed with a trembling finger to the corner. He scratched his head. 'That's where I put the bag the spawn came in,' he said. 'Rummy things, mushrooms. You can't keep 'em down.'

Personally, I now prefer prawns.


§ 6


The mushrooms were only one example of a great many early blunders. You see, I was still under the spell of seed catalogues. I would gaze with rapturous eyes at the photographs of some duke's garden in the South, over which generations of slaves had toiled, into whose rich soil coffers of gold had been spilt, and I would imagine that the same purple miracles, the same riotous abundance, could be achieved in my own few yards of newly conquered clay.

I wanted my garden to bloom like the gardens of the Arabian Nights. When my father, who comes from a long line of gentlemen farmers, adjusted his eyeglass, glared at the kitchen garden, told me that the soil would need to be turned in the autumn so that the frost could get into it, and that after the frost had got in, we could plant cabbages, I said that I did not want cabbages. I wanted gourds.

THE GIFT OF A GARDEN

'Gourds?' he said. 'What the devil for?'

'I want gourds,' I repeated. 'I can't tell you why I want gourds, because you are my father and you would not understand. But I want them, and it is my garden.'

I also wanted sweet corn. I also wanted *Couve Tronchuda*, principally because of its name. It sounded like a peculiar edition of Dolores del Rio. But principally I wanted gourds.

The gourds had large seeds like dry beans, and I planted them in all sorts of unexpected places, with the idea that they would pop out from the darkness, like faces. I hoped that people would be terrified of them, so I decided to scratch eyes and mouths on them when they came up. But they never came up. Only one appeared, looking like a rather rude fungus, and it was promptly eaten by a slug. However, the *Couve Tronchuda* flourished, and I wish that it had not, because it not only sounded like a Spanish dancer but tasted like one—very sweet and stringy. The sweet corn also did remarkably well, but one gets very messy eating it, and it is really much nicer in tins.

It was not till I experimented with seeds plucked straight from a growing plant that I had my first success . . . the first thrill of *creation* . . . the first taste of blood. This, surely, must be akin to the pride of paternity; indeed, many soured bachelors would wager that it must be almost as wonderful to see the first tiny crinkled leaves of one's first plant as to see the tiny crinkled face of one's first child.

In both cases, it is to be supposed, the predominant emotion is incredulity. 'Was *I* really responsible for this?' asks the young father, as he holds the child in his arms. . . . Sometimes he is not entirely convinced that the answer is in the affirmative.

40

§ 7

My first experiment was with a lupin which flowered unexpectedly in the garden three months after my arrival.
When the flowers were over, the pods split open, revealing
seeds, and in a mad moment I decided to plant seeds. 'This
is crazy,' I said to myself as I tipped out the small black
pellets. 'Quite mad. Do you seriously think they will come
up, for you? Do you honestly imagine that this creative
miracle is actually going to occur?'

I really did ask these questions, simply because seeds
that had failed to receive the baptism of a penny or sixpenny packet seemed, somehow, not quite authentic. Of
course, the conscious mind proclaimed that all seeds had to
come, originally, from flowers, and that therefore these hot,
ripe lupin seeds, plucked straight from a healthy plant, had
as much chance of success as any that could be bought at a
shop, even at Woolworth's. But the subconscious mind
demanded the packet. It wanted to see the beautiful blurred
picture on the cover. It wanted to read that they formed
'gigantic spikes of dazzling blue flowers', and other fearful
lies like that.

The conscious mind won. I said to myself, 'You are
being idiotic. This stalk, in front of you, was once a lupin.
The horrid things sticking out all over it are, without
question, pods. Inside the pods are small black pellets
which are not beads or eggs or sweets, but seeds. The
obvious course is to go back to nature, seize some seeds,
and put them in the softest, sweetest, most luxurious earth
you can find. It would not be surprising if quantities of
large aspidistras instantly appeared, put out their tongues,
and made fearful smells. On the other hand, it would not be
surprising if the seeds actually came up as lupins.'

The seeds did come up, as lupins, and it *was* extremely surprising. The surprise lingers to this day. I have just been for a walk in the garden—it is late June—and the seeds that I sowed some time ago are now grown to a whole border of plants, trembling into flower. The subconscious mind still cannot believe it. I suppose that it is experiencing the wonder and humiliation of all men who have assisted, in their meagre way, in creating something.

That is why I dragged in the subject of paternity. If it is possible to gain this exultation, this true and lasting delight from the seed of a cold blue flower, what might not be the frenzy were one to sow one's own seed, to have a son? Ah—but it isn't as simple as that! Sons are not as easy to grow as lupins. Apart from the fact that they frequently turn out to be daughters, you cannot count on their being true to type. The seed of a blue lupin will usually produce a blue lupin. But the seed of a blue-eyed man may produce a brown-eyed bore, especially if his wife has a taste for gigolos.

Well, you have read so far, and you are probably saying to yourself that this is all a vague muddle, with far too much irrelevant personal detail, and far too little about the garden itself. 'We can learn nothing from this,' you will say.

Please do not throw down the book just yet. For after a very few more pages you *will* learn something. I promise you that. If not, you can go and ask the bookseller for your money back.

*Chapter 3*

## MIDWINTER MADNESS

We are now in the depths of winter . . . my first winter at the cottage . . . and the first winter when I went mad.

The average gardener, in the cold dark days of December and January, sits by his fire, turning over the pages of seed catalogues, wondering what he shall sow for the spring. If he goes out in his garden at all, it is only for the sake of exercise. He puts on a coat, stamps up and down the frozen paths, hardly deigns to glance at the black, empty beds, turns in again. Perhaps, before returning to his fireside, he may go and look into a dark cupboard to see if the hyacinths, in fibre, are beginning to sprout. But that represents the sum total of his activity.

I wrote, above, that on this first winter I went mad. For I suddenly said to myself, '*I will have flowers in my garden in winter.*' And by flowers I meant real flowers, not merely a few sprays of frozen periwinkle and an occasional blackened Christmas rose. Everybody to whom I spoke said that this desire was insane, and I suppose 'everybody' ought to have been right. Yet everybody was wrong. For my dream has come true.

Now, one more moment of selfrevelation, and we can really begin. I *must* explain my love of winter flowers, in order that the charge of insanity may be refuted.

And yet it is so strong and so persistent—this love—that I sometimes call a halt and ask myself if it may not be, at

43

least, a little morbid. For there are curious visions that come to me, on blazing summer days, when the garden is packed with blossom like a basket. In an instant I seem to see the garden bare . . . the crimsons and the purples are wiped out, the sky is drained of its blue, and the trees stand stark and melancholy against a sky that is the colour of ashes. It is then that I see, in some distant corner, the faint, sad glimmer of the winter jasmine—like a match that flickers in the dark—and at my feet a pale and lonely Christmas rose. And I kneel down quickly, as though I would shelter this brave flower from the keen wind . . . only to realize, with a start, that I am kneeling in the sunshine, that there is no flower there, only a few green leaves and overhead, the burning sun.

I wonder why. And yet, perhaps I know. For this passion for winter flowers has its roots deep, deep within me. I have a horror of endings, of farewells, of every sort of death. The inevitable curve of nature, which rises so gallantly and falls so ignominiously, is to me a loathsome shape. I want the curve to rise perpetually. I want the rocket, which is life, to soar to measureless heights. I shudder at its fall, and gain no consolation that, in falling, it breaks into trembling stars of acid green and liquid gold. I can hear only the thump of the stick in some sordid back yard. The silly thump of a silly stick. The end of life. What does it matter that a moment ago the tent of night was spangled with green and gold? It is gone, now. The colour is but gas, a feeble poison, dissipated. Only the stick remains.

I believe that my love for winter flowers has its secret in this neurosis . . . if one may dignify the condition by such a word. I want my garden to *go on*. I cannot bear to think of it as a place that may be tenanted only in the easy months. I will not have it draped with nature's dust sheets.

That is why I waged this battle for winter flowers. Make no mistake about it. It *is* a battle. There is the clash of drama about it. People think that the gardener is a placid man, who chews a perpetual cud—a man whose mind moves slowly, like an expanding leaf, whose spirit is as calm as the earth's breath, whose eyes are as bright as the morning dew. Such ideas are very wide of the mark. A gardener—if he is like many gardeners I know—is a wild and highly strung creature, whose mind trembles like the aspen and is warped by sudden frosts and scarred by strange winds. His spirit is as tenuous as the mists that hang, like ghosts, about the winter orchards, and in his eyes one can see the shadows of clouds on bleak and distant hills.

§ 2

As soon as I had decided that I was going to specialize in winter flowers, I began to study the catalogues. Very crudely, at first. I used to turn to the lists of chrysanthemums and choose the latest flowering varieties, forgetting that they needed the protection of glass. Then I would get hold of the bulb lists and choose the earliest flowering bulbs, little knowing that the average bulb merchant was a master of deceit, and gaily advertised his wares as blooming in January when, in fact, they would not deign to thrust their green caps through the earth until the beginning of March. I knew all about the winter jasmine, of course, and I ordered a dozen of these. Also a quantity of clumps of Christmas roses. There my knowledge of winter flowers stopped. And so I began to write to various nurseries, ask⁄ing them what they could recommend.

The nurseries could recommend winter jasmine and Christmas roses. When they had made these two brilliant suggestions, their ingenuity appeared to be exhausted. The correspondence invariably trailed off into vague generalities. When I wrote to them that there must surely be *something* besides winter jasmine and Christmas roses, they replied with dark hints, saying that of course there *were* things, but it was doubtful whether they would 'do', and perhaps it might be as well to meet 'our Mr Wilkins'. But I did not desire to meet their Mr Wilkins. I wanted to be told about winter flowers.

Of course, I had written to the wrong nurseries. There *are* places which specialize in winter flowers, but I did not know about them.

For this reason my garden, on its first winter, was as barren as ever. A few snowdrops, of the feeblest variety, thinly planted. One or two sprays of jasmine. Not a solitary Christmas rose.

§ 3

It was during that first barren January that my passion for winter flowers developed into an obsession. I felt that some⁄where somebody was waiting to tell me something. But who? And where? And what? I threw the catalogues into the fire and watched their false pages curling into smoke. They were deceivers, those catalogues. I went back to London.

It was in such a state of depression that I strolled, one bleak January morning, into Messrs Hatchard's bookshop at 187 Piccadilly. I was after a copy of George Moore's *Confessions of a Young Man*, for my own copy was almost worn out, so passionately had it been fondled. I walked into the shop, muttered something about 'looking for a book', and went to the shelves where Moore lay, in lofty seclusion.

But as I looked up I saw that I had come to the wrong section. The books in front of me were all about gardening. They did not seem to be very attractive. They were mostly in wrappers which showed women in obsolete hats standing with guilty expressions by the side of immense hollyhocks. They had terrible titles too—like *Romps in the Rockery*, and *A Garden of Memorie*. I was about to pass on when suddenly I saw, right by my hand, a book with a title that made me catch my breath in excitement.

It was called *Winter Blossoms from the Outdoor Garden*, by A. W. Darnell.

Gingerly I stretched out my hand to take it. Would it vanish into thin air? No. It was real enough. However, as I took it down, I felt that surely there must be some catch somewhere. For months I had been vainly searching the catalogues and the encyclopaedias for even a few paragraphs about winter flowers. And here was a whole book devoted to the problem. Was the title a fake? Was it not a garden book at all . . . was it perhaps an awful collection of sentimental short stories? About thin, sickly children who grew ivy in slums, and all that?

I opened it. And as soon as I read the introduction, my anxiety ceased. Here is what Mr Darnell says:

Beyond the Winter Jasmine, Christmas Roses, and Laurestinus, but few of the winter blossoming plants described in the following pages are to be seen outdoors in the average gardens of Great Britain. In the hope that lovers of winter blossoms may be induced to grow such subjects more freely, and glean some of the pleasure that has been his, the author has compiled the following pages from voluminous notes made over a period of many years. These observations have taught him that given shelter, a warm soil, and a normal season, the smallest suburban garden may be made to yield sheaves of beautiful blossoms for table and room decoration throughout our winter months.

The commoner inhabitants of the amateur's garden such as: Roses, Chrysanthemums, Michaelmas Daisies, Primroses, Violets, etc., that frequently muster sufficient precocity or belatedness to supply a few blossoms on Christmas Day in mild seasons, have not been included, the space being allotted to less well known plants. Care has been taken to include only those plants which may be expected to give their blossoms during the months specified on the title-page of the book; they have, with but few exceptions, been repeatedly observed by the author in blossom year after year during that period.

This was so absolutely the book that I had been seeking that I bought it at once, and rushed out of the shop, forgetting all about George Moore.

§ 4

Let me observe, without delay, that I do not know Mr Darnell, nor anything about him. I would like to know him very much indeed, but I have not that honour. I have not even written to him. I only say this in order to relieve your suspicions that we are in some awful league together. He has not scratched my back, nor have I scratched his.

Nor do I expect to, though I should like to *stroke* his back, very gently and with a decently controlled ecstasy, for the pleasure and instruction he has given me.

In this book (which is published by L. Reeve & Co Ltd, Bank Street, Ashford, Kent) you will find nearly every-thing about winter flowers that is known to modern man. Its full title is:

*A Descriptive List of Exotic*
*Trees, Shrubs and Herbaceous Plants*
*That Flower in the Outdoor Garden in*
*The British Isles*
*During the Months of December, January and February*

(Presumably, these trees, shrubs and herbaceous plants will, with few exceptions, flower equally well in most North American districts. It would be interesting to know.)

I said, a moment ago, that Mr Darnell and I were not engaged in any unholy conspiracy together. I would re-inforce that statement by venturing one or two criticisms of his book.

For instance, on several occasions he is madly optimistic. Thus, on the very first page, there is a beautiful plate, drawn with his own hand, of the *Acacia baileyana*, which most of us call mimosa, though the Australians somewhat unkindly call it 'wattle'. 'How's that?' you will exclaim. 'Mimosa? Out of doors in the British Isles?' And then you will make that noise which one writes as 'Pshaw!' At least, that is the noise which I made, when I thought of those pale powdered tassels vainly endeavouring to with-stand the cutting winds of the Midlands . . . stretching their sensitive roots into the cold, sullen clay of Hunting-donshire.

Perhaps this is a little unfair to Mr Darnell. For if you

read the opening phrases of his first section you will perceive that he breathes about the *Acacia baileyana* an atmosphere of warmth and cosiness which the poor plant, alas, encounters but seldom in these climes. He writes:

> In many gardens in Devonshire and Cornwall, in spots sheltered from the north and east by a living wall of evergreen trees, but open to the sun's rays, grand specimens of this glorious tree may be seen in full flower in the month of January. . . .

Well, that may be so. But we do not all live in Devonshire and Cornwall. We are not all the possessors of spots sheltered from the north and east. We have not, all of us, a living wall of evergreen trees. We want something more definite than that.

Mr Darnell, as soon as he gets beyond the awkward letter A, which appears to have unduly exalted him, supplies us. He leaves Devonshire and Cornwall. He makes no more impossible demands. He caters for the Midlands, for the open spaces, for the hard, ungrateful soils, for the bitterest and sourest tempers of winter. Yet always his hands are full of flowers . . . and they are real flowers, too, as I have learnt from sweet experience. Sometimes they may not be so flamboyant, their petals may be nearer to green than to gold, and their beauty may be shy and timid . . . over their faces they may stretch green leaves to shield them from the wind, or they may droop diffidently to the kindly earth, afraid to rear their heads too high. But they are flowers, all the same. And they flower as Mr Darnell states, in December, January, and February. Let us make their acquaintance.

§ 5

If you are a great expert, with a case of medals from the Horticultural Society on your mantelpiece . . . if you have written treatises on the *Ionopsidium acaule* (which, by the way, is well worth growing) . . . if you have a huge, drooping moustache and a huge, drooping head gardener, then you had better throw this book aside. I am not writing for you. I really have not the least idea for whom I am writing. For the flowers themselves, I expect. For the really simply, absolutely trustworthy winter flowers that may be guaranteed to spangle the garden with blossom whatever the weather, whatever the soil, and whatever the inter-national situation.

First and foremost among these I would place the winter aconite. By some extraordinary oversight Mr Darnell does not mention it at all, which is the only serious criticism I have to make about his book.

The winter aconite is included in nearly every bulb catalogue. That is about all the publicity this brave and radiant blossom has ever gained. It is just 'included'. It is never starred, as it should be. It is given a tiny paragraph, down at the bottom of the page, with a curt note saying that it is 'one of the first spring flowers. Effective in borders. Fifty shillings a thousand.'

It is *not* 'one of the first spring flowers'. It is a midwinter flower. It is *not* 'effective'. It is dazzling. And, from my experience, it would come up if you planted it on an iceberg.

I am sorry to get so hot about the winter aconite, but I hate to see these lovely things neglected. I hate to think of all the bare, gloomy spaces in English and American gardens in mid-January, when they might all be made as gay as a buttercup field.

*A buttercup field in mid-January!* That is what the aconites will do for you, if you buy enough of them. For the aconite is like a large, brilliant buttercup with a green ruff round its neck, and nothing will stop it from flowering. Its brave gold is untarnished by rain, by snow, by the fiercest degrees of frost. I once planted some aconites in low ground under trees. Shortly after Christmas the ground was flooded. Then came the frost, and a thick sheet of ice covered the whole area. Yet the aconites pushed their way through the earth, expanded their blossoms, and gleamed beneath the ice, like a Victorian posy under a glass case.

They are particularly lovely when there are a few inches of snow on the ground. Their stems are just tall enough to lift the blossoms above the white coverlet. The effect is of gold-spangled satin. But they are lovely too on the mild days, for then they open very wide, and one sees how essentially innocent and childlike they are, which makes their courage and endurance all the more remarkable.

You cannot have too many aconites. They cost, as I said before, about fifty shillings a thousand. A thousand will make a brave splash of colour, which lasts a month. If you can afford ten thousand, you are mad not to buy them. There are so many exciting places where you can put them . . . in the hollow of a felled tree, by the border of a pond, in a circle round a statue, or immediately under your window, so that you can press your nose against the glass, when it is too cold to go out, and stare at them, and remember that spring is on its way.

§ 6

After the aconites, I place, in order of excitement, the *Chimonanthus fragrans*, which is better known by its charming name of Wintersweet. There is a delightful picture of it in Mr Darnell's book, showing a creamy yellow flower, prettily striped with red. This picture does not lie. As Mr Darnell says,

> From a well established specimen, planted against a warm wall, we may expect to gather long sprays of its pretty, highly fragrant flowers in the very depth of winter with absolute certainty.

My plants—I have a dozen of them—have only been 'established' for three years, and they have not the shelter of a warm wall . . . only a thin wooden fence protects them. Yet last year the spare brown branches were lavishly starred with blossom soon after Christmas. If they were cut in bud, they lasted . . . with the discreet assistance of a tablet of aspirin . . . nearly a month. Their perfume was as sweet and delicate as anything you could desire.

Do not forget the importance of picking many winter flowers in bud. It is a secret which brings astonishing rewards. Most people, for example, do not realize how exquisite the common *Jasminum nudiflorum* can be, for indoor decoration, if it is properly treated. They see it on their suburban porches, tattered and brown and windswept, with a lot of tiresome twigs surrounding the flowers, and they hardly ever bother to cut it and give it shelter.

Yet, if you go out and run your fingers over the shrub, you will find quantities of young branches bearing an abundance of buds. Some of these buds may be barely formed; they may show you only a gleam of yellow with a reddish-brown tip; they may be cluttered up with a lot of dead wood. Be brave; Slice off those branches. Carry them indoors. Trim off the dead wood. Place the result in water. Leave it for a week, in a dark, warm cupboard. When you return you will find that the jasmine has broken into the gayest blossom . . . a bright, sturdy array of blossom that lasts, literally, for weeks. Then, as you tuck some asparagus fern into the vase and transport it proudly to your desk, you will feel inclined to ask the question, 'Who said that it was cruel to cut flowers, when these are as happy as primroses in a sheltered corner?' And, one might add, as expensive looking as any spray of orchids.

§ 7

And now, quickly, to the next winter flower, the witch-hazel. (I refer to the *Hamamelis mollis*, by far the most vigorous variety.)

It is a melancholy thought that the millions of tired shop-girls who wearily smear their faces with watered extracts of this enchanting plant, every night, should know so little about it. A very melancholy thought indeed. For the shop-girls, as they dab on to their parched skins its healing essences, are not reflecting upon the true, sweet source from which the healing comes. No. They are only recalling that the cold cream, in which the magic lurks, is also being applied by a quantity of Mrs Vanderbilts and Lady Dianas.

It would be better if there could dance, before their tired eyes, the impudent, shining sequins of the *Hamamelis mollis*. The feathery, spidery, yellow exuberance of this darling plant! For was there ever such bravery, such delicious effrontery, as is displayed, on many quiet walls throughout England, by the witch-hazel in midwinter? Oh, it is much to be praised, infinitely to be exalted, this strong and delicate flower! There is something theatrical about it. To discover it, on a dark day, glistening epigrammatically in a forsaken world, magnificently pert and yellow, is so inspiring that one's hands automatically begin to clap, as though one were applauding a witty actress who was tossing her pretty head at a damned difficult situation.

I shall never forget the thrill I had when I saw my first witch-hazel in bloom. It was a bitter day in early February, and I arrived at the cottage just as it was getting dark. I was tired and depressed. Work was going badly. There was a slump on Wall Street, a pain in my leg, and a fierce north-east wind. I will not pretend that all these mental and physical ills were completely cured by the witch-hazel. But at least it made me forget them until the next morning.

I was Making the Tour as usual, and for once in a way I thought I would cut it short. The witch-hazel was situated at the farthest end of the orchard wall. It was really hardly worth while going to look at it, on a night like this. After all, I had watched it for weeks, and there had never been a sign of life. The buds remained like cloves, apparently sealed with a seal that would never break until spring.

Then I said to myself, 'I must not get into bad habits. If I cut the Tour short now, I shall always be cutting it short. A spell will be broken. Things will never be the same again. I shall go to the farthest corner of the orchard wall, see the witch-hazel, curse its barren twigs, and go in to have a drink.'

I went. And there, in the gathering darkness, with the high, strange wind roaring through the great branches above me, I saw that the twigs of the witch-hazel had broken into golden stars.

It was a miracle. Surely there is no need to emphasize that. It was akin to the barren fig tree. It was . . . but we must curb our excitement. There are more winter flowers waiting round the corner.

*Chapter 4*

## MORE WINTER FLOWERS

Even if you invested only in the winter aconite, the winter-sweet, and the witch-hazel, you would have plenty of flowers in the middle of January. All of them, however, would be yellow flowers. So let us introduce some pinks and blues.

The pinks you may obtain, with absolute certainty, from several heathers, though the *Erica carnea* is much the hardiest and most impudent. You can have whole months of thrills from the *Erica carnea*. It begins to drop hints of what it is proposing to do as early as September, but the hints are so quiet and discreet that one pays small attention to them. Then, as the autumn progresses, the little greeny-white buds swell slightly, and towards the beginning of December there is an authentic tinge of pink in them. This tinge deepens quickly, until at last, round about Christmas time, the bells flush to a lovely rose colour. And this colour is maintained until spring is well on its way.

They are adorable, these clumps of winter heather. Actually they seem to welcome the snow, for it enhances their sweet complexions. They demand no care, they crave no shelter. Their one request is that you should plant them in good, peaty loam. Plenty of it. Not merely a little top dressing over a hard bed of clay. If you do this for them, they will do the rest themselves. I think that it is fun to plant them at the extreme end of the garden, as far from the house as possible, in order that you may have an excuse to make long expeditions and be able to see their welcome colour gleaming from afar.

There are several other ericas, with which you might well experiment. But the *Erica carnea* is the only variety which I can heartily recommend from personal experience.

§ 2

If you want to begin with something that is quite fool‚ proof, you cannot do better than invest in a few roots of *Petasites fragrans*\*, which has the pretty English name of winter heliotrope. Some people sneer at the winter helio‚ trope. They say the flower is dingy, and that the roots have abominable habits, being inclined to spread indiscrimin‚ ately into the garden next door. The people next door should be very grateful if the roots *do* spread into their garden. For the flower is not dingy . . . it is a little pale and humble . . . that is all. Besides, one does not grow the winter heliotrope for its beauty of form. One grows it for its beauty of scent. It has a most exquisite fragrance. If you cut it and carry it indoors it will scent a whole room. I always put a few flowers in my winter bunches for this reason alone.

However, there are far finer blues, far lovelier blossoms than the winter heliotrope, which is best regarded as a dis‚ embodied perfume.

---

\* By and large, these pages have not been pruned of their juvenile excesses, but this is one piece of advice which the reader is earnestly requested to ignore. In no circumstances should he plant *Petasites fragrans*. It has taken me a lifetime to live down my praise of this pestilential intruder and I am glad, at long last, to take this opportunity to disown it.

The best of all is the *Iris stylosa* (or the *Iris unguicularis*, if you are feeling high-hat). It is a real sky blue—not the deep blue of summer, but the brilliant paler blue of a frosty January day. The lower petals have gold patches in their centres, spotted with purple. If you want a finer flower than this in winter, you had better go and lock yourself up in your greenhouse and sing hymns.

However . . . the *Iris stylosa* has peculiar habits. It takes a long time to decide whether it is going to like you or not. It is rather like a temperamental prima donna. I speak as a veteran of three years' experience, which is the average period required for the *Iris stylosa* to settle down. Here is the record of my own plants:

First Year. Twenty clumps planted in June. Two were dead by October. The rest survived but did not produce a single flower.

Second Year. Suddenly, in the middle of May, three plants put out large blue tongues at me in the shape of fine and authentic flowers. They were entirely out of order in flowering at this time. They seemed to be saying, 'So you thought you were only going to allow us out in winter, did you? This'll learn you.'

Three more plants died that winter. In January two very feeble blossoms appeared.

Third Year. All through the spring and summer the remaining fifteen plants put on a prodigious amount of leaf. By this time I had given up much hope of ever getting any flowers from them. However, I took a hint from a friend who told me that they liked a coarse soil and that I had been feeding them too well. So I sprinkled a lot of gravel over the roots, which seemed the best way of coarsening the soil, and also helped to drain it. Whether this was what they had been waiting for, or whether they

were already 'established', without the gravel's assistance,
I do not know. In any case, the first bloom appeared at the
beginning of December, and by Christmas Day all the
plants were flowering. Some of the stems were a good nine
inches high, and nearly all the flowers were fine and
brilliantly coloured.

Do not, therefore, be rude or unkind to your *Iris stylosas*
if, at first, they do not appear to be trying.

## § 3

However, even the *Iris stylosa* is beaten for loveliness of
colour by the glowing purply blue of the *Crocus imperati*.
Most people regard a crocus as a spring flower . . . if it
were ever to come up before March they would think that
something very odd was happening, and would go round
muttering about sun spots, or observing that one never knew
what to expect, now that the atmosphere was so disturbed
by all this radio.

Well, certain crocuses *like* coming up in January and
February, and the radio and the sun spots have nothing
whatever to do with it. You may say, 'What does it matter
whether they come up in January or in March, provided
they do come up?' However, if you were capable of asking
that question, you would not be reading me at all, for
unless you long to defeat winter, to make your gardening
year an *endless* chain of blossom, this would all be a sorry
bore for you.

To return to the *Crocus imperati*. You will not find it in
the average bulb catalogue, though some of the bigger firms
list it. However, even when they do condescend to mention
it, they hide it away, as though it were in disgrace, and they

seem to have no fixed idea about its price. Some merchants will charge you as much for a dozen as for a hundred, so it behoves you to make adequate inquiries before you buy it. However, buy it you must. For nothing can be lovelier than its purple centres with their striped lilac exteriors. It comes up without fail in January, and even when the sky is a dirty frozen grey it opens its bland and innocent blossoms, like a child that does not understand the meaning of danger.

There are many other crocuses (Mr Darnell mentions over a hundred), but the few that I have tried have proved difficult and recalcitrant, and it is almost impossible to obtain them at a reasonable price. The only one with which I had any success was the *Crocus sieberi*. But they were neither so early nor so pretty as the *imperati*. They did not come out till the middle of February, and most of them were white.

§ 4

We are almost at the end of our blues—for I am not writing for specialists or millionaires, and it would take too long to describe all the little plants which are scattered throughout my garden in sheltered corners. I am assuming that you have only a little money and a sullen soil, and that you do not live at Cornwall or Charleston, but near Manchester or Minnesota. If you do live near either of these places, it is difficult to see how you can possibly exist without the assistance of the *Daphne mezereum*.

This plant is not really a blue at all . . . it is a pinkish-purple. And when you have once seen it in flower, you will not wish it to be any other colour. However, you will not see it in flower at all unless you take a deep breath and learn this by heart:

The Daphne mezereum loves its roots in the shade and its head in the sun. The secret of its successful cultivation is a cool root run, deep and moist, but well drained, for it is very short lived in hot dry soils.

This is bitterly true. I had six Daphnes and only one has survived, because this was the only one which was properly planted. The soil was dug very deep, and a protect⸗ing arm of evergreen honeysuckle shaded the roots. The branches were sheltered by a western wall. Against this wall, in the second year, the blossoms shone divinely. They began to come out at the end of January, and by the middle of February the bare stems were thickly spangled with the flowers, which smelt as sweet as freesias.

But if we are in search of scent . . . nothing can equal the *Lonicera fragrantissima*. Being translated, this is honey⸗suckle. It is strange that in this England of ours we should always think of honeysuckle as linked with harvest, and summer skies, and sultry lanes through which the towering hay wagons lumber. Honeysuckle makes most people recall lemonade, and country girls in bonnets, and parched grass, and all the rest of it. However, I am perverse, so it makes me think of icicles. For there were long icicles dripping from the rain gutters on the sparkling January morning when I first found my winter honeysuckle in flower. The drops fell, like truant diamonds, from the icicles on to the frozen, creamy petals. Yet the flower was not deterred. It shook off the drops and continued to emit its fantastic sweetness. By the time the sun was high, the scent was quite over⸗powering.

The flowers are not, of course, as large as those of the summer honeysuckle. I cannot talk learnedly about corollas, lips, lobes, and axils. I can only say that the blooms are extremely pretty and look as if they had been quarrelling, for they are usually placed back to back. As far as I know they are not fastidious about soil. I merely put mine into the common clay, which had been roughly treated with a little sand and loam.

The flowers last for a fortnight if you cut them in the bud. And they send out such a perpetual stream of fragrance that you will long to rush about the house waving scarves and doing spring songs, protruding your lips and breathing with suspicious violence.

§ 5

Are you bored?

Indeed, I hope not. For the flowers' sake, not for my own. At the risk of out-winnying the pooh, it must be admitted that I always think flowers know what you are saying about them. If I see a scraggly lupin, I like to pass well out of its hearing before delivering any adverse comments on it. For how do we know what tortures it may be suffering? It surely can be no more pleasant for a lupin to have to appear with tarnished petals than for a woman to be forced to walk about with a spotty face. One does not say, 'Oh, look at that awful girl covered with pimples!' Why, then, should one stand over flowers and hurl insults at them? Besides, the flowers' condition may be all your own fault, which cannot be said of the girl's complexion, unless she is a particular friend of yours and you have been keeping her up too late at nights.

I can therefore only hope that some of my love for winter flowers has been transmitted to these pages. If not, it is a bad lookout for you. We have not done with them yet.

I am writing a floral autobiography, so I am confining

myself strictly to the flowers that I have grown myself.
Moreover, I promise to include only those which can be
absolutely guaranteed to come up in midwinter, with a
minimum of shelter and care.

One of these is the *Corylopsis spicata*. This is a lovely bush
covered with little yellow bouquets that smell exactly like
cowslips. One is bound to admit that, if the winter is very
severe, the flowers will not appear before March. However,
in a fairly mild season they will come out at the end of
January. The *Corylopsis spicata* revels in sand around its
roots. I poured a whole sackful round mine, with the
happiest result. The average nurseryman, when asked for
the Corylopsis, will flinch and look the other way, as
though you had made a highly criminal suggestion to him.
However, if you persevere, he will eventually talk sense, and
will 'procure' one, even if he has not got it in stock.

On no account must you neglect the *Sternbergia lutea*.
This is an *early* winter flower, as opposed to most of the
others I have mentioned, i.e. it flowers from the end of
October until Christmas.

People call it the winter daffodil, but it is really much
more like a large and peculiarly brilliant crocus. For this
reason it is best planted in the grass, near the house, if
possible. But you should see that it is not placed in the drip
of the trees, because, though its petals may be frozen with
impunity, and though it will stand any amount of wind (in
which it differs strangely from the ordinary crocus), it hates
being dribbled upon.

Because I have not space to tell of many more winter
flowers, please do not assume that I have mentioned even a
hundredth of those which you may grow with an assurance
of delight. There are, for example, quantities of saxifrages
which may be counted upon to produce their tiny starred

The Garden Room

blossoms throughout the darkest, most shivering days. Of these I can personally recommend the *Saxifraga ciliata*, which is rather like a lovely white cowslip. With any luck you will be able to pick it on New Year's Day. It will offer you the prettiest thanks if you cover it with a sheet of glass when the weather is exceptionally rough.

Nor can I pass on without mentioning the *Forsythia intermedia*, a true winter shrub if ever there was one, for even in London its bare branches are covered with golden-yellow blossoms in mid-February, while I have had it in bloom, against a sheltered wall, before the end of January.

Nor, again, the *Cyclamen coum*, nor the *Berberis japonica* . . . but if I go on like this, there will be no end. I must therefore content myself by a few very pedestrian observa-tions on two of the commonest winter flowers of all, the Christmas rose and the snowdrop. It is very seldom that one sees either of these growing in anything like their proper size or abundance in English gardens.

The average Christmas rose is a sickly, squalid-looking thing. Half its petals are black. The stalk is only about an inch high. It looks as if it had a fearful cold in the head. Nobody could possibly go into raptures about it.

Yet I have grown Christmas roses as white as lilies, with stalks a foot long. Christmas roses that were so fair that they were like some radiant gardenia. I once had a bowl of such fine specimens that people thought they were orchids.

The secret is very simple. Firstly, you must grow them in deep shade. Then they will be forced to produce stalks. Put them in a wood, or a shrubbery, or under a thick ever-green. Secondly, you must protect them with a cloche, i.e. a little tent of glass, which you can buy from any garden shop. Some people think this is cheating, but if you could only see the result, you would risk the damage to your soul.

Now about the snowdrops. Most people are abysmally ignorant about snowdrops. They buy feeble little bulbs that come up late and never reach a decent size. In January, when the ground outside my window is white with snow‐drops almost as large as cyclamen, I have often opened my newspaper to read a letter from some benighted woman saying that she picked three snowdrops from a sheltered position in her Devonshire garden, and isn't it wonderful? It is. It is wonderful that she and the editor should be so ignorant.

If you want huge snowdrops, of a white that dazzles and of a shape that is perfection, and if you want to have them very soon after Christmas, there are only two things that you must do, and one thing that you must remember. Firstly, you must buy the variety *Galanthus elwesii*. It is, of course, a more expensive bulb, but you would be expensive, too, if you looked like that. Secondly, you must plant it at least six inches deep. I have not the vaguest idea why, but you must. And the thing you have to remember is that they will not be so large in succeeding years as they are in their first year. They will be large, but not gigantic. Nor would you trouble to be gigantic if you had made so superb a début. You see, I will not hear a word spoken against my snowdrops.

They are heavenly, when they are cut and set in a glass bowl, so that their fresh green stalks are seen with the water bubbles glistening around them.

If you want snowdrops for massing under trees, there are all sorts of cheap varieties. However, they are at least six weeks later than the *elwesii*, and I myself will have none of them. I shall probably go bankrupt, with my tastes. But I would rather be made bankrupt by a bulb merchant than by a chorus girl.

## Chapter 5

## GARDEN FRIENDS

I seem to have broken into technicalities rather earlier than I intended. However, it was the fault of the winter flowers, which lured me on with their cold blossoms, like ice maidens.

We must return to the story of the slow and painful transformation of a wilderness into a garden. We must tell how the rock garden was made, how the little wood came to be planted, how the greenhouse was changed from a sort of glorified meat safe into a flowery, perfumed place of magic. The very thought of these things makes me want to bounce up and down on my chair and blow out my cheeks with pleasure.

However, if we are to be honest, it must be admitted that these achievements, which will shortly be described, were not all my own work. To some of them I was inspired, to some goaded. Constantly, in the background, there flitted friends and relations, and I think that it is only fair to pay tribute where it is due. (Incidentally, I hope that I may be able to wipe off a few old scores.)

Let us therefore meet some of these gardening friends.

A garden can make or mar a friendship. It brings out all sorts of hidden virtues and unsuspected vices. By no means all of my friends are gardeners, and I never say to people, 'Would you like to look at the garden?' because any lover of gardens, even if he sees only a lawn and a solitary herbaceous border, will ask to see it himself.

But one's friends who *are* gardeners . . . how a garden shows them up! It is as though a curious light were reflected from the petals of the flowers—a light in which the emotions are sharply revealed. I saw this light most clearly on the face of a middle-aged lady whom I will call Miss Hazlitt, and I believe I am not exaggerating if I say that it was divine.

She was the first woman who ever stayed with me in my cottage.

§ 2

She was lying in Charing Cross Hospital when I saw her. It was twelve years since we had met, and I fear that I had done little to deserve that she should remember me. Perhaps my tardiness as a correspondent was partly due to a certain embarrassment.

Religious people trouble me . . . possibly because they have a gift which I cannot find, nor buy, nor cultivate. But it was impossible to be troubled by Miss Hazlitt, even when she expounded the doctrine of Faith Without Works, in her sweet country voice. 'If you would only have *faith*!' she would cry. Once, in a rare exasperation (more at myself than at her), I said to her, 'You might as well say "if I would only have red hair, or a tenor voice, or blue eyes" . . . you either have these things or you don't . . . you either believe or disbelieve.' She shook her head, and smiled, and put her hand on mine. I could not resent this. One does not resent the actions of a saint.

Only a saint could have borne without resentment the grotesque and squalid course of events which had led her to Charing Cross Hospital. She had suffered for years from neuritis in her right arm. This had made it difficult for her to play games with the children whom she was teaching. Her employers had shaken their heads, dropped hints that perhaps she was growing a little old. . . . She was very sensitive, and when the local doctor told her that the neuritis was caused by her teeth, which should all be extracted, she gave notice, scraped a little money together, and had the teeth out.

At least, she thought that she had her teeth out. Actually, the dentist was criminally incompetent and left many of the roots in. She grew worse. Her money was almost gone. After many humiliating vicissitudes she was brought to the hospital, and it was here that I found her.

She was lying in a little ward that contained, besides herself, two working women, and a Swedish girl who lay with a waxen face, the fumes of ether still about her. Outside, the noise of the traffic roared perpetually, and the October rain lashed the panes. Yet, over Miss Hazlitt's bed there seemed to hover an aura of serenity. She was toothless, she wore a rough pink nightdress, her hair was lank, and her face was drawn. She looked happier than I ever hope to look.

I gave her a little bunch of roses, sat down on a hard chair, talked inanely. It was then that I learnt the last blow that had been dealt her. Instead of being out of her agony, she was beginning it. Almost the first words she heard, when she awoke, were: 'Your mouth was in such a bad condition that we could not finish the operation. You will have to have another . . . perhaps two.' This meant that she would not be able to take up the new position which a lucky chance had offered her.

I asked her to come down with me to the cottage as soon as she was well enough to be moved.

§ 3

You may call me sentimental, moonstruck, what you will, but I swear that the flowers welcomed her. The date was October 5th, and I copy two notes from my diary: The first was written before she arrived.

> Today marks the end of summer time, and indeed the garden is reflecting it too. Early fallen leaves are whirling down the crazy pavements, the grass is a sadder green, and some of the flowers are beginning to have their complexions tarnished.

On the same night, as Miss Hazlitt lay upstairs in bed, I wrote:

> I never picked a finer, sturdier bunch of roses than today, nor a more flamboyant collection of daisies. The Japanese anemones are still lovely, and so are the Michaelmas daisies. The dahlias are still glorious—a mass of cold but promising buds.

It is ridiculous, of course, for I am trying to write a truthful chronicle, not an Algernon Blackwood extravaganza. Yet these are actual extracts from my diary, and the difference in their tone is due to Miss Hazlitt, and only to her.

She *knew*. She knew flowers not only by their names— English and Latin—not only by their families, or their structures, or their habits—she knew them in their essence. It is extraordinarily difficult to explain what I mean, but if you had seen her bend over a winter iris, you would realize what I meant. She pressed the ground about its roots, she fetched some gravel and scattered it on the earth, she helped it to shelter by slightly altering the position of the rock behind it. All these things could have been done by any gardener who is aware that the *Iris stylosa* needs 'a coarse, well drained soil in a sheltered position'. But she knew more than that. There was a magic in her touch. At any rate, the iris over which she had bent was the only iris which bloomed that winter.

On the day after she arrived she was a new woman. I rejoiced. Yet my gratification was tempered by a certain apprehension. I knew that as soon as she was strong enough I should have to endure a religious cross-examination. I would not have minded this, on my own account, but I dreaded it, for fear of hurting her.


§ 4


She had been with me for three days, and I was still un-saved. The heart-to-heart talk had not yet taken place. Every time that we walked through the garden I felt that it was about to come.

'How can anyone look at that rose and fail to believe in God?'

This, I felt, was a flank attack. I looked at the rose and saw a huge earwig sitting in the middle of it.

'Or the devil!' I pointed to the earwig.

'Yes, yes, indeed,' she said eagerly. 'We *must* believe in the devil.' (I wish I could recapture the yearning, the tremulous sincerity of her voice.) 'We are meant to believe in him. To believe in the devil is half-way towards believ-ing in—*Him*!' She had an extraordinary gift for making the capital H articulate.

I grunted and tried to change the conversation. There was a lusty spray of groundsel at my feet. I bent down and tugged it up.

'These foul weeds . . .' I muttered.

'Oh, but weeds are *wonderful*!' cried Miss Hazlitt. The tone of her voice robbed the remark of any sense of silliness or affectation. She meant what she said, with every fibre of her being. She went on: 'My father made a collection of Devonshire weeds which he presented to the Exeter museum. My sister Anna and I helped him to collect them. There was so much to learn, and they were often difficult to find, but some of them were so beautiful that we enjoyed it and felt it such a privilege to work with him.'

She refused to see ugly things . . . or perhaps it would be truer to say that she really did *not* see them . . . that her long training in looking on the bright side of things had made the dark actually invisible to her. One or two hideous little red brick bungalows had been put up in our village. I lamented their presence to her, one day, when she came in from a walk. She smiled at me. 'I did not see them,' she said.

With anybody else I should have been extremely irritated by that remark—as irritated as I am when a Christian Scientist tells me that I have not got toothache. But I was not irritated with Miss Hazlitt, for I knew that she was telling the truth.

§ 5

Toothache!

It was this grotesque and undignified affliction which gave her the cue for the little sermon which must inevitably be preached.

I will not endeavour to transcribe that sermon. Even if I could remember it, I should make it sound foolish. Perhaps it *was* foolish, divorced from her sweet accents. Yet there was a passage which can be transcribed without loss or humiliation, for in its stark simplicity it seemed to challenge the whole world in which I move and have my being . . . and perhaps the challenge may apply, equally, to you.

We had been talking . . . and talking. Words . . . they echoed and died away, and they seemed to mean nothing. The lamp flickered. On the one side there were poverty and pain and faith; on the other, there were plenty and health and . . .

I said to her, in desperation: 'But when you "came to", after the operation . . . when you woke up, in that awful agony, and they bent over you and they said, "We're very sorry, but you'll have to go through all this again . . ."'

'Yes?'

'When they told you the whole horrible business would have to be repeated . . .'

'Oh, I was so *thankful*!'

She broke in unexpectedly. She was leaning forward and her hands were tightly clasped.

'You were . . . what?' I said it dully. I did not understand.

'Oh, but you *must* see. I was so thankful!'

'That it was all to happen again? That loathsome business?'

'Yes . . . yes! Because it meant that Christ was testing me!'

## § 6

The garden still waits.

The wood and the greenhouse and the rock garden . . . still unchronicled! But it is not my fault. One thing leads to another. First it is a spray of winter jasmine that sends me off to chase its golden stars . . . then Miss Hazlitt intervenes, with her quiet smile. Soon, I do indeed believe, we shall be able to get down to business, and drop the wisest hints, and confess the most awful failures (though we shall confess them with a slightly supercilious accent, since they belong to such a distant era). But first we must finish our introduction to the persons who influenced the development of the garden.

Which is the cue for the entrance of Mrs M.

Mrs M. lives not fifty miles from me, but whether to the north, south, east, or west, I prefer not to say.

She is the only gardener I know who never, for one instant, recalls Ruth Draper. (I apologize for introducing that lady's name, but it had to come out, sooner or later.) Never does she walk down a border and say, 'You should have seen this six weeks ago . . . the wallflowers were a *mass* . . . weren't they a mass, Ada? . . . a positive *mass*.' Nor does she pause in front of a collection of feeble shoots and say, 'Of course, if you'd only come next month, I don't know what you would have *said* about these dahlias . . . what could he have said about the dahlias, Ada? . . . Nobody *knows* what to say about them!'

Mrs M. is not like that. I have tried to catch her garden off its guard, without success. I always seem to arrive at the crowning hour of something or other. I have a feeling that as my car draws up at the door the stocks blaze into their ultimate, purple flames, the last of the lilies open their scented lips, the final rosebud sheds its virginity and flaunts itself in a Southern breeze. Things are always at their very best when I visit Mrs M. Perhaps if I stayed a little longer, till dusk fell, I might detect a weariness among the lilies, the stocks might droop, and on her hard pavements I might catch the echo of rose leaves falling. But I can never stay long at Mrs M.'s. She annoys me too much.

She is damnably efficient. She spends next to nothing on her garden and gets astonishing results. She shows you a blaze of delphiniums. 'All out of a penny packet,' she croons. You pass a bank flaming with golden broom. 'All from seed,' she declares. 'A shilling packet I bought years ago.' In the rockery is a sheet of purple cyclamen. It grows so profusely on the hills outside Rome that the little boys stuff bundles of them on the backs of their bicycles, in the same way that English little boys load their backs with bluebells. 'Just a few roots I stuffed into my suitcase after my visit to Italy last year,' she murmurs.

And one is sure that she went to Italy for about ten shillings, and picked up a Granacchi or a Bronzino for a couple of lire, and had a suite of rooms for which she paid half a crown a night.

She bullies one. The first time she came to see me she cried, 'Oh—but you must have a lavender hedge. Why haven't you got a lavender hedge? And I can't see any scarlet lupins. You *must* have scarlet lupins . . . so easy to grow . . . I have masses . . . I'll send you some seeds.'

If she does, they will go down the drain, damn her.

'And your rock roses . . . where did you get them?'

Scenting a compliment, I told her.

'How much did you pay for them?'

Again I told her.

'But that's *monstrous*!' She poked her umbrella contemptuously into the middle of my best clump. 'It's daylight robbery. You shouldn't pay a quarter of that. And, in any case, why do you want to pay for them at all when you can get quantities wild near Sandringham?'

'But Sandringham's fifty miles away.'

'You've got a car, haven't you? All you need to do is to take a trowel and a fork, get into your car, and come back with enough to stock your garden.'

'One day the Queen will catch you at it and put you in the Tower,' I observed bitterly.

Whereupon, to my disgust, she broke into a high, hard laugh and said, 'How funny you are! You must write that down!'

Well—I have written it down, but not quite in the way she expected.

Mrs M.'s most irritating trait is that she is always right. When I was beginning my little winter garden, she went round it, shaking her head, and saying in tones of the utmost relish, 'Oh, I'm afraid this will never *do* here . . . it might be all right in Cornwall . . . but here it will never *do*.'

'Never do what?' I asked. She makes one deliver feeble jokes like that.

Of course, the things which she had indicated didn't 'do'. But I feel that at least part of their failure was due to the fact that Mrs M. had cast an evil spell over them. Her spirit was like a chill breath, withering everything which it touched.

Mrs M., in short, was a witch. We had better leave it at that.

*Chapter 6*

# HOW NOT TO MAKE A ROCK GARDEN

We have dallied long enough with Miss Hazlitt and Mrs M. But the dalliance really was necessary, for it was entirely through the goading of Mrs M. that I made my first great experiment—the rock garden.

By 'first great experiment', I mean my first real structural work. I had weeded and dug and planted, but I had not built or scooped or trifled with the landscape. I was now destined to trifle quite a lot.

When I first came to the cottage I decided that there would not be a rock garden at all. Partly because there seemed no place where such a garden could be made, but principally because, in my ignorance, I did not greatly care for rock gardens.

I have not a 'rock-garden mind'. Until quite recently I associated rock gardens with the horrors of the English Riviera . . . visualized them as gaunt, damp rubbish heaps on Southern promenades, over which there brooded a few diseased palms, while in front of them passed an endless procession of nursemaids, wheeling perambulators in which revolting infants glowered and spat.

Rock gardens seemed to be the monopoly of garden gossip writers, who were always telling one to tidy up the saxifrages and throw snails over the left shoulder. I had, in short, the gloomiest views about rock gardens, and as previously stated, it was only by accident that I ever possessed one.

77

It happened like this. The first summer which I ever enjoyed in my cottage was phenomenally dry. Day after day one looked up to skies of enamelled blue, praying for rain. But no rain came. Sinister cracks appeared in the herbaceous borders. The roses dropped flushed, exhausted heads. Even the pansies protruded purple tongues over the crumbling earth, demanding mercy.

For several anxious weeks I scrambled about the neigh-bourhood in search of water. There was a pond in a distant field which was often raided, at dusk, when its owner was safely in the local pub. I would set off, accompanied by any friends who were staying with me, and make many guilty excursions to this pond. How exciting was the gurgle of the water as one thrust the pails into the cool mud! How exquisite its smooth glitter as one poured it into the welcoming tank in the greenhouse! Till late at night we would labour, the sweat pouring off our foreheads, scurry-ing silently over the fields, cursing softly as the pail made an indiscreet clatter, thinking always of the dry, dying roots which we were so soon to succour.

Very pretty and adventurous, you will agree. But also extremely inconvenient. After a few nights of scurrying and being thoroughly boyish, we were bored and decided that it was really far more agreeable to sit at home and play bridge and drink brandy like civilized persons. It was therefore decided, as we laid away the last pail, somewhat sulkily, at midnight, that the water problem must be solved by the creation of a pond.

§ 2

It was the creation of this pond which led, by steps which

will shortly be explained, to the creation of the rock garden. First, however, please note that the episode of the pond was the one occasion on which I ever triumphed over my father. *I* said that if one dug a very deep hole in the earth, a pond would eventually come and sit in the hole. *He* said that no pond would come, that the earth would fall in, and the water would run away. Well, the earth did not fall in, and the water did not run away. Indeed, the water rose at such a rate that we had to dig trenches to prevent the whole garden from being flooded. But that is another matter. The fact remains that I was right about the pond and my father was wrong. He never passes by it without slightly curling his nostrils and making a noise strangely like that charming Victorian interjection—'Pshaw!'

The pond was dug by a young man from a neighbouring village. There was a legend that he was very lazy, and that he must be watched if any work was to be got out of him. And so I would be constantly popping out of the house and peering at him over the hedge, in the fond expectation that my awful presence would galvanize him into great activity. Unfortunately, it had precisely the opposite effect, for he conceived an almost morbid fancy for me. As soon as he saw me sternly regarding him, he would drop his spade, fold his arms, and gaze up in a sort of ecstasy. The fiercer my expression, the more captivating he appeared to find it. 'Always got a smoile for a poor chap, 'aven't 'ee, sir?' he would croon . . . or words to that effect. I learnt, from other sources, that this affection was genuine, and that he continued to sing my praises when he got home, to the great annoyance of his wife. So I decided that it would be better not to pop out any more, but to trust to his affection from a distance.

Before the pond had reached any appreciable depth I had to return to London, and it was more than a month before I was able to be at Allways again. Judge, therefore, of my surprise when I discovered, as I hurried over the field, that I had created not only a pond but a mountain. This mountain towered over the pond in a most menacing manner. It had not previously occurred to me that if you dig a large hole, the earth from the hole will ascend at the same rate that the hole descends. It occurred to me very forcibly now, and I did not like it at all.

Now, at all moments of crisis in my country life, Mrs M. has a habit of popping up, and I had hardly seen the mountain, and was still wondering where I could possibly put it, when a footstep on the other side of the hedge betrayed her presence.

'Ah . . . good evening! Going for a climb up Mont Blanc? He! He! Ho! Ho!'

I turned and said with grave distaste, 'Good evening, Mrs M.' Then I averted my eyes from her, and drew from my pocket a piece of paper on which I pretended to make notes. I did not wish to make notes, and actually I only wrote the word 'William', over and over again. But I wrote it very firmly, frowning as I did so, in the hope that Mrs M. would go away.

Mrs M. did not go away. Far from it. She actually slipped through the hedge as though she had been invited. I wrote 'William' once again, very hastily, and folded up the paper.

She stared at it inquisitively. 'Making notes?'

I shook my head and smiled.

Baffled, she snorted. Then, very heartily, she said, 'You'll have a job getting all this earth away, what?'

'Getting it away?'

'Well . . . you're surely not going to leave if here, like this?'

'Not like this . . . no.' My mind was working with desperate speed to try to get some valid reason for keeping the earth. Now that I had given Mrs M. the impression that I was not going to move the earth, I was determined to keep it there.

Then suddenly I had an inspiration. 'This,' I blurted out, 'is the beginning of my rock garden.'

And it was.

## § 3

Mrs M. stared at me with undiguised suspicion. 'Rock garden?' she cried. 'What do you mean . . . rock garden?'

'By a rock garden,' I replied, 'I mean a garden containing a quantity of rocks.'

'But you haven't any rocks.'

'Not yet, no.'

'Where are you going to get them?'

I had not the least idea where I was going to get them, so I said, in a sepulchral voice, 'They Are Coming', rather as though the skies might open at any moment and deluge us with a cascade of boulders.

'Yes, but where from?'

'Yorkshire.' This was partly guesswork and partly memory, because I remembered reading in some book of a man who had a quarry of stone in Yorkshire which he used to export.

Mrs M. snorted again. 'That'll cost you a pretty penny,' she said. I could hear signs of fierce envy in her voice. She swung her string bag backwards and forwards, and glared at my mountain. Then she said:

'But you're surely not just going to stuff a lot of rocks on all that mud?'

'Stuff them? No. I shan't stuff them.'

'Well . . . throw them, then. You've got to have some sort of design.'

'I have.'

'What is it?'

'It is being Done For Me,' I said.

'By whom?'

I could think of nobody but Sir Edwin Lutyens, who designed Delhi. So I said, 'You will catch cold, Mrs M., if you stand in the wet grass.'

I am glad to be able to record that she did.


§ 4


I was therefore committed to a rock garden. I spent a restless night, cursing myself for being so easily irritated by Mrs M. But on the following morning, when I again visited the pond and its accompanying mountain, the prospect did not look so black. The site was promising. A fair slope led down to the pond. Two green arms of a hedge encircled it. And over the pond towered the mountain, which had only to be slightly sat on, and carven into shape, and decorated with roses, cunningly disposed, to be transformed into a rock garden.

So I fondly imagined.

I ordered the rocks. I was told that it was cheaper to order a truckful, which would contain about eight tons. It seemed a great deal, especially as they had to come all the way from Yorkshire. However, I was assured that if less were ordered 'it would come out much dearer in the end'. This commercial principle is usually to be distrusted, for we learn by bitter experience that it is not cheaper to order, for example, ten yards of silk for pyjamas when only three are required, or to buy a guinea bottle of hair oil when the three-shilling size would do just as well. For it usually happens that we take a hatred to the silk, while the oil goes bad. However, it was unlikely that the rocks would go bad. Besides, there constantly rose before me the sneering face of Mrs M., who did not believe that any rocks were coming at all.

She believed it, well enough, a few days later, when she had to drive four miles out of her way because the road in front of my cottage was completely blocked by the collapse of an enormous vanful of best quality, fully weathered Yorkshire rocks. She believed it still more when she discovered that she would be deprived of the services of her odd man, who had secretly deserted her in order to earn double pay in transporting my rocks across the field. He had transported them with such energy that he ruptured himself and was confined to his bed for three weeks.

At last the thing was done. All the rocks were safely ensconced in the mountain—the big ones at the bottom, the small ones at the top. Looking back at this adventure, it seems almost incredible that I could have been such a fatuous and ignorant optimist as to imagine that this was the way to make a rock garden—without any plan, without even an adequate preparation of the soil. Yet, I did imagine it . . . until I saw it in being. Then I realized that a very big and expensive mistake had been made.

The thing was horrible. It was utterly out of keeping with the quiet and rambling beauty of the rest of the garden. I tried looking at it from this way and from that, half closing my eyes and putting my head on one side. I regarded it before and after cocktail time. It looked much worse after, which is a proof that alcohol stimulates the æsthetic sense. No amount of self-hypnotism could persuade me that I liked it.

It reminded me of those puddings made of sponge cake and custard, which are studded with almonds until they look like some dreadful beast thrown up from the depths of the sea. It had no sort of design. It was so steep that the earth was already showing signs of falling away in the slightest rain. The best I could say about it was that it made a very good shelter from the wind.

Had it not been for Mrs M., I should have destroyed it overnight. False pride made me keep it there for several days. But there are stronger emotions than false pride. One morning, a few days later, I went out, saw the hideous thing, and decided that it could remain no longer. Urgently we summoned the same man who had put it together. By the following afternoon the earth had all been taken away and deposited in a neighbouring field. There remained only a quantity of rocks, scattered about the grass.

## Chapter 7

## THE OTHER SIDE OF THE PICTURE

And now I found myself confronted by the first real problem of my gardening career.

Here were the rocks, the grass, the pond. Here was I, standing in a flat field, wondering what on earth could be done with them. How could they possibly be made to fit in with the landscape? How could one ever hope that they would ever look anything but a lot of rocks in a field? For days these questions presented themselves. And no answer was forthcoming.

Now, when you ask yourself a question and do not receive an answer, you must do something about it. You must not sit still, in a paralysing silence. So I decided to do something as quickly as possible. The thing I did was to order three Scotch pines.

I ordered three Scotch pines for several reasons. Partly because it was November, and partly because I like Scotch pines, but principally because Scotch pines 'went' with rocks, and I hoped that they might help me to find some sort of design.

They did. One was planted on the very edge of the pond. That suggested a little hill behind it. The other two were planted a little distance away. Which suggested a tiny valley, leading to a second hill. Thus, a vague idea of a topographical outline had been born. That was the first hurdle which had to be surmounted.

However, there were many others. The Scotch pines were duly placed in their appointed positions. We began to delve and to build. Then we remembered that the pines would eventually grow, and cast shade, and we had to move them to a different position. More delving and more building. Then we discovered that the roots of the Scotch pines were too near the water and would probably rot. They had to be moved again. They were moved, in all five times. An expression of poignant fatigue hovered over their branches when they reached their final resting place.

Then we found that we had not enough rocks. We ordered more. Then it transpired that the top soil of loam and sand was not nearly deep enough, that it was only a feeble coating over the hard clay. All the rocks had to be taken up again, more earth had to be removed, more cart- loads of sandy loam delivered. Oh, it is great stuff, this rock gardening! It would be unutterably tedious to narrate the innumerable stages through which we progressed. I can best sum it up by suggesting a few elemental rules for the guidance of those who are even more ignorant than myself.

When you are making a Rock Garden:

1. You must be bloody, bold, and resolute. By this I mean that you must stand at a little distance from your slope, visualize a certain broad design, and decide there and then to carry out that design, cost what it may. Perhaps you want a little valley, that rises gently to a little hill. If so, you must mark the outline of that valley, there and then, with sticks or stones, or whatever may come handy, and get your gardener to come along to help you scoop it out. Long before you have attained the desired outline you will feel sick of the whole thing. You will feel that you have descended into the bowels of the

earth before you have done much more than scratch the surface. But you must stick to it. Otherwise your rock garden will have no design at all.

2. You must be monstrously extravagant with your rocks. By which I mean that you must push them really deep into the earth. It is agony to have to do this, because a big rock probably costs about five shillings, when you come to reckon up the price of its transport, the labour of the men who put it in, etc. It would be much more soothing to stick the rock on the top of the slope so that you could say, 'Look at my enormous rock! How rich I am to be able to afford such enormous rocks!' But if you do stick the rock up like that, you will eventually take a hatred to it. Also, nothing will grow on it, and, anyway, it will certainly fall down. So, really, you must bury it so that only a mossy nose sticks out. It is maddening to have to do a thing like that.

However, as the garden writers would say, '*It is advisable to follow the dictates of Nature, which, being natural, is the amateur's wisest guide. Nature, whom the Greeks worshipped, is just as possible to reproduce in the humblest suburban garden as in the lofty palaces of the duke. The rocks should be buried to two thirds of their cubic capacity in rich, well seasoned loam, to which a small proportion of sand has been administered.*' Garden authors really do write like that. I envy them their style. There is the echo of a healthy, well spent life in every paragraph.

3. Having obtained your design and buried your rocks, your next task is to exercise phenomenal restraint about the things which you put in. I have always been a fervent advocate of birth control, but since I have been the owner of a rock garden my fervour has increased a hundredfold. The prolificacy of the common saxifrage

87

is positively embarrassing. The speed with which the rock rose reproduces itself brings a blush to the cheek. Violas appear to have absolutely no self-control, and as for the alyssum . . . well, if *we* behaved like the alyssum, Australia would be overpopulated before the year is out.

Forgive me . . . I ought not to have spoken disparagingly of the generosity of these delightful plants. It is really rather caddish to sneer at a saxifrage which climbs so bravely from rock to rock, bearing its sweet standards aloft, carrying to the barren lands a rosy glow of hope. How can a decent man *check* the glowing flame of violas, that burn ever more blue in successive dawns, spreading their cold fire in secret places? These are valiant flowers, and gay, and sturdy, and it is only one's own decadence which urges one to decry them. For us, the rocks are not so easily scaled, nor the darkness so sweetly illuminated.

§ 2

You will find, as you wander through your garden life, that each form of gardening has its separate and peculiar charm —that one corner of your garden will evoke a mood quite distinct from that which pervades you in another. A large garden is like a large house, with rooms variously decorated. There are rooms which soothe, and rooms which stimulate; rooms that are only made for work, and rooms that are only made for play. The clearest analogy that occurs to me is between the kitchen and the kitchen garden: in both these places there is the same feeling of comfort and security. The same tranquillity lurks in the smell of sultanas on a shelf as in the cool tang of a cabbage in a roughly dug bed.

The charm of a rock garden is essentially Lilliputian. To extract the keenest pleasure from it you must be able to diminish yourself—you must acquire the talent of shrivel-ling yourself up into a tiny creature that is able to walk, in spirit, under the tiny saxifrages, and shiver with alarm at their heavy weight of blossom, to climb, in your mind's eye, the mossy stones, and grow dizzy on their steep escarpments. This is the whole genius of the rocks: the power they have to swell out and out, until they are full of menace.

Endless adventures of the spirit are possible in the rock garden, if you have an hour to spare. There is every stimulus to the imagination. The smallest pool in a rock's hollow becomes a great lake, and a clump of violas is transformed into a pathless jungle. In the valley where the rock roses grow the sun never comes, but it is wild with splendour over the crest of the Aubrietias . . . far, far away. And thus, when you are designing your rock garden, though you must be sternly practical in many things, it is as well sometimes to allow your fancy the freest flight . . . to place certain plants simply for their 'adventurous' value, i.e. to put a miniature pine, six inches high, at the top of a small mound, so that you may have all the fun of thinking that it is a forest giant on a mountain summit.

The first really big experiment I ever tried in my rock garden was the result of just such a childish excursion. It was concerned with a group of Chionodoxa. (If you look it up in the *Encyclopaedia of Gardening* you will find that its other name is Glory of the Snow, that it is of the order of Liliaceae, that it is a hardy, deciduous bulbous plant, and that it was 'first introduced' in 1877.)

The experiment, as I say, was due to a happy accident. One day I was weeding. There were a lot of peculiarly loathsome docks, against which I had declared war. Docks are the worst weeds of all, because, just as you are pulling them up, they make a sickly sucking noise, and break in half. The root remains in the ground, and you find yourself clinging onto the leaf. Whereupon you have to tramp off to the tool shed, arm yourself with a trowel, and return to the scene of action, only to find that you have forgotten where the abominable dock root is lurking. In a rage, you scrape up a lot of earth, feeling like a dog that has lost a bone, and if you are lucky you will find, after ten minutes' search, an obscene sprout that you imagine to be the dock root. It is only after you have thrown it into the hedge that you realize, with horror, that you have destroyed your best gentian. The only person of my acquaintance who ever said a good word for docks was Miss Hazlitt. She told me that if you rubbed their leaves on your skin after you had been stung by a nettle, the poison would disappear.

Well, I was bending down over the docks for quite a long time, and when I occasionally looked up, I saw the world upside down. And then, all of a sudden, a little lump of earth detached itself from the top of the slope, and rolled slowly down to my feet. It was only a very little lump, the size of a plum, but in my Lilliputian mood, it seemed immense. I stepped back quickly, as though to escape from an avalanche. As soon as I thought of the avalanche I thought also how wonderful it would be if I *could* simulate an avalanche here, with flowers of white and frosty blue, foaming down from the summit to form a great pool at the bottom.

It occurs to me that this is possibly a very long and elaborate explanation of a very minor event . . . minor even in the chronicle of my garden, for the avalanche when completed was only a few feet long. However, it seems that one becomes Lilliputian in one's style merely by thinking of the rock garden.

I spent one of the happiest mornings of my life planting the bulbs of the Chionodoxa. They were such *nice* bulbs. Round and smooth and clean, like nuts. I would have eaten one of them, had I not been so conscientious. Moreover, on the day when I planted them, I was in a particularly good 'shrinking' mood. I had only to narrow my eyes and to think hard for a moment, to become two inches high, to gaze in becoming awe at the rocks over which my hands were spread. There are some days when it is terribly difficult to shrink properly. Try as one will, one remains six foot high—a cumbersome human in an overcoat, with cold feet and a trowel. But today . . . ah, my body was as volatile as the ghostly scarlet leaves of the maple near by, that stained the October sky with swift blood-stains.

Never was there such fun. I made a little plan of it all. At the top of the slope I laid a mass of bulbs to represent the gathering snow. In order that the illusion might be perfect, I chose the smallest bulbs for this position and packed them very tight. Then, where two rocks jutted out, I made my avalanche split in two. There would be a foam of blossom on either side, breaking here, flowing there, sweeping turbulently over the brown soil. And then, where the main rock jutted out, I seized bulbs by the handful, and jammed them in all round, in order that there might be a fierce jet and spray of blossom. This accomplished, I paused. But not for long. For there were many minor rivulets to be created, many pale streams to bring into being, wandering in irregular lines through the small boulders, till they ended in a little pool of earth into which I placed the last of the bulbs, hoping so earnestly that one day the pool would be blue, and restless with blossom.

For many weeks I visited that patch of sloping ground where the Chionodoxa lay dormant. My diary is full of impatient entries about it. Thus:

*November 30th.* No sign of Chionodoxa. Feel very depressed. Doubt if shall ever succeed in anything.

*December 15th.* No sign of Chionodoxa. Why do I live in this damned country? Had a letter from Willie Maugham today. They are bathing at Antibes.

*January 18th.* No sign of Chionodoxa. If the government goes on spending money at this rate, there will be a flight from the pound.

*February 3rd.* No sign of Chionodoxa. My hair is coming out. Went yesterday to hair man. Says must have treatment. Will cost twelve guineas.

*March 3rd.* No sign of Chionodoxa. Perhaps I should feel better if I had a real religion. But how *can* one have a real religion if one *wants* to have one so much? I mean, does not the *desire* in itself nullify the authenticity of the creed . . . which means nothing . . . but I am so terribly tired that I cannot phrase things properly.

*March 10th.* Signs of Chionodoxa! Really, at last, three wart-like objects have appeared. They are so late that one ought to have hit them on the head and told them to go back and come again next year. But one doesn't. Is one weak?

*March 20th. Two Chionodoxa out!* Ah, but it was worth waiting for! The most beautiful blue. Like the blue of a church window on a cold spring morning when the sun is behind it, and the starlings are shrill outside the porch. But I must not go on like this.

I must not indeed. If I am to keep any remnants of my soul intact, for future serial publication, I must shut up that diary with a snap. Yet I cannot shut it up before I recall those early delights in my avalanche—delights which were endless in the lengthening twilights of spring, as I bent down and looked up at the nodding spray of blossom, descending just as I had planned, a rivulet here, a cascade there, and a grand torrent in the middle, over the central rock, all outlined against the deep, quiet skies of April. For my avalanche was an avalanche that really succeeded, that swept into my memory forever.

§ 3

It would be absurd presumption on my part if I were to attempt to offer any hints on the creation or the maintenance of rock gardens, since my own knowledge is so very limited. But in its very limitation lies a certain value. If you have only been doing a thing for a few years the memory of early blunders has not lost its sting, and the memory of early triumphs is still fresh about you.

My first triumph—or rather, my first little splash of colour —was an Aubretia. It sounds comparatively tame but I do pray you not to neglect the Aubretias, for, of all the flowers I know, they are the kindest. There are few months in the year when you cannot find some colour on them. I write in October, when my Aubretias still hold many trembling purple stars, and I remember that from March to May they gave me delight with their thick cushions of blossom.

But their floribundity—if there is such a word—is only a small part of their claim to our respect. They are, of all plants, the easiest to increase. Tear off a piece of root, press it in the earth, and it unfailingly thrives. This, at least, has been my experience. Moreover, the flowers are far more valuable for cutting than most of us imagine. People see the frail tiny petals, they explore downwards and discover a straggly stalk that is like a thread of cotton, and they shake their heads, thinking that the petals would be shed before dawn, and that the narrow stalk would not absorb water. They gravely misjudge the Aubretia, who think these things. For those petals are fastened as with hooks of steel, and the stalks have an efficiency which their appearance belies. I have picked the most delicate-looking Aubretias side by side with other flowers that seemed far more sturdy. The Aubretias were always the last to die.

Of saxifrages there are many, but the very earliest I know, which comes into bloom in February, is the *Saxifraga grisebachii*. It is not always very easy to get. Nurserymen have an awful habit of writing to say that, 'Owing to the recent troubles in Turkey, our stock of this item has not been replenished.' Or they say, 'In view of the national situation, this item has, unfortunately, been destroyed by mildew.' However, if you persevere, you will be able to get some plants.

You will be well rewarded for your trouble, because this saxifrage will light its pale pink torch before the winter days are done, and soon its flame will be reflected in many flickers of answering fire, until one mild spring day the whole rock garden seems to burst into a dazzling blaze. However, you have to exercise a great deal of tact with the *Saxifraga grisebachii*. It hates damp and so should be planted fairly high up, where it cannot be dribbled on. It is also wise, during very wet seasons, to put a sheet of glass over it. Some people seem to think that this is a lot of trouble, but personally I think it is great fun—like making a little house

94

for the flower, in which it can shelter and keep dry and warm. Also, if you put some small pieces of limestone in the soil around it, you avoid any risk of mildew.

I will not give a long list of plants, because half the fun of making a rock garden lies in the search which one makes through catalogues, choosing flowers without really any knowledge of what they are. It was in this way that I discovered *Calandrinia umbellata*—one of the perkiest, gaudiest flowers you ever saw. It comes out only in full sunlight, but when it does . . . phew! You have to shade your eyes, it is so bright. It likes a very dry soil, and you can grow it easily from seed. However, you have to be careful that you do not put it near any red rock roses or purple Aubretias, because it is a brilliant magenta-crimson and will fight violently with any other colour within fighting distance. People have a habit of saying airily that 'flower colours never clash'! I should like them to have heard what a certain scarlet geranium of my acquaintance said to a neighbouring fuchsia, last spring. They might then alter their opinion.

## Chapter 8

## MIRACLES

Where were we? In summer or winter? It is difficult to say. We may, however, assume that by now the garden was in running order, that the rock garden had at least been moulded into its permanent shape, and that the hardest spade work had been done. For some months, now, there was peace, in which things simply grew, and made delicious smells, and looked adorable. One felt like something in a symbolic picture, clad in shorts and resting on a pitchfork at the close of day, with a lot of hollyhocks (out of drawing) in the background.

But the tranquillity of this agreeable interlude was disturbed, from time to time, by the most astonishing happenings. Let me hasten to add that the disturbances were welcome, because the happenings were nearly all of them delightful. And they were so entirely unexpected that they fully deserve to be called miraculous.

Everything is, of course, a miracle. I am a miracle, and so, I must reluctantly allow, are you. But whereas you and I are used to ourselves—know exactly how our hair curls and how our hands are shaped—the garden miracles are more fresh and exciting. Every gardener has a strange and romantic tale to tell—if you can worm it out of him—of blue flowers that come up yellow, or of a white lily that sinned in the night and greeted the dawn with crimson cheeks. In the strong heart of every gardener some wild

96

secret stirs, of seeds that were sown on barren ground and brought forth an hundredfold. And in this class comes the story of my first miracle—the miracle of the vine.

Ah! The vine! One is exalted even by the sound of that word. It is so beautiful . . . so cool and pure. It is like a soft high note blown on a far-off flute. How Poe must have loved writing:

*The viol, the violet and the vine . . .*

It is a like a triple echo of fantastic music, dying away in a sleepy hollow.

The leaves are beautiful, as well, flamboyantly designed with a fine romantic flourish, flushed when the hour comes with a hectic red, as though something of the virtue of the grapes had stained them with their own sweet shame. You may take a thousand vine leaves in your hands, and never will you discover a pair which is patterned in the same shade of red, nor decked in the same design. A vine leaf is a fine thing . . . an aristocrat . . . it curls disdainfully on the slender stem and flaunts its flushed cheeks to the dying suns of September.

And here, in the grape clusters, is the whole sting and sweetness of beauty . . . its bloom and its opulence . . . its poison and its dark fire . . . its gentle, self-sufficient grace. There are some flowers and fruits that have beauty of form, or of colour, or of association, but a cluster of grapes has all these beauties, and more. There is the radiance of much remembered poetry about it . . . and a misty promise of happiness to come. Yet even if these things were not so, even if one saw, for the first time, the heavy purple fruit hanging sudden against the white sky, one would be amazed by the discovery of a new glory.

I cannot honestly say that I ever saw any 'heavy purple

fruit hanging, etc., etc.' But I certainly saw something. And I saw it very suddenly, on a thundery morning in August, when the skies grey-white, as though they were scared of the wild spirits which leapt behind their sober curtains.

§ 2

My father called to me from the garden.

'Here! Come out and look at this!'

There was a note of urgency in his voice. I threw away the book I was reading and hurried out. My father was standing in the little arbour which leads into the Secret Garden. I went to him and looked.

I do not know if one's heart ever really stands still, but mine at that moment stood as still as it is ever likely to do, until it stops forever.

For there, underneath a tangle of ivy, sweetbriar, honey-suckle, and jasmine, was a little bunch of grapes. True, the grapes were green and not much larger than peas. But the bunch was perfectly formed, and it hung its head deli-cately, as though it were diffident that it had been discovered.

'Grapes!' I whispered.

'And how they're alive at all, beats me,' observed my father.

He had every reason to be surprised. The very survival of this vine was a miracle. For its roots were mixed up with those of a rank and greedy laurel. Its stem was being throttled and eaten by a rapacious ivy. Its slender branches were buried, tangled, and overcast by a thick roof of many creepers. Hardly a leaf of that vine can ever have seen the sun. Why, there was even a flourishing elm tree, high above the thicket, casting so thick a shadow that the sturdiest of the creepers had grown pale and anæmic.

Add to all these things the fact that we had suffered the worst summer within living memory . . . a summer of endless rain and biting winds.

Yet, in the cold and the darkness, in the face of fierce competition, the little vine had produced a bunch of grapes. If that is not a miracle, I should like to know what is.

§ 3

We took the vine under our care from that day. I was for building a little tent round it, or sheltering it with an umbrella, or . . . if these pleasing devices proved impracticable . . . for procuring a small glass bulb and pushing the grapes inside it, so that they would have their own house, and would be able to feel that somebody was taking an interest in them.

However, my father intervened. One can't be whimsical for long when my father is about—a fact for which the reader should be duly grateful, or I would come to every chapter trailing clouds of whimsicality. He cast great scorn and derision on my suggestions for tents, umbrellas, and bulbs, and said that the first thing the poor vine needed was a little air.

We proceeded to give it air. With shears and clippers and scissors (for now the whole household was gathered about the rescue of the vine, and every available instrument was in use), we hacked away at the encroaching creepers. The gardener dealt with the briar. My mother sliced off little bits of jasmine, rather regretfully, for my mother is not a born slicer. My father hacked grimly at the ivy. I shinned up the elm and tore off huge branches in a frenzy. At least the branches seemed huge, in that enchanted moment.

Light and air flooded in. I could swear that I saw a swelling in those tiny pallid globes. A deepening of the bloom about them. And we discovered many other clusters, hanging coyly in the gloom that we were turning so quickly into light. It was really like rescuing prisoners from the Bastille. As each thick and sullen parasitic branch was torn away one had a sense of a prison door opening . . . a gust of fetid air in one's nostrils . . . and through the strange silence the thin, querulous plaint of the condemned.

Well . . . the work was done. The last creeper was torn away. Fastidiously, and with a sad little sigh, my mother clipped the last leaf that was shading from the grape cluster the strange rays of the agitated August sun. And then, more than ever, we saw the miracle of the whole thing.

For the stem of the vine was diseased . . . pitted and pock-marked by the horrible hold of the ivy. The leaves drooped from the long assaults of the cloying briar. There was a fetid atmosphere over this brave plant. And yet . . .

My father brought us all down to earth. His gruff voice broke the silence. He said:

'Of course, it's the pig wash. That's what it is. The pig wash.'

I gazed, with ill-concealed distaste, at this parent of mine. Here he was, in this sacred moment, which was really Biblical in its simplicity, profaning the air with filthy words like 'pig wash'. Moreover, he went on:

'No air. No sun. Nothing. Therefore, there must be some explanation. The only explanation lies in the roots. The roots have probably stretched down into the stream on the other side of the hedge. That stream's always being polluted by the pig wash that comes down from the farm. Damned insanitary. I always told you it ought to be filled in.'

Whereupon he left his shears on the grass and went into the house to have a glass of beer. I remained staring at the grapes.

'Pig wash,' I thought. And shuddered. Then I realized that I was being silly. For do not all lovely things spring from dirt? Is not dung the ultimate essential of poetry? Filth and the fine frenzies are linked by more than mere alliteration. Thus, in this mood of sensuous worship, I kissed the grapes and bade them good-bye. And I too went in to have a glass of beer.

## § 4

The winter passed. Spring. Summer. And next summer the grapes came to harvest. The vine responded to the affection that was lavished on it.

Affection, indeed, it had in plenty. Our first task had been to remove the roots of the laurel. They were so close to those of the vine that it was only after the greatest diffi-culty that they were disentangled. While the roots were still exposed, we dug in quantities of bone manure, to reinforce the tonic of the 'pig wash'.

Then, in the spring, when the tiny flowers were forming, I spread a net of thin muslin over the whole vine to take the worst edge off the late frosts. You would have been surprised to see how effective a shield it made. Frost is a strange, queer thing, fickle, volatile, easily discouraged. It was very greatly discouraged by my muslin. In the morn-ings, before breakfast, it would waste all its bitterness on the muslin, freezing it stiff and snow-white, while underneath, the little grape flowers bloomed gaily, untouched. You see I wanted them to have a good start in the race for sunshine, when summer came.

They had their start. As the warm days came, so the grapes formed, swelled, flushed, stored their sweet juices, blushed with the delicate bloom of adolescence. There was an awful moment when I found a huge and depraved thrush pushing its hideous beak into one of the grapes. I rushed at the thrush, which winked at me, languidly fluttered away, and sat on a branch just out of reach. After that disturbing episode we got a net to keep the birds off.

In September there were sixteen clusters of perfectly formed grapes. They were close-packed, of a deep purple, and of a heavenly bloom (except in those places where one had been unable to resist the temptation of fondling them). Grapes, grapes, *grapes*! I got a crick in the neck looking up at them. And when we cut the first bunch, and put it on a silver dish, and pressed our teeth into the cool skin so that the juice trickled out . . . when we found that they were sweetly flavoured, with real skins and real pips . . . well, I repeat, for the tenth time, it was a miracle.

§ 5

The grapes, of course, suggested that they should be made into wine. I have not yet attempted to do so, although the idea is quite practicable. Several bottles of good, strong red wine are to be tasted in a cottage in the village. They were made some five years ago, and though the vine from which they came was much bigger than mine, my own vine would produce at least two bottles.

This leads one to the conception of a dinner composed entirely of things one had grown in one's own garden. It would be, you must admit, the most delightful dinner imaginable . . . to prepare, if not to eat. The wine we have settled. The bread would be rather a bore, but if one sowed the potato patch with corn it should be possible to make at least one loaf. Salted almonds could be served, for I have several almond trees, and even in wet summers there are always a few which ripen. Hazelnuts there would be in plenty, and vegetables galore.

It would be, of course, a vegetarian dinner. However, we could have an omelette. Not that I have a hen. But we could hire a hen for the occasion, so that it could come into the garden for a little while in order to satisfy the requirements about everything being grown on the estate. Then, after it had laid some eggs, it could go away again, because I do not want a lot of animals all over the place. I am sure that hens are charming, but I do not happen to want them. Nor cows. If we *had* to have cream for dinner, I would allow a cow to come in, be milked, and depart. But I do not like cows in my fields. People are always telling me that I ought to have cows to eat up the grass, but I will not have them, for several reasons. Firstly because cows do not eat up the grass properly. They leave the thistles and nettles. I do not blame them for this, but merely state it as a fact. Secondly, cows make it impossible to take the dog out. They have a ridiculous and unreason- able hatred of dogs. Thirdly, cows are very untidy in their ways. And I do not like having to glare about the ground to see that I am not approaching a danger spot. Therefore, if we *had* to have cream, I should let the cow come in for just long enough to be milked on my property, and then, as far as I am concerned, it could go and drown itself.

Thus, you observe, we could have a delicious dinner with wine and bread and omelettes and heavens knows what else, all off the estate. Which would be a miracle indeed. 'Hell, it *would*!' said a rude American, who is sitting near me as I write.

§ 6

We now come to yet another miracle. I refer to the pond. It was mentioned, earlier in the book, as a small stretch of water lying at the foot of the rock garden. So I suppose it is. However, if you knew as much about it as I did, you would agree that it is a whole collection of astonishing phenomena.

Consider the case of the goldfish. A kind friend pointed out to me that one of the drawbacks to any pond was its habit of producing, every season, enough mosquitoes to sting the entire neighbourhood. He added, however, that if one put fish in the pond, the fish would eat the mosquitoes up, and all would be well. When asked, 'What sort of fish?' he said, 'Any fish.' So I got goldfish, which are really the only fish I know.

I bought twelve tiny goldfish at Woolworth's. They looked so pale and feeble. It seemed likely that if any eating was to be done, the mosquitoes would eat the goldfish. But perhaps the goldfish would be able to dive if they saw a particularly huge mosquito approaching. Or perhaps, since they were so small, the mosquitoes would not notice them.

The goldfish were in a cruelly small bowl. They could not swim without bumping into each other. They looked as if they were gasping for breath. I took them up into the country in the train, with a sheet of perforated metal over the top of the bowl. A lot of water came out during the journey, so that there was a perpetual pool at my feet, which caused newcomers in the carriage to stare very haughtily at me.

Dusk was falling when I tramped through the field, bearing the precious bowl. Just before I emptied the fish into the pond I held the bowl aloft. The rays of the dying sun glinted on the glass. In glowing enamels the green trees were mirrored. The sky was an arc of grey crystal. And through it all moved the goldfish, rhythmically, backwards and forwards.

I emptied the bowl into the pond. A quick stream of gold and silver, a few bubbles and a group of rings spreading over the black surface of the water, and then the goldfish disappeared. Completely. Not one could I see, peer as I might. A little resentfully I thought that surely one, at least, might have had the decency to swim to the surface, blow a bubble at me, and say, 'We like your pond very much, thank you. Good night.' However, not one did come.

Days went by. Weeks. Months. And still I never saw the goldfish. When the winter came, the pond was often covered with ice two inches thick. I used to go down to the pond, on these occasions, to break the ice, partly in order that the goldfish might have some air, but principally because I think that it is very pleasant to break ice—to see the jagged cracks, to take a piece of ice and hurl it on the surface so that it breaks with a million slippery, delicious tinkles. For I had really given up all hopes of the goldfish, in view of their complete disappearance, and the only thing that made me feel they might still be there was my gardener's assurance that, if they were dead, they would float on top. They showed no signs whatever of any tendency to do that.

Spring came. One day I was walking by the pond when I saw a gleam of gold. I stood very still and held my breath. Another gleam. The goldfish! But what utterly different goldfish . . . large, and brilliant, and all a-glitter! Nor was this all, for swimming about with the goldfish were quantities of other fish . . . even as I stood there I could count over sixty. And the amazing thing about these fish was that *they were all black*!

On tiptoe I went nearer to the pond to see that I was not deceiving myself. No . . . there they were. They were tiny fish . . . about the size of the goldfish when they had first made their début in the pond . . . and they were as black as your hat. This seemed to me the most peculiar phenomenon. Where had they come from? There was no stream feeding the pond. There was not a trickle of water leading into it. The only water which ever went into that pond came from the sky, and it could not, surely, have rained fish? The sole explanation was that the black fish were the children of the goldfish.

Yet there was something a little scandalous about this explanation which prevented me from accepting it at once. It seemed incredible that goldfish should have black children. Had a black fish got into the pond, and had something unholy been going on? But where, *where* could the black fish have come from? Had one of the goldfish Negro blood in its veins? It all seemed inexplicable. I asked my father, and he said he had never heard of anything like it, so that it shows that there really was a problem, because my father seems to have heard of most things to do with animals.

Then, slowly, the mystery cleared up. Or, rather, the objects of the mystery began to disappear. For one by one the little black fish began to turn gold! It was like a fairy story. At first there was a bronzed gleam on two or three of the fish. Then one day I noted an authentic speck of gold. Soon after that half the fish in the pond were piebald, while about twenty had shed all trace of black, and were going about in coats as brilliant as the original goldfish. Today there are several hundred beautiful glittering creatures, who disport themselves with the utmost grace, and do not flicker a fin, however abruptly you come upon them.

§ 7

Of course, one could go on like this *ad infinitum*. For example, I have only to look out of my window to see a miracle. It is an old, hollow, shredded trunk. Its bark is like rotten black cardboard. Tap it and you hear only a dull, unresilient thud. Were you to throw such stuff on a fire, it would hardly crackle, so far do its dim roots stretch into the dank and musty past.

Yet, through this sad and deathly passage, there flows a stream of eager life. For this is a jasmine, and high above the father trunk the branches take on a strange green life. Old, old as the jasmine may be, it still spangles the early September days with quivering stars of silver, darts and foams and sheds its sweet spray over my wall on many bright mornings. It is tenuous yet strong, delicate and dainty, but there is steel in its passionately curling branches. Steel, or some magic elixir that conjures up these starry flowers from a source so evidently moribund. It is the mystery of birth in death.

The birth of plants would form a theme for many sermons. My last miracle is concerned with the birth of a rose geranium. To a professional gardener it will not be a

SUMMER

miracle at all, but to many men it may seem as strange as it did, in those days, to me. For the average man's ignorance about the processes of reproduction in plants is far deeper than the average child's ignorance of similar processes in human beings. He seems to imagine that trees are brought in a black bag, and that crocuses fall from the mouths of storks. The only plant with whose genesis he is really familiar is the mistletoe, owing to the somewhat embarrass⁄ing ordeal which all mistletoes have to endure before they can establish themselves in life.

Of the mysteries of cuttings and layerings and divisions he knows nothing. It is a great pity. I do not mind sexual ignorance in the adolescent—in fact, I prefer it to the hideous precocity which certain shrill educationalists wish to thrust upon the modern young. I think that the actions of sexual intercourse are, by the ordinations of anatomy, essentially grotesque, ugly, and indecent. No amount of purple romantic veils can conceal this elementary bio⁄logical fact. I grow hot and restive when I read novels about heroines who lie down on banks of heather, submit to a long embrace, and then discover, to their great surprise, in the following October, that they are about to have a baby. Certain very definite and very ludicrous things have to be done before one has babies. One cannot have them with one eye on the sunset and the other eye on the *Oxford Book of English Verse.*

Plants do things much more delicately. I did not realize how delicately till the episode of the rose geranium.

The air was full of bronze whirling leaves, the rooks cawed distractedly, and underneath the great chestnut tree there echoed the perpetual plomp, plomp of nuts falling, splitting open when they hit the road, and sending the polished nuts spinning into the wet grass. I went out into the garden and stood facing the wind. I was excited. I remember that I was humming the prelude of César Franck's Prelude, Aria and Fugue. It is a grand thing to hum when there is a tang in the air and the sense of a dark cloak soon to be drawn over the world. Then I saw the rose geranium.

It was shivering. One blossom endured bravely on the end of a stalk. It looked like a little hat . . . the summer hat that some wretched woman might hold on her head if she were caught in a thunderstorm at a garden party. The flower seemed to be appealing to me: 'Take me in, take me in, take me in . . . the frost is on its way . . . soon it will be here to kill me . . . take me in!'

I bent down. What was one to do? I did not dare to root up the whole plant and put it in a pot. That seemed too drastic a business altogether. Yet something had to be done. The rose geranium was a lady in distress. One could not pass on and leave her bewailing in the storm, clinging onto her little pink hat with tired green fingers.

Then dimly through my mind floated the word 'cutting'. Why should I not take a cutting of the rose geranium and put it in the greenhouse for the winter? Well, if you are a professional gardener you will be quite justified in asking impatiently, 'Why not, indeed? What is all the fuss about —a simple geranium cutting? Ridiculous!'

But you must remember that this was my first autumn in the garden. I had never 'taken a cutting' before. And though I had heard that it could be done, was indeed done, on a very large scale, the idea, when one came to put it into practice, seemed so fantastic that it made me tremble with apprehension.

Do you not realize that the whole thing is miraculous? It is exactly as though you were to cut off your wife's leg, stick it in the lawn, and be greeted on the following day by an entirely new woman, sprung from the leg, advancing across the lawn to meet you. Surely you would be surprised if, having snipped off your little finger and pushed it into a flower-pot, you were to find a miniature edition of yourself in the flower-pot a day later? Even if you were prepared for it, your wife would think the whole thing highly suspicious, and might institute proceedings for divorce.

Yet this phenomenon, which sounds like the wildest fairy-tale when you apply it to human beings, does not arouse the least interest in many gardeners, who yawn as they snip off their cuttings and push them into the appointed loam.

I am quite sure that I did not yawn as I snipped off the little branch of the rose geranium. For one thing, I was afraid that the gardener would see me and tell me that I was doing it all wrong. I did not care whether it was wrong or not. I wanted to do it all myself. So I went furtively to the greenhouse, found a pot, filled it with the richest earth I could find, and put it in.

The stem sank into the earth. I pressed it down to make it firm. I gave it a little water. Then I stood and watched it. It did nothing. It merely stood quite still, sweetly green. A faint echo of its scent drifted upwards . . . a scent that made one think of sun-kissed lemons, and roses after rain.

Then I pulled myself together, beetled my brows, squared my shoulders, and, like a strong silent man, seized the pot and hid it. And rushed out into the night.

On the next day I went down to the greenhouse very early. The rose geranium was drooping. My heart sank. I said to myself, 'It is ridiculous to imagine that it could be as simple as all that. It *must* be more difficult. One probably has to take the cutting off at a special place, on the stem, and put it in a peculiar sort of earth, and say "Ena mena mina mo" over it till it goes to sleep.' However, I gave it some water. It should have every chance.

The day after, the rose geranium had picked up. My spirits soared. But only for a brief space. For was it not quite possible that its life was only being prolonged artificially, by water? Would the leaves not have been just as fresh if the stem had merely been placed in a vase? How could one tell if the plant was really forming root? Only, apparently, by pulling it up to see. This, by superhuman effort, I refrained from doing.

And so, for another ten days I remained in an agony of doubt. The watering was continued, and after each drink the little pot was put back in its hiding place, behind a box of seedlings. But gradually, as the second week drew to an end, I began to feel more assured. When a whole fortnight had elapsed it seemed almost certain that something really was happening. The plant grew perkier every day, and even if it had been in a vase of water, its leaves could not have been a fresher green.

It was at the beginning of the third week that I knew. For as I was watering it I suddenly saw a tiny new speck of green protruding from the stem. Awed, I bent down and scrutinized it. I knew every detail of the rose geranium, and this was something that had not been there before. A moment's examination proved that it was, beyond doubt, a new shoot. In other words, the plant had taken root!

Well . . . there we are. Today I have a dozen flourish-ing bushy geraniums that have all sprung from the little cutting which was taken years ago. You will tell me that it is all very commonplace. Perhaps. However, for me it is so miraculous that I am going to draw a line, very quickly, at the end of this chapter, before I am tempted to break into blank verse.

## Chapter 9

## THE EDGE OF THE WOOD

It has been impossible in the last few chapters to keep to any system of chronology. However, we can return to it now, because we are about to enter my wood. And it was not till the third autumn that the first tree of the wood was planted. Till then, there was only an empty field, bounded on one side by the lane, on the other by the garden hedge, and elsewhere by similar fields, flat and placid, dotted with occasional elms and willows.

A word about this field. It consisted of about three acres of grass. I was very proud of it. If you stood in the extreme centre of it and shut one eye, it looked enormous. One had a sense of owning broad acres, and sweating minions, and delicious things like that. However, one could not spend one's time standing in the middle of a field, shutting one eye. People would think it peculiar. So I decided to do something with it.

Up till the moment I had done nothing with it except plant it with mushrooms which, as you may remember, did not come up. And so I decided that I would turn it into a wood.

To me all woods are enchanted. I cannot imagine being lonely in them. Nor can I share that strange psychic uneasiness which Algernon Blackwood, in several stories, has drawn from the forest's depths . . . that curous *malaise* of the spirit which some men feel when the branches are thick about them, and a thousand green arms hide the blessing of the sun. There are those who shiver and throw uneasy glances behind them when they plunge from the open country into the narrow, tortuous corridors of the trees . . . and many will skirt the borders of a wood rather than enter its dark recesses. But I feel that the trees are my friends, that I could wander naked among them, without hurt, and sleep unharmed among their sturdy roots.

Besides, there are so many exciting things to be grown in a wood. Violets among the cool mosses at the trees' roots, and spindle, that exquisite shrub which damascenes the dark November days with rosy spangles . . . the 'apple blossom of November', it should be called. There are anemones and bluebells for the spring and many brilliant berries for the autumn. And the whole sense and spirit of a wood is at once aloof and protective, for it retreats from you and yet it shelters too . . . brushing your cheeks with a sweet caress in spring, laying in autumn a pale, petalled carpet of fallen leaves at your feet, lacing the winter skies with an iron grille of frozen arms.

However, though I longed for a wood, for its own sake, I was actually impelled to begin the planting of it sooner than I had intended, owing to a chain of circumstances over which I had no control. The first circumstance was Mr Greenarm.

§ 2

One day I received a mysterious telegram from my gardener which caused me to hurry up to the cottage without a moment's delay.

When I arrived, I rushed out into the field and saw that there was every cause for alarm. Just beyond the little iron fence, within a stone's throw of my bedroom window, a small plot of ground had been pegged out for building. It transpired that the person who was going to build was Mr Greenarm. And all you could say in Mr Greenarm's favour was that he would have been a better poacher if he had not been in an almost perpetual state of intoxication.

This was horrible. The field, it is true, was not mine, but I felt that I had a moral right to it. Besides, I had hoped to buy it one day. Was it too late? I felt absolutely no moral scruples, because there was mile after mile of similar property in the district which Mr Greenarm could have bought equally well without plumping himself down on me. I must admit, however, that even if this little piece of land had been the last piece on earth, I should have endeavoured to prevent Mr Greenarm from securing it. For I knew the sort of place he would build. A three-roomed bungalow with a bright red roof and sanitation which is better imagined than described.

For the next twenty-four hours I worked feverishly. I discovered that Mr Greenarm had not actually signed his contract. It might be possible, said the solicitor who acted for the landowner, to persuade him to go a little farther down the road. 'And of course,' said the solicitor, 'I fully appreciate the fact that you would probably improve the district more than Mr Greenarm. . . . Oh, indeed? Did you? Are you? No, I do not know the Prime Minister personally, but if you say it is possible that he may be coming up to stay with you . . . yes, I should be delighted. Perhaps my wife too? Most kind.'

You see, in my desperation, I suggested that at any moment I was going to be descended upon by Ramsay MacDonald, Charlie Chaplin, Lord Rothermere, and Marlene Dietrich, who would all be enchanted to meet the solicitor, but would undoubtedly view with grave distaste the proximity of Mr Greenarm. It was therefore arranged that on the following day the solicitor should come out to Allways in person and discuss the whole matter on the spot, with Mr Greenarm and myself.

§ 3

I am afraid that when I saw, and smelt, Mr Greenarm I was seized with an extreme distaste for the lower classes. He was very small, with eyes like a malign ferret, and a thin red moustache that looked like a prawn's whiskers. He spoke in a low, whining voice.

When I was first introduced to Mr Greenarm, in my field, I tried to be very bluff and hail-fellow-well-met, as though he were some elegant and charming person whose acquaintance I had long been seeking.

'Ah, Mr Greenarm!' Even as I said it I wondered how such an astonishing aroma could possibly come from any living creature.

'Huh!' he said.

'I see we're both after the same bit of land, what? Ha! Ha!' I glanced quickly round to see if it could possibly be some very unhealthy pig which was responsible for the aroma. But no. It *must* be Mr Greenarm. So I took out a handkerchief and for the remainder of the conversation spoke through it in muffled tones, occasionally turning my head and taking a deep breath.

'It's 'ard luck,' said Mr Greenarm, 'when a working man can't buy a little bit o' land.'

'Come, come,' said the solicitor, 'you know quite well that I've offered you a dozen similar plots at a reduced rate.'

THE EDGE OF THE WOOD

'Very 'ard luck,' repeated Mr Greenarm.

Booming through the handkerchief, I inquired, 'What exactly was it about this particular plot that you liked so much?'

'I've got to be near my work, 'aven't I?'

'Now, really,' interposed the solicitor, 'six of the plots I showed you were a good half mile nearer to your work than this.'

'And supposin' I don't always work in the same place?' he demanded querulously. This was so strange and baffling a question that neither of us could think of an adequate reply.

I removed the handkerchief for a moment, took a deep breath, and said, 'But I still don't see why this *particular* plot of land . . .'

'I've took a fancy to it,' observed Mr Greenarm.

This was really dreadful. For here was a reason with which I entirely sympathized. After all, Mr Greenarm was entitled to take a fancy to a piece of land just as much as I was. The whole thing was really very difficult. Here he was, standing in the middle of my field, with folded arms, saying that he had taken a fancy to the piece of land, and smelling like nothing on earth. It was too complicated.

The solicitor saved the situation:

'Nonsense!' he said sharply.

Mr Greenarm scowled at him. 'It's 'ard luck when a working man—'

'Nonsense!' repeated the solicitor. 'You talk as though you were homeless. You already have a house on the hill over there.'

'I don't like that 'ouse no more.'

I regarded Mr Greenarm with increasing respect. He certainly had the courage of his whims.

117

'Perhaps not. But at least you've *got* it. You want to build another. You've been offered exactly the same sort of land, with the same hedges, the same trees, the same water, or lack of it—'

Mr Greenarm looked up to the sky. 'That's as may be. But the fact of the matter is this 'ere gentleman don't want a working man as a neighbour.'

This was so poignantly true that I almost dropped my handkerchief.

'Working man!' snapped the solicitor. 'I'm a working man. We're all working men. Don't talk to us about working men, *if* you please.'

I felt that Mr Greenarm was being bullied. And in spite of his fierce perfume, I did not want to hurt his feelings.

'Really,' I protested, 'you've got it all wrong. It's nothing to do with *you*.' I took a deep breath, gulped, and went on. 'I should feel exactly the same if—well, if the Prince of Wales wanted to put up a bungalow there.'

This, unfortunately, had an effect upon Mr Greenarm very different from that which I had intended. It appeared to arouse him to a frenzy of resentment.

'Prince of Woiles?' he cried. 'What's the Prince of Woiles want in this village?'

'He doesn't want anything. I was only saying . . .'

''Asn't the Prince of Woiles got henough 'ouses of 'is hown halready?'

'Of course. I merely meant—'

'Yus. You *meant*!' Infinite scorn radiated from Mr Greenarm. 'You *meant*!'

He glared at us both. Then he said : 'Very well, gentlemen. If that's the way it is, I'll take my money elsewhere. Yes, *sir*. Elsewhere. You can keep your bloody land!'

And then, without further warning or argument, he

lumbered off. A skunk-like effluvium lingered after him.

'Quite,' said the solicitor. 'A highly undesirable neigh-bour.'

'Highly,' I agreed, thinking how very appropriate the word was.

§ 4

However, in spite of the rout of Mr Greenarm, it is possible that I might not have bought the land, nor planted the wood, but for the international situation.

It was a question of seeking shelter. I wanted somewhere to hide in. Things looked so dreadful everywhere. When-ever I opened the paper I saw that my pitiful little holdings in various industrial shares had slid still farther down the slope. Everything seemed to be cracking up. England was unutterably weary; America was in the throes of a nervous breakdown; Germany had consumption; Italy was suffer-ing from delusions of grandeur; Spain was about to be sick; Russia had delirium tremens; and France had an acute attack of hysteria following indigestion. The world seemed vulgar, irrational, and dangerous. And so I said to myself, selfishly, 'I will make my wood and hide while there is yet time.'

There was something very fascinating in this idea. I planned to glower out at the world through the branches. Then, if I saw anybody awful coming along, I would rush behind a tree trunk and pretend not to be there. When the revolution came, the mob would march down my lane, see the wood, and pass by. If they happened to see me and chase me, I could climb a tree and deliver a polite address on the economic situation, combined with a request that, as they went out, they would not trample on the delphiniums.

My mind was therefore made up. I bought the field. The wood should be planted at once.

§ 5

It was a lovely day when I entered the nursery gardens. A yellow September day that smelt like the rind of a lemon. My heart beat fast with excitement as I drew up at the gate and walked down the empty drive. All around me were flourishing shrubs and trees. In my pocket was a fat wad of notes, earned by writing faintly insulting articles on "the modern girl". All that was lacking was somebody to come and take my order.

I wandered about, down empty avenues, through deserted shrubberies. I have since discovered that one always does this when one goes to a nursery garden. Nobody is ever there. However, on this, my first visit, the absence of human life struck me as a little odd. I felt like pulling the branch of a weeping willow and crying, 'Miss.' At last, turning a corner, I saw an enormous young man crouched in a peculiar position in a small green bush. I could not help recalling one of the most significant of Lear's limericks, and slightly changing it to suit the situation, I advanced towards him, murmuring:

> *'There was an old man who said, "Hush!*
> *I perceive a young man in this bush!"*
> *When they said, "Is he small?"*
> *He replied, "Not at all!*
> *He is four times as large as the bush!"'*

I told the young man that I would like to order a wood, if it pleased him, and it appeared to please him so much that he put his fingers in his mouth and produced an ear-splitting whistle. Instantly, the gardens came to life. It seemed as though managers slid down the trunks of trees and clerks dropped like walnuts from the topmost branches. Eventually from this gathering there detached himself a small man of evident authority, who was the top man of all. We will call him Mr Honey, because it is very like his real name, and it fits him perfectly.

Mr Honey talked exclusively in Latin.

The first thing I said to him, after explaining that I wanted to buy a wood, was that I liked 'that big bush with red berries over there'.

'*Crataegus pyracantha crenulata yannanensis,*' crooned Mr Honey.

I took a deep breath, and was about to reply when Mr Honey waved his arm to the right and murmured:

'*Ribes sanguineum splendens.*'

This, I felt, was enchanting. One had a sense of being a young disciple walking by the side of his master. Overhead there was the clear enamelled sky, all around were flowers and bushes, exquisitely displayed. And through the still air, as we walked, came the dulcet tones of Mr Honey, speaking Latin.

'*Cornus mascula alba variegata,*' he observed diffidently.

I racked my brains for a suitable reply. But all I could think of was '*Et tu, Brute?*' which is the worst of a classical education.

So I said, very weakly, 'I would have liked to see how big one can put in chestnuts.'

Mr Honey gave me a wistful smile. '*Cytisus scoparius andreanus,*' he whispered.

However, he showed me the chestnuts. He showed me a great many other things. And here is the bill for the first list of trees which I ever ordered:

| | £ | s. | d. |
|---|---|---|---|
| 4 Standard limes | 2 | 10 | |
| 4 Standard silver birches | 2 | 10 | |
| 2 Standard laburnums | 1 | 1 | |
| 2 Standard mountain ashes | 1 | 5 | |
| 2 Standard English elms | 3 | 3 | |
| 6 Austrian pines | 2 | 5 | |
| 4 Douglas firs, Colorado variety | 1 | | |
| 2 Rosa Moyseii | | 7 | |
| 1 Horse-chestnut | 1 | 1 | |
| 2 Standard cut-leaf birches | 1 | 11 | 6 |
| 2 Standard walnuts | 2 | 2 | |
| 2 *Abico colorados* | 1 | 1 | |
| 6 Nuts Merveille de Boluryller | 1 | 10 | |
| 1 Standard sycamore | | 10 | |
| 1 Standard *Maple dasycarpum* | | 10 | 6 |
| 1 Standard thorn, double crimson | | 10 | 6 |
| 20 stakes tar cord and hessian | 1 | 1 | |
| Foreman's time preparing and planting | | 15 | |
| Bus fare and out-of-pocket expenses | | 2 | 9 |
| Special delivery by road. Calling | 1 | 4 | 9 |
| 1 bundle and packing | | 10 | 6 |
| 3 stakes | | 3 | |
| | £26 | 14 | 6 |

It sounds very modest. It was. For, in those days, I had myself well in hand. Today, it is different. I have a dreadful suspicion that before I have finished with my wood it will cost me every penny of five hundred pounds.

§ 6

However, if you know a trick or two, there are ways in which you can fill out your wood with comparatively small expense. I have not yet reached the stage where I can record the exciting progress of the trees from the nursery, down the Great North Road, along the narrow lanes, into my little field. I must first explain the episode of the willows.

I had paid several visits to the nursery, and after each visit I left behind me orders for quantities of trees. In my soberer moments I began to worry about the bill. It would be terrible to have to write more articles about the modern girl. On the other hand, it would be still more terrible to have huge gaps in my wood. So I approached my father—as one does, in moments of crisis. My father is as poor as every﹅body else's father, nowadays, but he really does *know* about woods and trees and plants. Which is one of the most irritating things about him.

'I am planting a wood,' I said.

'Humph!' he replied.

'It seems to be very expensive,' I observed, 'to plant a wood.'

He looked up from *The Times*, glared at me, and said, 'Humph!' again.

'I wondered'—and I spoke as casually as possible—'if you could suggest any cheap trees . . . just to fill in . . . or something that grows very quickly . . . perhaps a peculiar sort of acorn?'

My father said, 'Humph!' for the third time and arranged to come up on the following week﹅end.

I am very glad he came up, because it was through him that I learnt many of the trees' more adorable habits. Up till now I knew practically nothing about trees. I had only old scraps of miscellaneous information. For example, I knew that ash buds were black in March. But I knew it not from observation but from Tennyson, and I knew it not from reading Tennyson but from reading *Cranford*. Do you remember the passage? It occurs in the chapter which is called 'A Visit to an Old Bachelor'. It goes like this:

We came upon an old cedar-tree, which stood at one end of the house—

'*The cedar spreads his dark-green layers of shade.*'

'Capital terms—"layers!" Wonderful man!' I did not know whether he was speaking to me or not; but I put in an assenting 'wonderful'. . . .

He turned sharp round. 'Ay! you may say "wonderful". Why, when I saw the review of his poems in *Blackwood*, I set off within an hour, and walked seven miles to Misselton (for the horses were not in the way) and ordered them. Now, what colour are ash-buds in March?'

Is the man going mad? thought I. He is very like Don Quixote.

'What colour are they, I say?' repeated he, vehemently.

'I am sure I don't know, sir,' said I, with the meek-ness of ignorance.

'I knew you didn't. No more did I—an old fool that I am!—till this young man comes and tells me. "Black as ash-buds in March." And I've lived all my life in the country; more shame for me not to know. Black: they are jet-black, madam.' And he went off again, swinging along to the music of some rhyme he had got hold of.

So now, whenever I go for a country walk with a friend in

March I always lead the footsteps, and the conversation, in the direction of ash buds, thereby gaining an undeserved reputation for literary erudition.

Valuable as is this information, however, it is far from exhaustive. There are a great many things to be learnt about a wood that have nothing whatever to do with ash buds. One of these things was taught me by my father as soon as he arrived. He examined the list of trees I had ordered, and said, 'Humph! Let's go and look at this field of yours.'

In the field he tramped about, making hissing noises. Then he turned to me and said:

'Why aren't you having any willows?'

I was unaware that I was not having any willows. So I said, 'I'm not very fond of willows.'

'What d'you mean—not very fond of willows?'

I did not really mean anything at all. 'I don't think they'd do very well here,' I suggested.

'Do very well? *Do* very well?' He snorted and waved his stick in the direction of the neighbouring fields. 'What's the matter with those?'

I looked where he was pointing. Dotted all over the fields were charming trees with leaves of glistening silver and thick gnarled trunks. I realized that these must be willows. Looking back on it, I find it difficult to believe that I really did not know they were willows. Today I think that I could tell the name of most trees that grow in the United Kingdom, even if you blindfolded me.

'Oh!' I said.

'Good God!' snorted my father. 'You don't deserve to have a property if you don't even know a willow when you see one. This place was made for willows. You could grow any amount of 'em.'

'I'll order some at once.'

'Order them? What d'you want to order them for? All you've got to do is to strip off as many branches as you want and stick 'em in the ground.'

'Stick them in the ground?'

'Certainly.'

'Do you mean that they'll grow, like that?'

He cast a despairing glance at me. Then he said, 'Come on, we'll go and find old W. He's got a pond with enough willows to set you up for life.'

We found old W., and we all set out in the direction of the willow pond. It was a cold, squelchy day, with a whipping wind. My father was in his element. His heart has always been close to the land. A natural current of sympathy seems to spring up, instantly, between him and any agricultural labour. He knows what to say and when to say it. Screwing in his eyeglass, he looks over a field and says something terrific about the turnips, and the agri⁄cultural labourer gives an admiring grunt and agrees. Or he prods his stick into some apparently innocuous clod and observes that it is . . . what? I forget the right sort of adjectives. I would give a lot to be able to talk like that. I think it is silly to be amateur about anything when one has an opportunity of learning. But I have not yet learnt about soils and the rotation of crops and all those exciting mysteries. I shall, one day.

When we arrived at the pond my father explained what he wanted.

'You can take 'em off here,' he said to old W., pointing to the place where the willow branch joined the main stem.

'Cut 'em, sir?'

'No, strip 'em,' said my father. He was evidently pleased that old W. did not know this particular trick. He began to explain.

126

'Strip 'em,' he said. 'Then shove 'em in about eighteen inches. We'll show you the places where they want to go. Of course, they'll need stakes to prevent 'em getting wind rocked. Now, about your fee for this little job . . .'

Whereupon my father and old W., with mutual relish and mutual respect, proceeded to bargain with each other. Having been accustomed to pay anything from a pound upwards, with numerous extras, for each of my trees, I was prepared to hear that I should have to pay at least ten pounds for the twelve willows. My respect for my father was never greater than when he finally settled with old W. to pay a shilling for each willow, with a pint of ale as a benefice.

*Chapter 10*

## IN THE WOOD

By the middle of November I had ordered about sixty trees. In addition to these, we had the twelve willows, by arrangement with Mr W. We also had a miscellaneous collection of my own which I had been secreting for months past. This collection included a small green shoot which I had grown in a pot from an orange pip, several peach stones, a rather disgusting-looking sycamore, and a few harsh and repellent trees from Harrod's in pale pink pots that had been saved from a dull Christmas party the year before.

However, all things considered, I felt that we were well on the way to a wood.

Now, I had observed, in the woods through which I have wandered, a regrettable lack of design. True, I desired nothing formal. . . . I needed no darkly eloquent avenues of yews, nor did I hanker after terraced groves of cypresses. (A lot of good it would have done if I *had* hankered!) But I had certain ideas which may be classified under the general heading of 'significant form'.

By 'significant form', as applied to my wood, I mean that I did very definitely desire to create, in time, certain vistas that should be aesthetically harmonious. If you choose to put it bluntly, I suppose that you could say that I wanted to put tall trees behind short ones, and light bushes against dark. But I do not choose to put it as bluntly as that. After all, I am writing this book, and so far this book has not

128

been at all blunt. It has whispered and rustled, and it will go on whispering and rustling . . . as long as I have any-thing to do with it.

'Significant form.' Often I have recalled that phrase, as I have stood at the gateway to my field, looking out on to the wood that is still in the making. I have seen a line of trees, and behind it the grey, ribbed sky. In the foreground a splash of lush grass. Green at one's feet, grey overhead, and in between the green and the grey is the black and silver pattern of the trees. These are the enchanted moments when one can play with Nature as an artist plays with a brush . . . when there is an imaginary pencil in one's hand, with which one traces, against the pale horizon, an ever changing network of branch and leaf. Here, behind this puny oak, we will plant a poplar . . . a gay green torch to salute the sun. There, in that space, we need the autumnal blaze of sycamores. And as soon as the first tint of colour has come into one's mind, there is an answering blaze from one's whole dormant imagination, and the mind's eye is dazzled with fairy flames of elms unborn, of unknown oaks and ghostly maples.

§ 2

Let us descend to facts.

When I first began my wood I decided to concentrate on a space about eighty yards square. It sounds absurdly small, but you have no idea how many trees such a space will swallow up. The more trees you put in, the larger seem the gaps between them.

I did not want my wood to be square, so I bulged one side of it in and out. People did not seem to get my meaning and asked me if the trees on that side were not a little out of place. I replied, somewhat impatiently, that I wanted the edge of my wood to look like a wave spending itself on the seashore. To which they replied that it did not look at all like that . . . it only looked like a few limes, chestnuts, and elms, sticking out a long way from the rest of the trees.

But gradually, as the edge filled up, they caught the idea. To help their blind eyes I filled a can with weed killer and traced a long, very wavy path all through the grass along the wood's edge. (This is a very good way of making a path in a field, in case you have never thought of it.)

To give the effect of spray, I ordered a quantity of double cherries, double almonds, weeping crabs, brooms, and half a dozen of that exquisite shrub, *Exochorda grandiflora*, popularly called the Pearl Bush. It is indeed well named, for the blossoms on a good specimen look like ropes of milk-white pearls swaying in the breeze.

Then I sat down and waited. Or rather, I stood up and waited. I have never known a winter pass more slowly. True, I had the excitement of the winter flowers, but even these could not entirely hold my attention. Moreover, I was constantly driven to distraction by the uncanny appearances of Mrs M., who had a habit of popping up unexpectedly from behind a hedge when I was wandering about stroking the tree trunks and looking for buds.

'Well . . . they're still there!' she would bark at me.

'Yes,' I replied, without encouragement.

'Haven't you finished counting them yet? Ha! Ha! He! He!'

The blackest glances never prevented her from laughing at this dreadful joke, nor did she ever fail to follow it up with:

'Quite a forest, haven't you? Ha! Ha! Ho! Ho!'

I said before that I was convinced that Mrs M. was a witch, and I was more than ever certain of it now. She was always asking if she might come into my wood, but I would never let her. I was taking no chances.

At last the leaves began to come out. First the golden-brown buds of the double cherry unfolded, then the lovely sticky pods of the horse-chestnuts, then the mountain ashes and the maples.

Looking back on that first year, I wonder if I shall ever find again the rapture which was aroused by those first pale flowers. Those few hesitant leaves, those sparse and spectral berries! Will the stronger, more lavish fruits of later years ever cause the heart to beat quite so quickly in gratitude and in anxiety?

What had I? So little that you may well laugh at it . . . nor shall I care if you laugh, for you cannot laugh away the memory of my delight. A few pink paper blossoms of the double cherry, some guelder-roses that might have come from a doll's house, one pink horse-chestnut flower—yes, only one, but it was at the very top of the tree, and it looked very grand—a little spring broom, some summer broom, about three flowers of a mock orange, a few thin threads of mountain-ash berries, one or two sprays of holly. In the flower and berry time, that was all.

Nor was there much in the tree line. But only one tree died. That was the big elm which, against the advice of Mr Honey, I had insisted on having transplanted from the nurseries. It was to have been my King of the Forest, but it died. As the spring grew later and later and gave way to early summer, and as its boughs remained black and leafless, my heart sank within me. I felt like a murderer. It had looked so strong and happy when I had seen it in the nursery garden . . . and now, it was dead. It is a dreadful thing to kill a tree, and often, when I am walking through the little wood, I shy and almost stumble, as though I had run into an unseen trunk. And then I realize I am walking over the grave of the elm that I had killed.

All the willows did wonderfully, much to the disgust of Mrs M. It was an unhappy spring for her. She made as much capital as she possibly could out of the death of the elm, but even she could not be entirely blind to the flourishing condition of the other trees.

She therefore made the most of the gaps. There was nothing at all in the centre of the field. So she would stare at the blank space fixedly and say:

'Quite a sight, isn't it?'

I agreed.

'They'll need thinning out soon. Ha! Ha! He! He!'

'They will, when I've put in all the things I've ordered for this autumn.'

She shot me a barbed glance. 'You rich young authors!'

Then she discovered some of my old articles on the modern girl. She must have read them in a dentist's waiting room, or somewhere like that, for she was far too mean to buy a magazine for herself. She had a strange instinct for choosing the one subject of conversation which was likely to irritate, and she realized that any reference to these articles irritated me. Therefore she referred to them on every possible opportunity.

Popping up over the hedge, she would say:

'What weather!'

'Awful, isn't it?'

'I've just been reading your fascinating article on what you would buy your wife. Tell me, do you really mean all you write?'

'I don't know. Why?'

'Would you really buy your wife a mirror so that she could see how old she was getting?'

'Whatever put that idea into your head?' I exclaimed. 'A mirror's the last thing I should buy any woman. Mirrors are congenitally incapable of telling the truth.'

Mrs M. shot out her rabbit teeth in a fierce grimace. 'But you said . . .'

'Oh . . . I see. What I said then has nothing to do with it. I've changed my mind.'

'But surely . . .'

## § 3

Enough of Mrs M. It is a shame to taunt her so. Everything seemed to conspire against her. Even the weather. For the first spring which followed the planting of my wood was one of the wettest that England ever knew . . . in fact, nothing could have been wetter, except the summer that succeeded it. Day after day I would rise from my bed, draw the curtains, and gaze out upon the driving rain. Normally, I should have been driven to a frenzy by this weather, but now, I could purse my lips, suppress a shudder, and say to myself, 'Well, it's very good for the trees.'

This, I must observe in passing, is one of the delights of being a gardener. Whatever the weather, however sportive the elements, you can always console yourself by the thought that it is indeed an ill wind that blows no plant any good. Even when the Great Earthquake came—do you remember it, in the spring of 1931?—I lay in bed, listening to the rattle of ornaments on the mantelpiece, and murmured to myself, 'This will make some nice healthy cracks in the new herbaceous border.' When the winter is hard and loath to depart, you can draw your overcoat tighter about you and gain comfort from the thought that no early fruit blossoms are being tempted to make a premature début. When the sun is bright and yellow there are, obviously, a thousand reasons for rejoicing. And even when the November winds are fierce and chill, you may allow your mind to dwell on the goodness which the ground is receiving from an early and plentiful diet of decaying leaves.

Of course, one does not always exercise this Pollyanna optimism. Often one frets and curses and despairs. But in this summer . . . the first summer of my wood . . . I did indeed gain much consolation, during the long and dreary rains, from the thought of those young roots, so thin, so delicate, so thirty.

## § 4

It is yet too early to tell of any real woodland enchantments. My wood is still only a glorified plantation. There are many gaps still to fill, when I can afford to fill them. But I have learnt a great many lessons, and before I leave the shelter of these trees in which we have been wandering, I would pass a few of those lessons on to you.

Firstly, do not buy your trees too big. This is a terrible temptation for the amateur. I had many arguments with Mr Honey about it. I used to see mountain ashes twenty feet high, and spiraeas the size of a grown man, and hollies that came up to my shoulder, and I would demand that they should be promptly transplanted to my field. Usually, he managed to dissuade me, but on the few occasions when I won the argument I always lost the tree.

Of course, if you are a Rothschild, and can afford to pay a hundred pounds to transplant half Northamptonshire, clinging in pained surprise to a solitary beech, you are in a different case. But if you are like me, you will get much better value for your money by catching 'em young. Besides, there are many consolations. Even if you cannot look up to towering branches, you can look down to tender shoots. There is something lamb-like and poignantly innocent about the shrill green of a baby walnut tree. And all the very young conifers are fascinating, for you can almost see them grow. Half the fun of a wood is this memory of growth . . . this happy mental catalogue of branches that began as babies, are now reaching manhood, and one day will shelter you as you creep slowly beneath them towards the dying sun.

Secondly, do not plant your trees too close together. These pieces of advice sound absolutely infantile, I know. You can find them expressed with a far greater wealth of detail in any sixpenny handbook. But I must emphasize my point. For the planter of a wood is so unreasonably impatient. There must be a thicket here, a close cluster there . . . it is all a flurry and a jumble. If you are old, then there is some excuse for this fluster. But if, like me, you have a reasonable expectation of forty years of life, there is no excuse whatever. After all, trees *do* grow. Branches *do* stretch out, and trunks *do* swell. They stretch and swell quite a lot even in five and twenty years. And it is then, I calculate, that my wood will be most precious to me.

Thirdly, distrust catalogues. I would not say this about flowers, but I say it most emphatically about trees. The average tree catalogue shows you, as an example of a tulip tree, a specimen that was planted by Queen Anne in Kew Gardens in 1708 and has been deluged with liquid manure ever since. If you order a tulip tree, on the strength of that

illustration, you will be bitterly disappointed by the slum‚
like stalk which is eventually delivered to you, by a sulky
car man, wrapped up in sacking (the tree, not the car man).
The only sensible way to order trees is to visit your nearest
nursery and see the actual tree you wish to buy. Then there
will be no disappointments. Moreover, you should visit
the nursery on every month of the year in order to see what
is out, what looks well in this month, and what flourishes
in your district.

Finally—and this is extremely important, though it may
sound frivolous—you should have a couple of cocktails
before making your tour of the nursery garden, because a
slight drunkenness clears the eye and frees the spirit. If you
visit a nursery entirely sober, you are inclined to linger too
long at the entrance and to hurry over the latter part. More‚
over, you will be inclined to haggle, and really it is useless
to haggle when you are gardening.

If you have one or two excellent dry martinis, well iced,
your visit will be far more satisfactory, not only to yourself
but to the proprietor of the nursery. For you will leap from
your car, see a divine splash of pink in a far corner, hail the
attendant with the cleanest face, and cry: 'I must have a
dozen of those!' And then you will dance off down the
nearest path, always followed by the clean attendant, and
you will swerve, instinctively, towards the lovely, coloured,
gracious things, and you will order them without stint.
The after effects are terrible, of course, but it pays.

Had I not been slightly intoxicated at the time I should
never have ordered my avenue of *Viburnum plicatum*. I saw
this exquisite thing on an evening in June, after several
toasts in an old inn. Do you know it? It is a lovely sister of
the guelder‚rose, which was always called 'the snowball
tree' by one's nurse. The guelder‚rose is, in itself, a sweet

creation. It hangs its gay wares in the stiffest breeze, and stretches its lively roots in the hardest soil. But it cannot compare in beauty with the *Viburnum plicatum*. The *Viburnum plicatum* is whiter, waxier, and of a far more poignant loveliness.

## Chapter 11

## THE PROFESSOR

Meanwhile, people were coming and going at the cottage.

Mostly they were young men who arrived in snorting cars, glanced at the garden through the window, and said in one breath, 'Awfully jolly, d'you weed yourself? Thanks . . . I'd rather have a sherry really.' I happen to to like young men like that.

Or there were young women who also arrived in snorting cars, looking adorable, glanced at the gardener through the window, and said in one breath, 'Divine, d'you weed yourself? No, thanks . . . I'm on a diet.' I happen to like young women like that.

There were also a few old friends who did not talk about the garden, but just went out into it quietly and loved it. They showed their love (and also their tact as guests) by spending whole mornings on their knees, pulling up weeds.

There were very few real gardeners, because I have learnt from bitter experience that real gardeners are not very good value on anybody else's garden. They are always thinking of their own. This sort of dialogue takes place:

Myself (showing the herbaceous border): There's nothing like this cosmos for September, is there? . . . I mean, for making a real show.

Real Gardener: You *must* see my pink larkspur. Heavenly. Do come down one day. It's only an hour from London.

138

Myself: I'd love to. These Japanese anemones are rather fine, I always think. I divided them from one root two years ago.

Real Gardener: Yes. And if you come down next week-end you'll be in time for my coreopsis.

Myself: My own coreopsis is . . .

Real Gardener: Oh, yes . . . I see . . . over there. You really must come. You change at Dorking.

Myself (harshly): All these dahlias were grown from seed.

Real Gardener: Yes . . . yes . . . you *must* see the amazing dahlia I've grown . . . and after you've changed at Dorking it's only twenty minutes, and I can meet you in the car.

I think that gardeners must be like parents. No parent wants to talk about anybody else's child. His own son's adenoids are far more charming to him than any other infant's achievements. And I would rather shake earwigs out of my own dahlias than pick the rarest orchids from the hottest of Sir Philip Sassoon's houses.

Real gardeners, therefore, were few and far between at Allways. They were mostly nice people who came and talked and drank and took the dog out for walks and were very pleased to go away laden with flowers.

However, in addition to these, there was the Professor. And I really think that he deserves a chapter to himself.

§ 2

'Why should a wheel be round? Why should it not be square or triangular?' That was one of the first questions he ever asked me, when I went to interview him years ago, for a Sunday newspaper. I was a raw young reporter at the time, and I felt that I had discovered a gold mine of copy. If a professor could ask such astonishing questions about a wheel, what might he not say about 'the modern girl'? Which was the problem chiefly agitating editors at the time.

The Professor, in those days, was more or less my monopoly. He is internationally famous now, but he still looks very young. He has a shock of jet-black hair, a charming absent-minded smile, and the largest spectacles any man ever wore. He is the most spiritual man I know. He is completely indifferent to food, sleep, and drink. He has a great contempt for his body . . . and for everybody else's body too. He thinks bodies are crude and hampering things . . . not nearly so pretty nor so clean as a nice engine. His only form of sensuality is smoking. A cigarette is never out of his mouth. As soon as one burns low, he lights another from its stump.

I met him at the railway station. He was at the other end of a long, crowded platform, but there was no difficulty in locating him, because everybody in the neighbourhood was turning round to stare at him. Not that he looked odd or eccentric. He was merely indulging his old habit of taking notes. And when anybody takes notes on a crowded railway platform, the British public instantly concludes that he is either a private detective or a lunatic. Especially when, in order to take the note, he stops abruptly, to the great perturbation of porters wheeling barrows, sets down his suitcase, sits on it, scribbles a few lines, and then as abruptly rises again.

He sat down for the third time just before he saw me, and wrote something on the back of a cigarette card. Then he rose, greeted me, and handed me a small package.

'Your invention,' he said.

I should explain that we have an arrangement that he invents something for me every time I see him. Since he invents at least ten things a day, this is no strain on him. He does not, of course, give me important inventions, though I am sure that he would do so if I asked him. He gives me the childish ones.

This time it was a cigarette of which the ash would not drop off. 'Last time I drove in this abominable car of yours,' he said, 'I noticed that it bumped so much that the ash dropped all over your waistcoat. The ash of this cigarette will never drop off. Though it might bend slightly, in a high wind.'

It did not even bend. It stuck straight out, all the way. And when I had smoked it as far down as possible, I lifted it up by its other end, like a little sausage. A lovely invention. But a poisonous cigarette.

## § 3

To walk round the garden with him was a perpetual delight. He always said the unexpected thing.

For example, as we passed under the arch over which my grapevine has clambered, he paused and pointed to a little green bunch of grapes that was basking in the long-delayed sunlight.

'Now, I wonder what a bunch of grapes *means*?' he said.

'What it means?'

'Yes. Is a bunch of grapes a cry of joy or a cry of pain? Is that bunch saying, "Hooray, look what we've done!" Or is it merely an evidence of pimples?'

'I refuse to allow you to call my grapes pimples.'

'Then we will take it that it is a symbol of joy.'

We looked at a *Rosa moyseii* . . . one of those lovely Chinese climbers which, in autumn, are hung with masses of long coral seed pods. He felt one of these pods with his white, bony fingers.

'Is this just a single seed? Or does it contain a whole mass of seeds?'

'Why, there are thousands of seeds in it,' I said. 'Rather a waste, when you come to think of it.'

'Waste? *Waste?* Pshaw! What rot!' He flicked the pod impatiently and frowned at me. 'Who are you, to say that nature's wasteful? People are always saying it. It's a sort of parrot cry. Well, what conceivable justification have you got for saying it? Just because nature may produce a thousand seeds in order to grow one plant, have we any right to assume that all the other seeds are wasted? We don't know—we haven't the least idea—what those other seeds are doing: whether they are falling to the ground and fertilizing it for the one chosen seed . . . whether they are affecting the waves of the ether . . .' He straightened himself and glared at me. '*The one thing of which we are certain, in an uncertain universe, is that energy is never lost. It is transformed, but it never disappears.*'

This was the theme of many conversations I had with him. He wanted to know what happened to the energy employed by my dog in running after a rubber ball. He could see absolutely no reason why I should pull up a weed, because a weed was a symbol of energy. When I observed that it needed a great deal of energy to pull up a bunch of docks he said it was I who was wasteful, and not nature.

The whole argument was a little beyond me. But I should like to recall one of his theories which he dreamily formulated that night as we stood in a field, watching the sharp yellow flames that forked up from a bonfire of dry bracken.

'That is what you would call Beauty, I suppose,' he said. 'And it worries me. It makes me sad. I don't know why it should make me sad, but perhaps it is because it is a problem which I shall never be able to solve by any scientific formula.'

'You must accept it,' I said feebly, 'for what it is.'

'Yes . . . but the sight of any beauty reminds me that I am a savage. Yes . . . a savage, with clumsy senses, and blind to a thousand things I should be able to see, deaf to a thousand things I should be able to hear. Just look at that fire. It is an example of energy, in a certain stage of develop- ment. The form of the energy is altering, but the elements are the same. The elements will be exactly the same when those bright logs are turned into dull grey ashes, and when the flames are dissipated into gas. Yet I shall come along, and shall see the ashes, and I shan't get any sense of beauty, though all around me, in the universe, are the elements which are disporting themselves so prettily at this moment. That's what I mean. It is all here, yet I can't see it. As though you had taken a word and jumbled up the letters and made it meaningless. We ought to be able to sort out the letters again and read the message without having to have them arranged for us as though we were children.' He turned away and added, almost to himself, 'However, I suppose that if we were given a gift like that, we should live in such a state of ecstasy that our idiotic bodies would not stand the strain. . . .'

At breakfast, on the following morning, he was still shaking his head morosely.

'It's a great problem, this garden of yours,' he said.

'Yes,' I replied. I was wondering if we should have to get in an extra man to scythe the orchard grass.

'A great problem,' repeated the Professor. He sipped his coffee and shook his head at a long branch of jasmine which trailed right across the window. 'That jasmine, for example.'

'Oh, that only needs trimming.'

'I didn't mean that. I meant, are we right to admire it?'

'Are we . . . *what*?'

'I mean, mayn't we be doing ourselves harm emotion-ally?'

'Oh, I see.' I realized that he was continuing his argument of the night before. 'Well, I don't think it does me much harm. I think it's a jolly good way to begin the day, looking at jasmine.'

The Professor frowned. 'It's so savage,' he muttered.

'On the contrary.'

'Intensely savage. For why should you admire it any more than you admire a beetroot or a bruise? Yesterday you went into raptures at the sight of a butterfly perched on a purple dahlia. Why? You wouldn't go into raptures at the sight of the caterpillar the butterfly came from, nor the cabbage that fed it. Why? Because you're a savage.'

'Well, you thought the butterfly was pretty yourself.'

'Because I'm a savage too.'

He threw away his cigarette and got up. As we walked into the study I strolled to the piano and played the opening bars of Bach's Italian Concerto. It seemed to match the hard brilliance of the morning outside.

'There, you see!' The Professor pointed an accusing finger at me. 'You're being savage again!'

'What, with Bach's Italian Concerto?'

'Certainly. It's all a question of stomach. All music comes from the stomach.'

'Really!'

'Listen!' There was that curious vibrating note in his voice which always came when he was very much in earnest. 'Music is rhythm, isn't it? Well, where did man get his sense of rhythm? *From the tides*! Why? Because the tides used to bring him his food. When we were jellyfish—to use a simple expression for life when it was still crawling out of the sea onto dry land—when we were jellyfish, the only thing that mattered to us was the regular ebb and flow of the tides. The tides brought us our dinner. The tides brought us life itself. And it is because of the memory of the tides that we love music.'

A fascinating theory indeed. A theory which demands that you should close your eyes, propel yourself into the past, and wander, in imagination, down some dim and steaming shore, straining your ears to catch in the sob of primeval waters the faint far echo of a saxophone.

However, the Professor did not allow me to dream about it. He had perceived several dandelions in the crazy pavement outside. And these he proceeded to attack, with regrettable savagery, and with a rusty trowel which Adam himself would have regarded as somewhat out of date.

§ 4

I am not often pleased to see Mrs M., but when, on the second day of the Professor's visit, she suddenly popped up from behind the hedge, with her rabbit's teeth glistening in the sunlight, I was delighted. For as soon as the Professor saw her he whipped out his notebook and made a note, gravely regarding her as he did so. And never did a more poignant expression of wild and baffled curiosity pass over any woman's face.

If there is one thing that Mrs M. cannot bear, it is a secret. By which, of course, I mean a secret which she cannot share. She has her own secrets—lots of them—which she cuddles close to herself in the most irritating way. When you are walking through her neat and damnably efficient house you may pause in front of a highly polished silver photograph frame containing the picture of a pretty girl and ask, 'Who's that?' Whereupon Mrs M. will wag her finger and chortle and say, 'Ah!' and refuse to tell you. The only way to worm such secrets out of her is by asserting, with steely calm, that you know the secret. For example, I once found out the name of an enchanting young creature by standing before the photograph and saying, over and over again, '*Not* a very good picture of Greta Garbo.'

'But it isn't Greta Garbo.'

'The man hasn't caught that wild look in her eyes.'

'But I tell you it *isn't* Gre . . .'

'Of course it's Greta Garbo. I know that hat.'

'Really. Considering I . . .'

'Quite. I expect they were sold out of the other positions. I must really write to Greta about it.'

After a little more of this Mrs M., in sheer desperation, told me not only the name, but the address, of the lady in question, and also her character. All of the information, unfortunately, was accurate.

This was an unpardonable diversion. But a lazy September sunlight gilds the paper as I write, and the air is heavy with dreams. One would say that there is a drug even in the flickering powder which the bees are stirring, in the purple hearts of the flowers outside my window. It is time to lay aside the pen, and sleep, and then come back, drink a cocktail, and try to catch again some of the bright sparks that still linger in the trail of the Professor.

## § 5

It is done. The cocktail, a very mild one, is drunk. But there is a tenderness in this fragrant month that lays one open to the slightest, the most delicate impressions. So that it might just as well have been a strong one.

When one is in this mood, Mrs M. is more than ever jarring.

I effected the necessary introductions. I laid particular emphasis on the 'Professor', because I knew that this would arouse Mrs M. to a frenzy of curiosity. It did.

As we walked round the garden she kept on trying to ask me, in an agitated whisper, what he was a professor of.

'Yes,' I would reply, in a loud voice, 'the asters are simply dashed to pieces by the rain.'

'Of course . . . of course,' hurriedly observed Mrs M., who was not in the least interested in asters. And then, as soon as we were round the corner, she hissed again, 'Is it science?'

To which I replied, with admitted ill manners, 'No. It's a geranium.'

'Really . . . I mean . . .'

'Ssh!' And I frowned at Mrs M. as though there were some fearful secret about the Professor which must never be divulged. It was all very childish, of course. But if you knew Mrs M. you would have behaved just as badly.

And all the time the Professor was gravely making notes.

The climax came when we reached the end of the herbaceous border in the orchard. A lot of new plants were flowering for the first time, and Mrs M., having been thoroughly thwarted, decided that here, at least, she could get back a little of her own.

'Oh, *dear*!' she cried. 'What a pity you put that fuchsia next to that Mimulus!'

'Why?' I demanded. I knew quite well what she meant, but Mrs M. does not inspire agreement. She meant that the fuchsia was a bright purple while the Mimulus was a very assertive browny-red. The two flowers destroyed one another. However, I was not going to allow Mrs M. to say so. I asked her:

'Don't you think they look nice together?'

'They *scream* at one another.'

'Oh, but I always think you can mix *any* flowers. Flower colours can't clash.' I have never thought anything of the sort, but—as previously stated—one will do anything to disagree with Mrs M.

What Mrs M. would have replied I do not know. For at this juncture the Professor again produced his notebook. Gravely regarding Mrs M. from under his black eyebrows, he scribbled something, sniffed, and put the book back in his pocket.

This was too much for Mrs M. She gave a shrill giggle and said, 'Sketching me?'

The Professor blinked. He seemed to be looking straight through her.

Mrs M. giggled again. 'I suppose I ought to be very flattered,' she continued in tones of mingled alarm and hatred. 'Ever since I came into the garden he's been taking notes of everything I said.'

Silence. She hunched up her shoulders, folded her hands in front of her, and alternately revealed and concealed her rabbit's teeth. She was breathing very heavily all the time.

Then the Professor broke the silence. He spoke with such charm and courtesy that even Mrs M. was momentarily disarmed. He said, 'I beg your pardon. But I have a bad habit of trying to remember things that interest me. You interested me just then.'

'Oh!' said Mrs M.

'Yes. It is really very simple why you are so distressed by those two colours. When the red hits you—'

'*Hits* me?'

'Hits you' repeated the Professor sharply 'you are at the same time hit—I use the word literally—by the purple. The wave lengths jangle. It is as though one wave length were designed like this . . .' and he drew a long curve in the air . . . 'and the other like this.' He drew a series of short curves. 'Your mind asks itself the question, "Which *is* it? I *will* get one of those vibrations." That is why you dislike those two colours in that border.'

I had my own theory as to why Mrs M. disliked the two colours, and that was because they happened to be in my border and not in hers. But I had no opportunity to say so, because at this point the Professor stooped down and lifted up a brick. He held it in his hand and stepped towards Mrs M.

Mrs M., in horrified fascination, retreated. Was she about to be killed? Or was she—in the words of the Sunday newspapers—on the point of being 'interfered with'?

The Professor settled the problem. 'If I were to drop this brick on your foot . . .' he began.

'*What?*' Mrs M. retreated still further.

He waved his hand negligently. 'A supposition, merely . . .'

'I should hope so, indeed!' hissed Mrs M., with a lightning glance at me, in which she managed to 'register' disgust, excitement, and outraged propriety. She could not

register any more emotions because she had to transfer her
gaze, very rapidly, to the Professor, to see what he was going
to do with the brick.

'I only said "if" . . .' repeated the Professor.

'Quite.' She revealed her rabbit's teeth, icily, for an
instant. Then her face set again, like a jelly, while the
Professor added:

'You would not say, in such circumstances, that the pain
had travelled from my hand to your foot, would you?'

'There's no knowing what I'd say.' And Mrs M., feeling
that she had delivered herself of a 'salvo', gave an unwilling
hiccup of laughter at her own joke.

The Professor blinked. Dreamily he said, 'No. You
would say that the pain was born when the brick reached
your foot. It is the same with light. Light is born when it
reaches the object it is to heat or irradiate. You cannot say
that "light leaves the sun". It does nothing of the sort. There
is no such thing as "light" . . . no such thing, I mean,
that you catch in space, and bottle, and keep. . . . It needs
*you* to bring it into existence.'

Mrs M.'s jelly face did not quiver. The Professor added:

'Do you realize,' he said, 'that when light reaches you,
the result is the same as the smell of an onion?'

Mrs M.'s jaw dropped. She glared at the Professor for an
instant. Then she closed her lips and turned towards me.
In tones of infinite elevation she said:

'I think this is a little beyond me.'

'Which is exactly what it is *not*,' cried the Professor, in
tones so extremely sharp that Mrs M. turned round as
though she were a naughty schoolgirl who had been caught
drawing peculiar objects on her slate.

'It is very foolish,' he said, 'to think that things are beyond
you when they are not. Besides, that is the whole of my

simile. As long as the thing that I am talking about, i.e. light, is *beyond* you, it does not exist. It comes to life, if you like the phrase, when it hits you.'

I wish I could recapture the rich texture of his talk, instead of being forced, so sketchily, to weave again a thin and imitative fabric. However, at least the sight of the little trio is still clear-cut in my memory. There was a bush of sweetbriar behind the Professor, that was starred with brilliant crimson berries. They seemed to be tangled in his hair. Mrs M. was standing by a white wall with the clean blue sky above her. She seemed grotesque in this simple, elemental design. I was bending down, endeavouring to persuade a worm to go away from the root of a pansy.

I felt that the conversation was getting too dangerous, so I said in a loud voice: 'This wretched worm's got no sense. It doesn't seem to understand what's required of it.'

'The worm has a great deal more sense than you imagine,' snapped the Professor.

'The *worm*!' snorted Mrs M.

'Oh, dear,' I thought, 'they're at it again.' And they were. For the Professor turned on Mrs M. and said:

'Yes, Mrs M. The worm feels your footsteps when it is underground far more acutely than you would ever feel the worm.'

Mrs M. shuffled her feet nervously. They were very large feet. She opened her mouth to reply, but the Professor got in before her.

'What do you know about insects? Nothing! That is why you think them stupid. Yet the spider's sense of touch is a miracle. And as for the dung beetle . . .'

I could not help looking at Mrs M. when this unelegant creature was mentioned. I am glad I did, for her left nostril shot straight up and stayed there, quivering.

The
Study

'The beautiful dung beetle . . .' repeated the Professor with something like ecstasy.

'The exquisite dung beetle . . . why,' he cried, '*it* makes provision for its young far more effectively than you would do, Mrs M.'

'Really,' gasped Mrs M., 'I fail to see . . .'

I should explain that the Professor had unwittingly hit Mrs M. on the raw. Her meanness towards her daughter Elsinore, an amiable anaemic who was learning to play the violin, in London, was proverbial in Allways.

'Quite,' observed the Professor. 'You fail to see. And when you do see, you fail to understand.' (In justice to the Professor, who is really the most courteous of men, I should explain that he was not really aware of Mrs M. as an individual. He was lecturing her as he would have lectured a class of rather tiresome students.)

'Your toe-nails, for example.'

And here I did *not* dare to look at Mrs M. The crisis had quite definitely arrived. One could only pray that nothing very appalling was about to happen. But it did. The Professor's voice went on, rising shrilly in the still air:

'Your toe-nails! Why do not your toe-nails shock you? Do you not realize that your toe-nails are extremely shock-ing? Do you not realize that a few years ago you were scratching roots out of the ground with your toe-nails?'

He ran his hands through his hair. 'Of course . . . I suppose I ought not to be shocked . . . but I am. Illogical of me. Because it's my own paralysing ignorance that makes things seem dreadful . . . my ignorance, I mean, of the universal scheme.'

And it was here that I looked up to find that Mrs M. had disappeared. I ran quickly after her. The Professor was still talking, quite charmingly, when I returned, twenty minutes later. (Mrs M. had been on the verge of hysterics and was almost inappeasable.)

The Professor looked up as I approached.

'Oh, there you are,' he said, with a vague smile. 'I was just working out rather an interesting theory.'

I felt a little confused and distrait, so I merely said, 'Oh?'

'About food,' continued the Professor blandly. 'It has always seemed to me very ridiculous that persons in different professions should all subsist on the same diet. Now, you are an author, I am an engineer, a chemist, and a lot of other foolish things. Doesn't it strike you that . . .'

But I cannot remember how he went on. The afternoon had proved a little too exhausting.

§ 6

It was the last day of the Professor's visit. The car was at the door. We wandered round the garden, mutely saying good-bye.

'Let me cut you a nice bunch of roses,' I said. 'Look, these dark ones are lovely . . . if you take them like this in the bud . . .'

'No . . . no . . . *please*!' There was a note of urgency in his voice which I had never heard before. I turned round in surprise.

His hands were spread out as though to protect the flowers. His forehead was wrinkled and agitated. He looked like a frightened little boy. Then he relaxed. His hands dropped to his side, and a slow, delightful grin spread over his face.

'Don't think me a fool,' he said, 'but I can't bear to have flowers cut.'

'I see.' Idiotically, I felt a little offended. I am always cutting flowers.

'It isn't that I'm trying to be aesthetic or anything damn silly like that. It isn't even that I care very much if the flower is hurt. There's so much pain in the world that one can't make every ache and agony one's own personal business. No . . . I only feel, when I stand over a flower with a pair of scissors, that the flower is looking up at me and saying, "What a *mug* you are! What a poor, God-forsaken *mug*! Don't you realize I'm living and you like me, and yet you want to bring about my death? For, the moment I'm cut, I die."'

'Yet some flowers last longer in a vase than in a garden.'

He gripped my arm. He spoke very tensely. And there was a wild wisdom in his words, which can only feebly be described. For he said:

'Yes. But we don't know what happens to the *plant* when we cut the rose. We don't know the influence, good or evil, which that action may have on the ether, nor on the roots under the earth, nor on the maggots that lie concealed in the leaves. We don't know to what extent we are impoverishing or modifying the quality of the air which we have robbed of its scent—and scent is tremendously important—we don't know how we have affected the ether radiations from the warmth of the sun.'

He paused abruptly and smiled again. 'Don't cut the flower, please,' he said.

I didn't.

As we wandered back towards the house, he summed up all his arguments, crystallized his philosophy in a few words:

'You see, I'm trying to get rid of the necessity of the Mascot.'

'The Mascot?'

'Yes. This is what I mean. Most of us find it impossible to think of anything without first doing something to our bodies. If we want to experience the pleasure of smoking we have to take out a silly little bundle of dried weeds and set them alight. We can't merely close our eyes and command the necessary sensations to affect us from the ether. They are all there, those sensations. But we cannot experience them without the little Mascot of dried weeds. It is the same with making love. We cannot cause the ecstasy to come to us. We have to worship a mascot in the shape of a body. It is the same with a rose. . . .'

He got into the car. 'They're all here . . . all your roses,' he said, and he tapped his forehead.

And that was the last I saw of him, smiling at me, his head full of roses.

## Chapter 12

## THE GREENHOUSE

I cannot remember the time when my family was not poor. There used to be money, but most of it went in the war, and after my father had sent my brothers and myself to school and to Oxford, there was little else that he could do. We had a house in Devonshire, which has now been turned into a hotel, and the garden there was exquisite, with some of the finest trees in the kingdom. But we could only afford one gardener, and it was as much as he could do to keep the grass in order.

'Why don't we have a hothouse, like the G.'s, so that we could grow grapes?' I remember asking my mother, when I was a child. She shook her head and said that hothouses were terribly expensive. I was deeply impressed. The idea grew upon me that a hothouse cost 'thousands and thousands'—that only a millionaire could have one.

Yet I have a hothouse today, and I am not a millionaire.

Here, I pause for a moment's reflection. I seem to be pausing a great deal . . . but then, there is some excuse, for the whole of this book is a wandering through a garden, a lazy pilgrimage. And at this place, I would record the curious fact that childish impressions of economics are never obliterated. If a thing was a luxury to a man when he was a child, it remains a luxury all his life.

That is why my little hothouse—though it does not cost nearly as much as the annual subscription to my club—

still fills me with faint alarm. I go out on frosty mornings
and see the pale, thin plumes of smoke coming from the
chimney, enter it and breathe deeply the temperate fragrant
air . . . and I tremble to think of the extravagance of it
all. 'This is folly . . . this is reckless squandering . . .' so
my subconscious mind tells me. It is to no avail that my
conscious mind reassures me, by the simple reflection that
the expense of the hothouse for a whole winter is not as
great as that of a single dinner at the Savoy. The feeling of
alarm remains. I feel as though I had invested in a yacht,
with a huge crew, and an appalling bill to foot every week.
All because I was told, years ago, by my mother, that
'hothouses' were 'terribly expensive'.

Yet it is worth it. Yes—the little greenhouse, with its
small stove and its single row of pipes, would be worth it
even if its upkeep involved my ruin.


§ 2


To go to the greenhouse when the weather is wild, to close
the door, to stand and listen to the wind outside, to the rain
that slashes the frail roof, to see, through the misted glass,
the black, storm-tossed branches of distant elms, to take a
deep breath, to savour to the full the strange and almost
uncanny peace which this frail tenement creates . . . to
me this is one of the truest joys which life has given.

There is a sense of escape, indeed a sense of Sanctuary.
Thus, perhaps, felt the fugitives as they clutched the altar
rails when the mob was fierce behind them. For here no
harm can come. No bitter wind can assault, no frost can
chill. I pray, indeed, that the storm outside may increase,
that the wind may rise more strongly, that the rain may

turn to sleet and beat a devilish but impotent tattoo on the crystal roof. All the sweeter, then, is the strange security of the greenhouse.

Listen! There are a thousand blustering echoes out yonder. There is a straining and a moaning in the wood, and a hissing in the hedge near by. Like the fitful beat of a cruel lash the rain is dashed against the panes, blurring them for a moment, and then leaving them water-clear, so that one sees through them a glimpse of tortured garden. And always there is the agitated treble of water gushing along the gutters into the black barrels below. But really . . . these sounds are nothing . . . they have no part in the scheme of things, as long as one remains in the green-house. In the greenhouse there is sanity and these sounds are made delusions, the ravings of a disordered mind. There is silence in here.

Silence, And yet, not quite silence. For, if you hold your breath and listen, you can hear the plants growing.

§ 3

When I first came to Allways, I took no great interest in the greenhouse. There were so many things outside it which claimed my attention. And so, on the first year, we did not even light the stove.

It was during the second winter, when I was growing excited about winter flowers, that the possibilities of the greenhouse began to dawn upon me. From the seedsmen's catalogues I discovered that many summer flowers could be brought to bloom in midwinter if they were sown in autumn, taken into the greenhouse with the first frosts, and kept in a gentle heat throughout the dark months.

And so these initial experiments were conducted with simple, hardy flowers . . . forget-me-nots, schizanthus, nemesia, and sweet peas. They all did beautifully, except the sweet peas. The temperature was never allowed to fall below forty. The schizanthus was the first to bloom . . . and I shall never forget the pride with which I transported a bunch of these orchid-like blossoms to London in mid-January. About three weeks later the forget-me-nots were ready. I had sown them in shallow earthenware bowls. They looked bluer than I have ever seen forget-me-nots before. The nemesia was rather late, but it was none the less welcome. The sweet peas failed completely. I have tried them for three years in succession and have not ever brought more than half a dozen blossoms into flower. Perhaps I maltreat them in some mysterious way. Yet, I do not know how. I sow them in the right soil, at the right time, and carry out the instructions as carefully as an anxious mother giving her child its first dose of cod-liver oil. But nothing ever happens.

On the third year I began to take the greenhouse seriously. For instance, I got the cyclamen craze. Up till then, I had only experimented in the *Cyclamen coum*, the rare and expensive outdoor variety which comes from Turkey and produces its tiny magenta flowers while the snow is still on the ground. I had not tried the large greenhouse varieties. These I now determined to grow from seed.

If you are a professional gardener you are entitled to snort with rage, and to throw the book away, saying, 'The insolence of it! Daring to write about a simple thing like that as though it were a miracle . . . when cyclamen are the simplest things to grow from seed!'

Very well. I don't care. I still think it is extraordinary. When I look at the cyclamen on my desk, with petals of

the palest ivory a cyclamen that looks like a flight of butter-
flies, frozen for a single, exquisite moment in the white
heart of Time. And then I try to think back from the
petal to the bud, from the bud to the curling stem, from
the stem to the first fan-shaped leaf, and from that leaf to the
tiny seed. And I cannot realize it. Here, in the folds of the
flower, are veins in which runs the cold sweet blood here
is a stem that rises swift and proud and a leaf of the most
delicate and fanciful creation. In its entirety it is a poem . . .
a poem that seems, somehow, to unite the formal rhythm
of the sonnet with the wild scamper of a Francis Thompson
ode.

A word of warning, however, must be issued to all who
first grow cyclamen from seed. You will read on the packet
that the seeds 'germinate' in from four to six weeks. This is
a black lie. Of course, you may say that by 'germination'
the seedsman implies some dark process which takes place
in the bowels of the earth. If so, I suppose the seedsman has
an excuse. But *I* mean, by 'germination', something that
one can actually see . . . a real cyclamen leaf pushing
through the soil. And my own experience, of some three
years, has taught me never to expect to see a cyclamen
protruding from the earth until at least three, and usually
four, months after the seed has been sown.

These gay and optimistic forecasts on the seed packets
cause one weeks of agony. When I first sowed the cyclamen
I hung over those seed boxes with fierce intensity, as the end
of the first month approached. All sorts of things happened
in them. Peculiar furry leaves sprang up, put out their
tongues at me, and vanished overnight. Were these cyclamen? Hell! Why didn't one know? Stately green spears
appeared, looking quite delightful, but less like cyclamen
than anything you have ever seen. Were these, however,

cyclamen? And if not, ought one to pull them up? Double hell! Why wasn't there somebody to tell one?

At the end of the sixth week, when the boxes contained a dazzling variety of sprouts, I was in despair. I was grateful, of course, to the sprouts. It was very nice of them to come up. But since none of them could possibly pretend to be cyclamen, my gratitude was not entirely unalloyed.

At the end of the tenth week I passed by the boxes with a faint sneer. I tried to autosuggest myself into a hatred for all cyclamen. 'Rather vulgar plants,' I muttered to myself. 'Too obvious. They make one think of bows and ribbons and fearful lattice-work pots. And hot hotel lounges. And tiresome women who live in flats with electric stoves and indigestion and a Pekinese snoring in the scullery.'

And then . . . one dank and despairing day, when the whole world was watery and chill, when the dawn was listless and the dusk came with sombre, shuffling feet, like an undertaker who arrives before the last breath has fled . . . I went out, in the fading light, and there, in the seed boxes, I found that the cyclamen had begun to live. Through the dark earth a dozen leaves, tiny but strong, had pressed. Oh . . . these were cyclamen, without any doubt . . . they held themselves sturdily against the fawning weeds . . . there was a fine flourish about them which set them apart from the rank usurpers of their place. And as I bent over them they regarded me gravely, as though they were saying, 'Well? Weren't we worth waiting for?'

§ 4

After the cyclamen I fell under the spell of the wild gipsy-like beauty of the cineraria. For they are the colour of

gipsies' scarves, these flamboyant blossoms, and there is a
gleam in their centres which is like the sun in a gipsy's eyes.
I did not know how lovely cinerarias could be, *en masse*,
till I saw them growing out of doors in Malta. It was April.
I had run away from England to try to get a little sunshine,
and had made the fatal mistake of imagining that the farther
south one went the sunnier it would be. Finding no sun on
the Riviera, I went to Algiers, which was like Manchester
in November, with muddy streets through which extremely
distasteful Arabs trailed vile rags. I stayed in Algiers one
day and took ship to Sicily. We called at Malta en route.
At last there was sunshine, but even if there had been none
I should not have cared, for it was here that I found the
cinerarias, turning the whole hillsides into sheets of flame.
I picked some of the dead blossoms for their seed and
carried it back to England. It 'took' beautifully, so that my
own flowers on the following year cost me nothing. And
their colour seemed all the gayer because they had come
from no packet, but from the hot, fragrant beds of a
southern garden.

A word about this habit of bringing seeds and plants
from abroad. When the experiment succeeds, one is
enchanted, but my own experience has been rather bitter
in this respect. In Sicily, for example, I rooted up quantities
of charming little plants from the brown hillsides: rock
roses, flax, anemones, wild cyclamen, a purple burrage,
and some curious pale yellow daisies. I could hardly wait
for the time to come when I should plant them, with
prayers for their safety, in the cool English earth. But before
that time did come there were many tribulations to be
endured.

Those plants made one long agony of the journey home.
I had tried to wash the roots clean, but it would seem that

they had a capacity for producing mud from their own insides, and a marked preference for my dress shirts as a place to deposit it. I endeavoured, for a short time, to carry them in a jam jar filled with water, but soon abandoned this ruse, because it led to several minor riots at railway stations. Fond mothers, imagining that the jam jars contained fish, snails, or even lizards, loudly demanded that I should exhibit the contents to their infants, and when I refused to do so (muttering that there was nothing in the jam jars but plants . . . not even a solitary newt), tossed their heads and pierced me with looks of intense suspicion.

But it was at the custom houses that the worst trouble occurred. One does not feel at one's best when one is awakened in the middle of the night by a large man with a black moustache who discovers a quantity of things like damp cabbage stalks wrapped up in a pair of old pyjamas and proceeds to dangle them in one's face, asking, in fiery tones, what they *are*. What are they? One does not know. It would be delightful to know what they were. Herbs. Yes. To eat? No . . . *no*! Yet an abominable official in Switzerland, in order to prove the valour of the Swiss gendarmerie, did actually bite through the stalk of an anemone. I hope he had a pain all night.

However, a few of the things survived, in spite of the heat of the wagon-lits and the teeth of the Swiss. Among them is a pretty little rock rose, of a brilliant orange colour, and a flax of so pale a blue that it seems impossible that it could ever have lived through such arduous adventures.

## § 5

All this is taking us a very long way from the greenhouse, which we can now enter again.

Cyclamen and cineraria . . . it must be admitted that there is nothing very sensational in either of these plants, from an exotic point of view. No member of the Horti-cultural Society is going to bite his beard in envy when he hears that I have grown cyclamen and cineraria under glass. Nor, probably, will anybody send me a medal when they hear that I have two very lovely mimosas that glitter like sequins on dark February mornings.

Of course, in this country, we do not really know what mimosa can be. Even in the South of France it does not grow to perfection. You have to go to Australia to see it at its best . . . and there it is indescribably beautiful. (Though why the Australians should call it by the ugly name of wattle I do not understand.)

The finest mimosa I ever saw grew in Melba's garden at Coombe, outside Melbourne. It was a good twenty feet high, and in September, which is the beginning of the Australian spring, it was so covered with blossom that it looked like an immense gold powder puff. One could stand under it and gently shake the branches, so that the delicate dust drifted on to one's head, and one enjoyed all the sensations of a blond . . . whatever they may be. Melba used to sit under the tree and sing the lovely bar-carolle of Massenet . . .

*'Dans ton coeur dort un clair de lune.'*

Her voice drifted up, like a thread of silver, into the thickly piled gold of the mimosa, and all around us was the sweet cloying scent . . . and far, far away the Blue Mountains, like brooding spirits on the horizon. Magical moments, indeed, and moments which return to me often in my greenhouse when my mimosas are in flower.

There are two of them. When I first bought them they

were about six inches high. They are now about eight feet, and since they show no signs of ceasing to grow, they rather worry me, for the mimosa is a proud plant and does not like you to bend its head or trail it in unnatural positions. However, time will doubtless discover a solution. Somebody might even give me a bigger greenhouse.

As I write of the mimosa I am reminded of another thing which you really must have in your greenhouse . . . a thing which I have seen in no other greenhouse but mine. This is a small standard laburnum.

Maybe it is quite common, and if it is, I apologize. My only excuse is that the idea of dwarfing an ordinary laburnum came to me spontaneously. By 'dwarfing' I may give a wrong impression, for no actual surgical operation is necessary. You merely take a baby laburnum tree, from three to five feet high, and put it in a pot. You can prune it to any shape you desire. The restriction of the pot prevents it from making any further growth, but it does not prevent it from flowering very abundantly. In the greenhouse, too, it flowers from four to six weeks earlier than out of doors. It looks very rare and expensive. If you take it up to town and put it in your drawing room, people will wonder where you got all your money, and will, it is to be hoped, jump to the conclusion that you are leading an immoral life.

Of azaleas, daphnes, grevilleas, begonias, gloxinias . . . of all the happy families of ferns, of the homely heliotrope and the excitements of early bulbs, one could write indefinitely. I have not space for these things.

However, the tale of one of my little experiments may possibly interest a few readers, if only because it may suggest to them a manner in which they can enjoy similiar adventures.

This experiment concerned a common field orchid. I am

not sure of its botanical name, but I refer to an orchid which grows very freely in my district. It is normally a deep purple, and the leaves are a glossy green, speckled with chocolate. In the summer the hedgerows are purple with these orchids. The school children pick great bunches of them, and call them 'flags'.

I had always loved these orchids, and wanted to grow them in my own fields, but they seemed impossible to trans-plant. I dug up quantities of roots, after the flowering time was over, and put them in precisely the same sort of soil, but there was never a sign of them on the following year. So I decided to see what they would do in the more luxur-ious accommodation of the greenhouse.

What they did astonished me. They grew to double the size, and they began to turn white! I had never seen such an orchid before, and it would not be strictly true to say that I have seen one yet. But if the orchids continue to fade at their present rate, they will be snow-white before another couple of years has elapsed. On the first year they were mauve, on the second pale pink, and last year they were white with only a faint pinkish fringe. They continue to increase in size, and their whole appearance suggests that they have long ago forgotten their connection with the open fields and intend to establish themselves as aristocrats in their adopted quarters.

This adventure with the orchid tempts one to speculate on the endless possibilities which are open to any man who takes the trouble to transplant wild flowers and give them shelter. I feel that there must be a thousand tiny flowers blooming, more or less unseen, in the fields and the woods, waiting for somebody to come along to give them a helping hand. Not, of course, that one would wish to treat all, or even a large proportion, of wild flowers in this way. Some flowers are wild by nature and would be as ill-at-ease in a greenhouse as a farm labourer in a drawing room. But there are others which seem to deserve better things than the cold winds and the rough soil which is their portion. Among these I would suggest the little purple vetch, the ragged robin, the scarlet pimpernel, and the speedwell.

## Chapter 13

## AND YET . . .

On our little village green, which is only a few yards square, the Terror lurks. It lurks in the shape of six or seven harmless youths with red faces, who stop talking when they hear footsteps approach, turn round, and stare.

They stare, no doubt, amiably enough. They do not make rude remarks, or giggle, or throw stones. But that does not make their scrutiny the less terrifying. I would rather walk naked into the House of Lords and say 'Pish' to the Lord Chancellor than run their gauntlet. There is nothing more embarrassing than meeting this little village parliament.

Do you remember those lines in the 'Ancient Mariner'?

> *Like one that on a lonesome road*
> *Doth walk in fear and dread,*
> *And having once turn'd round, walks on,*
> *And turns no more his head;*
> *Because he knows a frightful fiend*
> *Doth close behind him tread.*

It is said that Shelley fainted when first those lines were read to him. Every sympathy is due to Shelley, but surely no fiend behind could be more frightful than the fiend in front, i.e. the little group of village youths at the end of the lane who stop talking when they see one coming. I have known people make detours of a mile or more, over hedges, across ditches, and through wet fields, in order to avoid this scrutiny. I do not mind admitting that I have done it myself.

For on these occasions one has the feeling of walking alone in the world, before a glittering array of eyes. They are not hostile, they may not even be interested. They are just Eyes. And there is something appalling about a row of Eyes, staring, staring.

The person whom the Eyes observe is powerless. One is utterly lost. One begins to 'put on the expression' at least a hundred yards away. Chin up, hips swinging, mouth set in a slight smirk. There is a terrible feeling that possibly a button may be undone in some crucial place, but it is far too late to alter it now. What would the eyes do if one suddenly stopped in the road and began to look for undone buttons? They would probably shriek and rush wildly down some steep place to tell their mothers.

Meanwhile one's 'expression' grows. As the boys loom nearer, this expression assumes overpowering proportions. The smirk has now spread, and is quivering violently, in order that it may break at the right moment into a maniacal grin. The eyes are slightly glazed. The nostrils are arched. The feet, which have swollen considerably, make extra⁄ordinary dragging noises on the gravel.

All the time, the mind is tortured by problems.

Shall one say 'good morning'? Or pretend not to notice the boys at all? It would be possible, by a supreme effort of nonchalance, to turn the head away, just at the critical moment, and say a few bright words to the dog. However, supposing the dog chooses to go on in front, instead of walking behind? It would not then be wise to say a few bright words to an empty road. They would think one was mad. Nor could one, as a brilliant improvisation, shout to the dog to come back, firstly, because the dog would probably *not* come back, which would make one look an awful fool; secondly, because the words might be choked by anxiety; and thirdly, because, in any case, they would know that one did not really want the dog to come back at all.

At last it happens. The feet, unwillingly, have propelled the victim to the sacrifice. There is a blurred vision of red faces and listless mouths. Something inside barks:

'Good morning. Nice day.'

'Good morning, sir. Yes, sir.'

Like a robot, with a crimson face, one marches on. In a sort of wild gibber, a few words are spluttered to the dog. Perhaps, as a gesture of bravado, one may even put out a hand to pat the dog, but this subterfuge is not to be recommended, for usually the dog is just too far away to pat, so that the hand is suspended in mid-air, in a grotesque position.

One does not seem to be making any progress. The boys are still only a few yards behind. One seems to be all back. And is not one wobbling in a most peculiar way?

It is even worse, if one is with a woman . . . especially if she is only a casual acquaintance. Conversation suddenly dwindles. It is evident, by the stricken expression on her face, that she has perceived the boys at the end of the road. She begins to speak absently, in a hushed voice. She tugs at her hat, quickly brushes her skirt, and transfers her stick to her other hand.

She talks more and more wildly. On certain awful occasions I have been with women who have been so terrified that they have been driven to a hideous bravado, so that their voices have risen in shrill horror to the heavens, regaling the entire village with intimate details of their domestic lives. Usually, however, they go on mumbling in a senseless monotone, to which one replies with disjointed and utterly irrelevant rejoinders. Something like this:

*She* (as we approach the group, speaking in a strangled voice, with eyes on the ground): It will, I expect, won't it?

*Myself* (equally strangled, swinging stick far too fast): She was, of course.

*She:* No, I suppose not. Still, one never knows.

*Myself:* That's what I always say. She could have done if she wanted.

*She:* It couldn't, was it?

*Myself:* Yes, on the other hand, they are. (*Fortissimo*) GOOD MORNING.

And then, with trembling knees, we walk on. When we reach the haven of the cottage we both take to drink.


§ 2


The reason I introduced this irrelevance was because I have just been saved from a similar experience by Miss W. (who has not previously appeared in these pages). Miss W. is the only person I know who is completely unembarrassed by the silent scrutiny of the village boys. But then it is impossible to imagine Miss W. being embarrassed by anything at all.

Middle-aged, stocky, purple of complexion, her face glowing with amiability, she tramps about the lanes humming hymns. She is always dressed in the shabbiest of tweeds, her hair is a disgrace, and she is accompanied by two of the most abandoned mongrels that man has ever seen. Yet, she looks, and is, very evidently a lady.

When Miss W. approaches the village boys she does not

look in the least sheepish, and I am quite certain that she does not feel it. Sometimes she is so intent upon her hymn-singing that she does not even notice the boys' presence, so that she marches past them chanting, 'The day-hay thou gaha-vest Lorhord is ho-ver,' through her large purple lips, pausing in the middle of a verse to whistle to her dog, Spot. So that occasionally one hears singular observations of this nature: 'The damn you Spot da-hay thou come here is where the devil is that Lor-hord is good dog is ho-ver.'

Usually, however, she yells at the boys from the end of the road, waving her stick, and calling them affectionate abuse long before she has reached them. And when she does reach them, ten to one she will leap at the ringleader and smack him on his behind. I would love to be able to exchange souls with Miss W., if only for an hour.

§ 3

All this is leading us back, in a very rambling way, to women gardeners. Soon we shall be able to pay them a few long-delayed compliments. Before we do that, however, we must continue the evidence for the prosecution. Miss W. forms a very good excuse for beginning. For she is the only woman I have ever met who is not beset by two of the worst sins of women gardeners: firstly, a sort of wild stinginess, and secondly, a maddening mania for tidiness, at the expense of all design.

Miss W. is not like that. She is poor, and she has only a tiny garden, but it simply bustles with flowers. Every autumn, sackloads of bulbs may be seen arriving at the local station, all addressed to Miss W., and when she goes to collect them there is a gala-day at the station. She staggers about with sacks on her back, and if a bulb falls out she plays cricket with it, the stationmaster acting as umpire. On one of these occasions Mrs M. arrived, all dressed up to catch the train to London. However, before she caught it, she also caught a very well-developed Henry Irving daffodil bulb on her left nostril. And she wrote to the manager of the London, Midland & Scottish Railway about it.

How Miss W. pays for her bulbs, it is impossible to say. She cannot have much more than two hundred pounds a year, yet she cannot spend less than ten per cent of that on bulbs alone, and since she is equally extravagant with seeds and shrubs, the total proportion comes to about twenty per cent. One day, if I am very rich, I shall give her a whole cartload of tulips (though without any of the 'parrot' variety, which I cannot abide).

I wish more women were like Miss W. It is not that they refuse to spend money on their gardens, but that they usually spend it so unintelligently. Nine women out of ten go in for quantity and let the quality take care of itself. You cannot get the average woman to realize that whether she is buying seeds or bulbs or plants, the best is the cheapest. She will hunt for bargains as though she were at a remnant sale. To see a woman in a nurseryman's shop is quite embarrassing: she pays much more attention to the price labels than to the plants themselves.

Of course, there are angelic exceptions, but too often one hears this sort of conversation, as a woman shows her friend round her garden:

'How much did you pay for this deutzia?'

'Three and six.'

'But, *darling* . . . Toots Brothers have beauties at two shillings.'

'*No*! I can't believe it.' (Sighing.) 'Still, they *did* throw in this euonymus.'

'But, angel, it's dead.'

'Oh, yes, it's dead. But it's also free. This ophelia standard was three and nine.'

'They charged me four and three.'

'*No*! In that case I shall get some more. I hate the colour, but it *is* rather a bargain.'

And so on, *ad infinitum*. I always think that the shady Continental bulb merchants must send their catalogues exclusively to women. They will buy anything, provided it is cheap. Then, when the bulbs arrive, small, mouldy, and obviously inferior in every way, they do not seem to be in the least put out. All they remember is that they have saved a few shillings on the bill.

## § 4

The other feminine gardening sin from which I exempted Miss W. was the sin of excessive tidiness. Nobody could possibly accuse her of *that*! At all times of the year, her garden looks like a room which the maid has forgotten to tidy up after a particularly wild cocktail party. However, it is always so full of flowers that one does not care. What does it matter if the nemesia ought to have been pulled up weeks ago? One can hardly see it because the cosmos blazes so brightly. Who cares if the stalks of the madonna lilies are unsightly? They are almost hidden by this brilliant clump of delphiniums. If there are quantities of things which are dead, there are even more things which are alive. I know that Miss W.'s creepers need thinning out, that soon the jasmine will smother the wisteria, and that the

honeysuckle will kill the clematis. But of what con-
sequence is that? In Miss W.'s garden it is always a question
of the survival of the fittest. A rule which applies even more
aptly to the vegetable than to the animal kingdom.

Again, I say, I wish that more women gardeners had
Miss W.'s qualities. They are only too often so tiresomely
tidy. I speak with a certain heat, because I have suffered
from their activities in the garden almost as much as I have
suffered in my study. Just as a woman cannot realize that
when you are writing a novel it is necessary to have at least
a dozen separate piles of manuscript left in odd parts of the
room, including the floor, so she refuses to admit that if you
want beautiful flowers you frequently have to put up with
unsightly patches all over the garden.

Snowdrops, for instance. If you want your snowdrops to
come up, year after year, you *must* allow the leaves to remain
after the flowers have died. They will grow bushy and turn
brown—one knows that—but surely there is something
rather lovely in the thought that those leaves are absorbing
the sunlight and air, and sending fresh stores of energy to
the bulb below, to be stored up and used for the dark days
that will come again? Women (I am, of course, writing
only of the women I know) do not seem to see things
in that light. Their fingers itch to snip off the dead leaves.
And if you give them half a chance, they will.

§ 5

However, I really must stop this dreadful crowing. The
sun shines so brightly outside my window, and the
clematis looks so lovely, that for two pins I would draw a
pen through all that has gone before, though I do believe

that it is true. Oh, that clematis! It is like a silver fountain that springs from a dark green bowl, and hangs on the summer air with a mist of stars.

However, this is no time to talk about the clematis. Nor is it a time to apologize. For I have just remembered the episode of Mrs M. and the red-hot pokers. And if you are inclined to tell me that some of my opinions on women gardeners are unduly harsh, you may feel that I have some excuse for thinking as I do, in view of the constant proximity of Mrs M.

Here, then, is the tale of Mrs M. and the red-hot pokers.

For a long time I had been irritated by Mrs M.'s airy claim that she grew everything from seed. If you walked through her garden with her, you were gradually driven to a frenzy by that monotonous intonation: 'It's just a penny packet . . . but of course you have to *know* how to do it. Only a penny packet . . . however, naturally, it needs a certain technique.'

One autumn, this penny-packet business drove me to desperation. I had procured, at considerable expense, a collection of red-hot pokers (i.e. *Kniphofia*; synonym, torch lily). These red-hot pokers had done very badly. When they flowered they did not look even lukewarm. It would have been possible to bear this blow with resignation had I not happened to visit Mrs M. and to discover in her garden a whole bed of magnificent red-hot pokers.

They blazed with arrogance. They were of a curiously lurid shade of crimson. Their stems were tall and sturdy. Their leaves were bursting with rude health. They really did look red-hot, and it made me red-hot to look at them.

Mrs M. was chortling beside me. She had been intoning monotonously the merits of her penny packets. She said:

'Very fine, aren't they?'

I turned to her. 'You don't mean to say that these came out of a penny packet?'

'But, certainly,' said Mrs M. Then, as though she suddenly saw the gates of hell opening before her in answer to this fearful lie: 'At least, from a *packet*. From seed, I mean. Whether it was a penny, or twopence, or fourpence . . . I really don't know.'

These last phrases seemed rather funny to me, since I know, from ulterior sources, that Mrs M. always crosses the halfpennies off her cheques.

However, the sense of amusement did not last for long. For when I left her, the red-hot pokers began to proclaim themselves. They stung me to a sullen fury. They seared themselves into my brain. I could not sleep at night because of those red-hot pokers, which pursued me as vehemently as if I had been a religious person in the Middle Ages, whipped by the devil's fiery tail.

The weeks passed by. Autumn swept upon us with a whirl of threatening winds. Then, one day, the winds ceased, and the world was breathless, with that strange hush in which one seems to hear, over the hills, the iron tread of winter, marching on. And again I went to see Mrs M. I do not know what led me on, but I felt it necessary to see her.

'Yes,' the maid said. Mrs M. was in the garden. She was somewhere near the iris bed.

'Ah!' I said to myself. 'If she is somewhere near the iris bed, she is also somewhere near the red-hot poker bed.' I walked through the drawing-room, out on to the little terrace. As I wandered across the lawn I looked about to try to find something awful to say about her garden. But, as usual, nothing suggested itself. Her Japanese anemones were superb. (They were not any more superb than mine, but they *were* . . . well, I cannot ransack my head for adjectives . . . they were 'superb'. And yet adjectives come tumbling, naturally, in the wake of those delicate petals, for they were still and calm and proud, as though carved of ivory that had flushed to rose; they were at once cold and sweet, and the heart of every flower was gilt and powdered, as though in *maquillage* for some exquisite and secret fête.)

I averted my gaze from the Japanese anemones (which were superb but not more . . . however, that has already been stated). A purple flood of Michaelmas daisies swam into my heated vision. Then there were other daisies, tawny and grand, and a quantity of chrysanthemums, and a lot of things which I could not grow at all.

I walked on. The red-hot pokers, of course, would be finished now, so that no maddening blaze would assail me. However, their memory was fresh enough to be bitter.

And then I saw it. I mean, her. Or rather, I *do* mean 'it', for what I saw was only a piece of 'her' . . . and what I am really trying to say is that Mrs M. was presenting me to a substantial portion of herself which can only be presented when a lady in a thick tweed skirt is bending down with her head towards the north while one is approaching from the south. However, it was not this unconventional glimpse of Mrs M. which caused my heart to beat in sudden rapture. No . . . it was something else . . . something entirely unsuspected. I felt as Sherlock Holmes must have felt when, at the end of a particularly fruitless day, he suddenly discovered the finger-nail of a Siamese twin lying near the body, or something of that nature.

The scene is clearly silhouetted in my memory. In the background, the yellowing leaves of a chestnut grove. A thin straight column of mauve smoke climbing to a sky of steel, indicating that Mrs M.'s gardener was burning a bonfire. Bright red berries glimmering, like sparks, amid the dusk of immense, forbidding yews. In the foreground a stretch of dark earth, a bundle of browny-green stalks that were once red-hot pokers, the nondescript behind of Mrs M., and . . .

## AND

. . . and a row of large earthenware pots, still earthy from their recent upheaval, containing, in more than one instance, the authentic plant of a red-hot poker!

With glazed eyes, I regarded those pots. At first, the full significance of the occasion did not strike me. It was not till Mrs M. had turned round, flushed as deep a red as any of her pokers, that I realized the blackness of her sin. For here was Mrs M., whose lips had paid lying service to the lore of seeds, detected in the contemptible act of removing potted plants from her own border. Plants which she had actually bought in pots! No, more . . . which, having bought, she had failed to remove from their pots! A practice which, as you must instantly agree, is akin to such awful things as the white slave traffic.

I smacked my lips. This indeed was a moment to remember. The whole thing was revealed before me. I saw, on one . . . on two, three . . . yes, on *four* of the pots, a little label. True, the labels were faded and worn, but I managed, with the unusual clarity of vision which great passion engenders, to detect the Latin name for 'red-hot poker', and also the name of the firm which supplied them. Then exaltation was usurped by horror as the appalling nature of Mrs M.'s felony burst upon me. It was as though one had found a criminal, who for weeks had been

violently protesting his innocence, in the very act of dis-
membering the body.

I looked at Mrs M. She looked at me. We were frozen
in a moment of time. I tremble to think of the vibrations of
hatred, passion, fear, exultation, etc etc, which must have
twanged through the ether, between us, on that occasion.

I said to Mrs M.:

'Sowing some more red-hot pokers, Mrs M.?'

She glared.

I glared.

A chestnut fell in the distant grove.

I walked away. We both realized that this was a crisis in
our lives. The situation was crazy, unnatural, akin to a
wild tale of hobgoblins. But if you are a gardener, you will
realize that it was not only credible but inevitable.

I do not know what to do about it. The discord is still
unresolved. Indeed, it clashes so violently that the only
immediate solution seems to be that I should marry Mrs M.

## Chapter 14

## WHITE BEAUTY

Anybody who has ever owned an empty cottage will agree that emptiness can be very exciting. Lank, neglected holly-hocks look in through the window, and undisciplined spiders among the beams weave webs of fantastic delicacy, as though they imagine that this regime is going on for ever. The light lingers in pools of gold on the old brick floors, and is only reluctantly swept up by the black broom of night. There is great mystery in this emptiness, and the silence is stranger here than in the wide spaces outside— for in the garden, even on the stillest days, one can always hear a faint break of leafy surf from the green shores of the forest. But in the cottage there is only a sigh, now and then, and a tiny creak from the old beams, as though they were weary of stretching their black arms across the ceiling, century after century.

It is difficult to disturb this emptiness. It is as though one were trying to shout in a cathedral. But it has to be done. And I think the best way to set about it is to go to the principal room in the house, lock the door, sit on a packing-case, smoke a cigarette, and decide what the foundations are to be.

Now the principal room in my cottage is the Garden Room, in the front of the cottage. It has seven windows and is as completely surrounded by the garden as an island is surrounded by sea. I suppose I ought to describe this room in detail. But descriptions of rooms, in books, are almost as boring as descriptions of faces, and quite as useless. Who has not groaned, inwardly, when reading a novelist's long description of his heroine's features?

'Her mouth, perhaps, was a trifle too large . . .' (her mouth is *always* a trifle too large in all the best novels, which arouses the gloomiest suspicions as to the tastes of the average novelist) . . . 'and her nose had a faint upward tilt. Her eyes were her most striking characteristic.' (They always are.) 'And though not strictly beautiful', etc etc. The net result of all this is that the reader gathers that Mr Smith, the novelist, likes large-mouthed, turn-up-nosey women, who are not 'strictly' beautiful. Nor 'strictly' any-thing else, judging by the way they go on in the last few chapters.

It is the same with rooms. Unless the man is the Dickens of a genius, his loftiest descriptions help you less than an auctioneer's inventory. And so all I shall say about the Garden Room, where the adventure really began, is that it is large and squarish, with low ceilings and a feeling of sunlight dancing over floors of old red brick, through the seven windows.

§ 2

I sat in the Garden Room, in the beginning of things, with the door locked, and the smoke from my cigarette drifting through the empty airs. And it was all terrible, because the walls were distempered a sickly lemon colour and the beams were painted over, and the floors were covered with that dreadful linoleum which pretends to be parquet flooring and looks like the symptoms of the worst sort of disease. So terrible was this room, in fact, that it made me

THE GIFT OF A GARDEN

feel positively unclean. It made me long for something very cool, and very simple. And it drove me to white in sheer desperation.

The Garden Room was the first room which was white-washed, but the result was so triumphant that now every inch of my cottage is white—the pure white of snow and lilies.

Of course it is late in the day to sing the praises of white— to proclaim the fact that of all backgrounds it is the most restful, the most friendly, and the happiest to live with. For about two years ago 'Society' discovered white, and since then it has been done to death. There have been endless white parties, in which the women looked like glistening china ornaments and danced before banks of lilies on which the light shone through vases of alabaster. There have been all-white weddings, in which the best man wore a stock of white satin that reached to his stomach and the church was knee-deep in camellias, white carnations, and Ophelia roses. There have been white fêtes, and white pageants and white parades, and one young woman of my acquaintance, on her father's death, was bitterly disappointed because her mother would not consent to an all-white funeral.

'*Dead* white, sir?' said Mr Joy, rather doubtfully, when I told him what I wanted. Mr Joy is the local plasterer and undertaker. His wife keeps the village shop, and very well she keeps it too.

'Yes, as white as you can get it.'

'Won't that be a little cold, sir? Wouldn't you like a little dash of cream . . . to give you body?'

I intimated to Mr Joy that I should very much dislike a little dash of cream to give me body. I had quite enough body as it is, without any little dashes of cream. And I reflected on the strange ways of decorators, who, as a class,

are invariably so hostile to their clients' suggestions.
White is a comparatively easy matter, because if you go on
saying 'white, white, white', against all recommendations
of cream and body, you will eventually get white. But
when it comes to green . . . there one despairs. The only
thing to do is to mix the paints oneself. It is no use pointing
to those frightful little cards of colours which the painters
always show you, and saying 'I want that one.' You will
never get it. The colour on the card bears not the least
resemblance to the colour which will eventually sneer at
you from the wall. No—if you want green you must mix it
yourself. And I am sure you want the same green as I want,
which is the colour of young grass, fresh and living and
natural, with no trace of blue, and no suggestion of the
chemist's shop.

Anyway we got white, at last.

And now we can return to the Garden Room. It is
high summer, and the sun is a perpetual beneficence from
dawn till dusk. It dances far more freely now—up and
down, in and out, in every shade of gold, playing lovely
melodies of colour on its white keyboard, with the black
notes of the beams sounding sonorously through the whole
enchanted rhythm.

The foundations are laid. And now, the first discovery
is made.

§ 3

I was in the Garden Room one morning, rejoicing in the
whiteness and the sunlight, and the emptiness. I was lazily
weaving patterns in my head of the room which was to be,
patterns of curtains, and coloured glasses, and deep chintz
chairs. And then I happened to lean rather heavily against

the wall . . . and the wall sounded hollow.

It was in a corner between the window and the fireplace. There was no sort of reason why the wall should be hollow here. At first I thought I must be mistaken.

I stepped back—looked at the wall, stretched out my hand and tapped, very gently.

Echoes!

Tapped again, with a heart that beat swiftly.

Echoes again! Only tiny echoes. Reluctant, faint, and halting, as though summoned from dim and distant corridors—where they had thought themselves safe from the clamour of life.

It seemed almost cruel to disturb those echoes. They had slept for so long. The deep coverlet of time had been drawn so surely over them—their sleep had seemed so secure—they had forgotten the loud sunlight, and the silly birds, and the tramp of men.

Yet, I had to disturb them. I couldn't help it. An empty room—a hollow wall—one just can't leave these things to rest. That is one of the damnable characteristics of man. And so, with vulgar excitement, I rapped and rapped, assured myself that I was not mistaken, ran across the room, flung open the door, and shouted:

'Mr Joy . . . Mr Joy.'

With dreadful slowness Mr Joy descended. He lumbered into the room, saw the blank space, tapped it, said it certainly sounded hollow, but it would make a fine mess to open it . . . yielded to argument, fetched his tools, struck the new, glistening steel into the old wood.

I closed my eyes.

There was a rending, a dust of plaster, and then, at last, the boards came away, clattered to the floor, and it was revealed.

'It' was a perfect Sheraton alcove, painted a faded white, with five shelves, and a very delicately carved shell poised in a tiny ribbed ceiling. The whole alcove was no bigger than a man standing upright, but its design was exquisite. Its date, I should say, was about 1780.

However, this was not the main excitement. For on the centre of the alcove stood a lady in a white dress. She was a Staffordshire lady with a white hat, and white arms, and the only colour about her was in the green china grass at her feet and the pale yellow sheaf of corn under her arm. Even her lips were white, and so were her eyes, which stared out at us with a curious calm, as though she were not at all surprised at being wakened from her sleep of so many years.

'Well I never . . .' said Mr Joy.

'How did that alcove get there?'

Mr Joy shook his head. He did not know. And indeed, it was a mystery. For until the American had the cottage— (and the American would certainly never have entombed a lovely white lady in a perfect Sheraton alcove)—the cottage had belonged to three poor families. For centuries, so the legend ran, it had been inhabited by farm labourers, ploughboys and other charming men who work with their bodies. These were certainly not the people to go to the expense of building a Sheraton alcove into a Tudor cottage —and it obviously *had* been built in—nor would they be either so foolish or so unkind as to shut up such a pretty lady in it.

The mystery deepened the more one thought about it. And many strange fancies fluttered in and out of that cup-board, with white and aerie wings—of how there had once been a Lord of the Manor who had loved a village girl, and betrayed her—how he turned her parents out of the cottage and made wild love to the frightened girl on stormy nights, when the wind whistled through the tattered rigging of the elms. How there was a quarrel and angry words, and how, suddenly, she was lying there on the floor, in the white moonlight of the eighteenth century, lying so still that even the elms were hushed. And the wicked Earl—for he was obviously an earl—had her body taken away, and caused a starving genius to make a model of her, which he set in this lovely alcove. Then he walled her up, and locked the door, and stole away, chuckling, under the elms.

You will agree that there is substance there for plenty of dreams. But we have no time for dreams. There are too many facts, waiting to be told.

§ 4

I now had a pure white room, with a white alcove, a white lady, black beams, and a red brick floor. What should I do with it? To be simple without being 'artily' simple, to be 'cottagey' without being self-conscious, to introduce comfort without marring the ancient pattern—this was the problem I had to face. And like all problems, it was solved in an unexpected way. It was solved by the red brick.

When the linoleum was first torn up, and when one had recovered from the horror of seeing loathsome insects, whose very existence was an affront to God, squirming about between the cracks . . . when all was clean and calm, I sat down on my packing-case, and rejoiced in the red brick. 'It shall be red brick, and nothing but red brick,' I proclaimed, in my innocence. And when they suggested that it would be cold, I said 'a fig for the cold' or words to that effect. And when they also suggested that it would be noisy, I made the same reply . . . for I love the sound of footsteps on old brick, footsteps echoing outside closed doors, the footsteps of servants going their errands, of friends moving about the house—even the ghost of footsteps, heard in the mind only.

But 'they' were right. The red brick was cold. And noisy. After a few days of it, I had a chill and a headache. Apart from that, it seemed quite impossible to keep it clean. You washed it, and though it would glow like rubies for an hour or so, by lunch time it was dim and drab. You brushed it, and it produced an inordinate quantity of dust from between the cracks. Also—worst trait of all—it developed a distinctly 'olde worlde' appearance. Yes, even in the long drawn twilights of summer, when the dying sun was like a golden stream retreating, the old brick struck a jarring note. Perhaps it was a supersensitivity that created this illusion . . . perhaps it was only a vulgarized taste. But I shuddered to think how nearly the old brick resembled the linoleum that had vanished, how nearly it should have been spelt OLDE BRICKE.

From such shudders, such doubts, such fleeting ecstasies, was born the coco nut matting. I do not know how, or when, or why, or where. I only know that one day, at some minute that was not particularly sparkling on the jewelled clock of Time, I said 'There shall be coco nut matting.' And there was coco nut matting. And it was good.

## § 5

Now, this is fun. At least, to me it is fun. I did not realize, until I began to write about it, how the Garden Room had been built up . . . how it had evolved, slowly, like a puzzle, piece by piece.

First the white, then the alcove, then the coco-nut matting, that had the colour of unpolished wood, and felt charm-ingly rough underfoot, with a border of red brick at the sides.

And then, the blue Bristol glass.

There were four of these glasses. I had bought them for a shilling each, years before, in an old shop at Bristol, and I have felt guilty about them ever since, because I do not like striking that sort of bargain. However, if I had not bought them, somebody else would have come along. And anyway they were very lovely.

I took them into the empty Garden Room one evening at twilight, with the idea of filling them with flowers. By accident I set one of them against the window. And having done so, I sat down suddenly on the packing-case, with a thump, and forgot all about the flowers, and stared and stared at the blue glass.

This was perfect! Here, surely, was the ultimate blue! And yet . . . not the ultimate blue, for if one stared long enough, at this little glass set in the window, with the dying light about it, one saw a hundred whims and echoes of its own sweet nature. There was a blue that was caressed with green, where the shadows of the damson tree lay across it, and a blue that verged to black, at its edge, where the light faltered. There were spaces that seemed almost white, checked and spattered with dancing spirits, glisten-ing with a filigree of silver leaves. There was a blue that was like the blue of secret pools, where the sigh of the sea comes softly from over the rocks, and the sky looks down in wonder at its own beauty.

All these blues were blended in my piece of Bristol glass.

The light faded . . . the stars began to come out . . . the silver signs of the nightly carnival of heaven . . . the birds grew weary, threw their last plaintive notes across the meadows, rolled up their song-books under their quivering wings, and shut their eyes. A door opened, and from an immense distance I heard a voice saying something about dinner. But the smell of the flesh-pots drifted only faintly to me. There was still a little blue left in the glass . . . a deep deep blue . . . the blue of fathomless lakes, in which one star shone, like a lovely diamond. At last even this blue was quenched.

And I suddenly realized that I was very hungry.

## § 6

This is becoming more and more like the House that Jack built. Still, we must reiterate. First the white, then the alcove, then the coco-nut matting, with its fringe of red brick, and then . . . the blue Bristol glass.

And from that blue, everything else in the room radiates. It sounds frightful, and more arty than words can describe, but it was like that, and I believe that it is the best way to do things. For once the blue glass was set in the window, to my endless delight, the rest followed quickly.

For weeks I went about London clutching the blue Bristol glass, wrapped up in a piece of brown paper, and many was the delightful hour I spent unwrapping it in china shops, and furniture shops, to compare it with plates and fabrics. 'Compare' is not really quite the right word, for I used to ask the glass questions.

'Do you like these curtains, O blue Bristol glass?' I would say.

And always I received an immediate answer. You would be surprised at the number of curtains it did not like. It took me a whole week to find a stuff with which the glass said it could be happy . . . but it was worth the trouble. For the material chosen was one of the most charming cretonnes you have ever known—a very simple design of blue cornflowers stamped on a pure white ground.

Sometimes, it seemed, the Bristol glass decided that it did not want blue things at all. It sternly vetoed any suggestion of blue in the chintz, for example, choosing a pale grey, with a misty design of yellow birds. It also chose, without hesitation, a pair of large, white, glistening china cocks, with yellow beaks, and observed, as it chose them, that it would like them put very close to it, on the old French Provençal table.

But usually, it demanded some echo of its own colour, and as I always obeyed, the room is full of blue echoes, that drift from chord to lovely chord as the pale fingers of the light caress them . . . the golden fingers of the day and the silver fingers of the night. There is a blue sky, for example, in a delicious little Early Victorian plate I bought in the Caledonian Market, which is painted with the picture of a young man felling a tree with a tiny hatchet and a ferocious expression. Underneath this picture is printed, in blue letters, the admirable observation:

*Light strokes fell great oaks.*
*Industry pays debts but despair increases them.*

The blue Bristol glass gave its instant approval to these highly moral sentiments.

There are also many blue echoes on my egg. I must explain my egg. It was originally a large, smooth, oval stone which I found in a field, one September morning, and bore home rejoicing, because it seemed exactly what I wanted to prop open the door of the Garden Room. But when I put the stone down by the door the blue Bristol glass for some unaccountable reason said 'I don't like that stone.' I could not think why, because it was quite a nice stone, of the ordinary brownish colour which stones usually affect. Still, the blue Bristol glass did not like it, so the stone was removed to the toolshed. And that, I thought, was the end of the matter.

But it was not the end. For the door creaked, and swung backwards and forwards, and had to be propped open with chairs which made abominable scrapy noises on the brick. I hankered after my stone. I used to go out and look at it, and wish I could have it back.

Then one day, I had a brain wave. I went into Peterborough and bought some white paint and some blue paint. Then I came back and made the stone white all over. When it had dried I painted large blue spots on it. The result was enchanting.

For I discovered that, by a happy chance, I had laid an egg.

I have always wanted to lay an egg. It seems, really, the one activity against which nobody could possibly protest. To go out into a field, to peck a piece of grass which nobody wants, and then retire, to meditate, and suddenly to go pop, and wander off, with complete unconcern, leaving a beautiful clean egg on the grass . . . you must admit that there is nothing to be said against this behaviour.

Well, at last I had done this thing. And I took my egg into the house, and laid it before the blue Bristol glass, and the blue Bristol glass said 'You have laid a very nice egg indeed. You can put it on the floor to prop open the door.'

And everybody who comes into the Garden Room, and

sees my egg, says, 'But it looks exactly like an *egg*!' Which makes me laugh.

I could write a great deal more about the Garden Room, but there are so many other things to tell you about that I suppose I had better stop. I do hope you have some idea how it looks? How the blues drift in and out, a note here, a note there? And how the Bristol glass presides over everything, giving the whole room its blessing?

If ever anybody were to break my blue Bristol glass . . . but I daren't think of that. This has been such a happy chapter. Let it remain so. For tragedy looms ahead.

## Chapter 15

## ENTER MRS WRENCH

Tragedy entered with Mrs Wrench.

The long interregnum of Mrs Wrench has not previously been mentioned. Partly because the matter was extremely painful to the writer, but principally because she played no part in the story.

It is now very necessary to refer to this lady, because it was she who was a very potent influence in the cottage during these early days.

Mrs Wrench was a Scottish widow, and needless to say, she came with the best possible references. Each employer for whom she had ever worked spoke of her in such ecstatic terms that it seemed difficult to understand how they had ever allowed her to be torn away from them. She was as honest as the day, as clean as a nut, as capable as Mussolini, and her cooking was a dream. So loud were the praises of the sheaf of letters which she sent me, and so varied were her accomplishments, that if a letter had arrived stating that Mrs Wrench was, in addition, a trapeze artist, and a Dame of the British Empire, I should not have been at all surprised.

Needless to say, her arrival was awaited with impatience, tinged with trepidation. Those letters had made me nervous. They had not said anything about Mrs Wrench's conversational abilities, but I was so worked up by these advance notices that I was quite prepared for the advent of

AUTUMN

some highly curved widow, smartly dressed, spitting *mots*, and tralalaing French songs as she condescended to make an omelette. I saw myself miserably following her about the house, picking up her lipstick as she flicked an incomparably efficient duster over my humble bed.

It was therefore with considerable relief that I saw, stepping out of the village Ford a large, homely-looking woman of about fifty-five, with straight red hair, and very long limbs, dressed in simple country clothes. Her features were somewhat gaunt and forbidding, but that seemed as it should be. She was obviously extremely strong, because she used only one hand to carry a suitcase which had made the chauffeur stagger under its weight. A fleeting recurrence of the fear that she might, after all, be a trapeze artist, assailed me as I hurried to greet her. But these fears were soon put at rest.

Mrs Wrench, apparently, was extremely normal. She looked at the stove and said she could 'manage' it. She examined the lamps. She could 'manage' them, too. As we went over the cottage, and examined each detail, she said she could 'manage' it. She also said that she could 'manage' coffee after dinner. As I left her, I felt that at any moment she would say that she could 'manage' *me*. Which filled me with gloom, because I am pliable and weak, and my back was specially designed for the accommodation, in large quantities, of old men and women of the sea.

But, no. Mrs Wrench did not want to 'manage' me. She constantly asserted that she would soon 'get into my ways'. She also asserted that 'nobody could say she didn't try'.

Therefore, though I felt that I could never cherish any very tender emotions about Mrs Wrench, she would do well enough.

§ 2

It would be difficult to say how the first signs of hostility manifested themselves. The causes of these domestic battles, like the causes of great wars, are obscure and far to seek. Master and man, mistress and maid—they begin as allies, for a time they work peaceably together, side by side, and then, gradually, there are frontier incidents, skirmishes, and at last, pitched battles, in which the maid, more often than not, is left in undisputed possession of the field.

Everything, it seemed, was going along very nicely. The odd man from the village (also a Scot) reigned calmly, if somewhat autocratically, over the garden. Mrs Wrench reigned in a similar manner over the house. She was clean, honest, and a fair cook, although her Yorkshire pudding always had to be buried in the garden. She also said, with an irony which was not at first apparent, that she *liked hard work*. And as I was seldom at the cottage for more than a week-end, and then usually alone, I did not detect any undercurrent of double meaning in this phrase.

However, there was a very deadly undercurrent.

Here the reader must be convinced, if he is to bear with me in sympathy, that Mrs Wrench's duties were by no means superhuman, and could, indeed, only by a vivid stretch of the imagination be described as onerous. For in those early days I was not able to spend nearly so much time at the cottage as I do now, and during most of that time I was alone. Besides, as we have seen, the cottage was nearly empty. Its accommodation, with the exception of the servants' quarters, consisted only in three small bedrooms (two of which were seldom used) two small sitting-rooms and one tiny hall. That was absolutely all, apart from what is euphemistically termed 'the usual offices'. These 'offices' indeed, were far from 'usual'. In fact they were so unusual that many people, when being taken over the house, gaily exclaimed, before I could hurry them past the door, 'Now *this* is the room I want for my sitting-room!' And then the sudden vision of an impolite object in a dark corner made them change the subject very hastily indeed, and remark that there was nothing like old oak, was there? To which I always replied that no, there really was nothing like it. After which, with mutual distrust, we would resume our tour of the house.

Of these five little rooms which Mrs Wrench had to look after, four were, at the time of her domination, furnished so simply that they could hardly be described as 'furnished' at all. The Garden Room, it is true, was gradually taking shape, but my study held little more than a table, a chair, and a piano, while the bedrooms contained only a steel bed, a cupboard, a rug, and a washstand, on which reposed a pitcher filled with amber-coloured rain-water. They could all be 'done out', by an energetic housemaid, in the course of an hour.

Therefore, the idea that Mrs Wrench could possibly be overworked never for one moment presented itself. And it was not till after a long series of incidents, small in themselves, but all pointing in the same direction, that I realized what was the matter.

It began with a curious phrase which constantly came to Mrs Wrench's lips. This phrase was, 'I was having five minutes.' She would say, for example, that the vicar had called during the week. 'I was having five minutes, after dinner, so he took me by surprise.' Or perhaps there had been a telegram which she had not known whether to open or not. 'But I was having five minutes when it came,' she would say, 'so I was able deal with it all right.'

At first this singular phrase went in at one ear and came out at the other. It meant nothing at all to me. It did not suggest, as it ought to have suggested, the first rumblings of approaching thunder. No—it was merely an odd note, like some constantly recurring refrain in a long poem. Like, for example, the extraordinary couplet which echoes through the work of Blake:

> *The caterpillar on the leaf*
> *Repeats to me my mother's grief.*

A wild couplet, that, to which, in all solemnity, we may apply the tragic adjective *insane*. Such was Mrs Wrench's constant assertion: 'I was having five minutes.'

A very minor incident gave to this phrase, for the first time, its full significance. . . I arrived, with a friend, an hour earlier than usual at the cottage.

I was feeling very happy that afternoon. The country was a paradise. The fields were dancing with buttercups, the hedges aflame with the sweet white fires of may. Over the wall the lilac leant its tipsy plumes, giving itself in lazy wantonness to the breeze. Every thrush was a nightingale, that day, and every starling a lark. And many were the thrushes and starlings and sparrows who fluttered into the air as I opened the gate of the secret garden, took a deep breath, and said, 'I am home.'

And then, framed in the window, a black figure appeared. Mrs Wrench. Black not only in vesture but in countenance—a countenance made all the blacker by flaming red hair above it. She advanced heavily.

'You're early,' she said.

'Why yes. . . .'

Was it imagination, or did a cloud pass over the sun? '*I was having five minutes,*' said Mrs Wrench.

She stared at me reproachfully. I stared back.
She turned and went.

§ 3

I sat down on a tree stump. The phrase echoed through my
mind. My friend, whom we will call John, was still
fiddling with the car outside, so I was undisturbed.

Five minutes. Where had I heard that phrase before?
Anyway, five minutes *what*? It could not be prayer or
meditation, because Mrs Wrench, as she often observed,
with her raven croak, had no use for the church or the
clergy. 'I know too much about 'em,' she would say, as
though she had spent years of research on ecclesiastical
abuses.

Five minutes *what*? Was she, perhaps, engaged in some
illicit enterprise? Coining? Or even worse, taking in other
people's washing? Was she drinking? But no—she was a
teetotaler.

I could no longer ignore the obvious. Mrs Wrench
meant that she was having five minutes respite from the
toils of slaving for *me*.

And yet . . . it seemed impossible. I had not been at the
cottage, during the last six weeks, for more than three
nights. Last week-end I was up for Sunday night only. It
was now Saturday. She could *not* mean what she seemed
to mean. Impatiently I jumped to my feet. She must be
sought out, and this dreadful problem must be solved.

She was in the kitchen, washing a salad. As I opened
the door, I suddenly remembered that I had no particular
cause to see her. So I said, on the spur of the moment, 'Oh,
Mrs Wrench, *have* you seen the bluebells in the orchard?
They're too lovely.'

Mrs Wrench inclined her head. 'Yes,' she said, 'I took five minutes off to go and have a look at them.'

That phrase again! I was as one hypnotized.

'Yes,' she went on, monotonously, 'I left everything, and went out, and I must say they're beautiful. Of course, I haven't seen them for a day or two, what with one thing and another, but I felt I just *had* to go and look at them.' She paused. And then, with the face of gloom which she always reserved for the delivery of an aphorism, she added, 'All work and no play makes Jack a dull boy. That's what I always say.'

## § 4

So it was true! I had been blind not to notice it before. And as I walked round the garden a whole flock of little memories pursued me, all revealing themselves, for the first time, in their full significance.

One of these phrases was 'it gives me a chance'. Every Monday morning, when leaving I would say good-bye to Mrs. Wrench and tell her that I would be up again on Saturday, to which the invariable reply was, 'Oh, yes that'll give me a chance.'

Idly, in the car, I had often wondered what she meant. A chance to do *what*? To go away? Or entertain? Or stay in bed? No longer did I toy with these illusions. It was glaringly obvious that Mrs Wrench meant that she would be given a chance to clean out my bedroom.

Again there was the phrase, 'I've got round.' Constantly, this was the first remark she made to me. 'I've just got round!' she would say—and I, poor innocent, concluded vaguely that she had been out for a walk, or had been in the kitchen garden when she heard the car. But no, she meant that during the week she had just been able to make the exhausting tour of my bedroom.

Now, a woman would, presumably, have seen these things long before, would have detected the delicate echoes of discontent, and opened immediate hostilities. However, my sex being of the gentler variety, I did not wish for hostilities. I wanted everything to go on quietly and peace-fully. I wanted 'a good time to be had by all'.

There seemed to be no real reason for battle. It was surely only a matter for a little tact . . . a little adjustment? For, in all truth, Mrs Wrench's position was *not* one of slavery. She was, to begin with, as strong as a horse. She ate enormously. She slept perfectly. For at least four days of the week she could stay in bed, if she so desired. I thought of the countless wretched general servants, in grimy London homes, who descend from their attics at six in the morning, who sweep, and brush, and cook, and run their breathless, soul-destroying race against time, day after day, year after year. If the 'family' are ever out to a meal, in such house-holds, it is a red-letter day for these poor damned souls. God forbid that I should ever subscribe, directly or indirectly, to the perpetuation of such slavery. I would rather make my own bed, and sweep my own floor, and boil an egg over an oil stove than be served by the toil of such creatures. But surely, Mrs Wrench's position could hardly be compared with theirs?

I decided to go and ask John what he thought about it. I found him in his bedroom, surrounded by piles of silk shirts, bottles, and tissue paper.

'I'm unpacking my own bag,' said John, rather loftily. 'I always do.'

I took a deep breath and was about to reply to this out-rageous lie, when I checked myself. For I recalled that John

was a Socialist, with exactly five thousand a year. He thinks
that nobody ought to have more than exactly five thousand
a year. (His last aunt died six months ago, and he has
nobody else to leave him any money, poor boy.)

'Besides,' added John, taking out a large *flacon* of lemon
verbena bath essence, 'one can never find things if one
doesn't put them away oneself. Where shall I put this?'

I looked at it greedily. 'We might pour a little in the
pond. The gold fish would probably grow horns.'

John, making no reply to this suggestion, put the bottle
on the chest of drawers. There was already a formidable
array of these bottles. They all had gold tops and little
labels on which one read, 'The Hon. John —, Hair Lotion
Number 47A', etc. Why John wanted these things, nobody
can imagine, for nothing could be thicker nor yellower
than his hair. However, I understood the purpose of the
bottle of 'Iced Orange Water', for use 'after shaving'. John
does not like shaving at all. He shaves, indeed, with
extreme petulance, because he hates to be reminded that he
is growing up. The 'Iced Orange Water' was therefore,
presumably, a consolation for this odious task.

The 'Iced Orange Water' being safely disposed of, John
sat down on the bed.

'I think I shall leave the rest of the things till after tea,' he
said. 'I can't imagine why Forsythe always wants to deluge
everything in tissue paper.'

Which made me realize that although John might un-
pack, he certainly didn't pack.

The mention of Forsythe gave me an excuse for introducing the subject of Mrs Wrench.

'Forsythe does everything for you, doesn't he?'

'What do you mean "everything"? He has practically
nothing to do.'

'No—well—however—anyway he does everything. And he doesn't complain?'

'*Complain*? But my dear fellow, we're *friends*. Real friends. That's the secret of it. When I went over to Paris last week-end, I allowed him to lunch at the same table as I did on the boat. At the same table.'

'Yes . . . you told me that before, several times. What I wanted to say was that Mrs Wrench is complaining.'

'What about?'

'The work. She thinks there's too much to do.'

'There probably is a great deal.'

'But, my dear John, I'm hardly ever here.'

'No—but when you are, there's a great deal. Besides it isn't only the work. It's the way you treat people. Now Forsythe . . . I always take him into my confidence. He's a friend.'

'And he lunched at the same table on the boat when you went to Paris, I know.'

'There's no need to be silly.'

'Well, how am I to take Mrs Wrench into my confidence? What can I talk to her about?'

'She's a woman,' said John loftily. 'She isn't a machine.'

'I wish she *were* a machine. Machines don't look at you with a frightful expression as soon as you press the button.'

'Supposing *I* talk to Mrs Wrench . . .'

'For heaven's sake, no!'

This almost broke up the conversation. However, peace was restored by my agreeing to John's suggestion that we should do our utmost, during the week-end, to make Mrs Wrench's job as easy as possible. John confidently prophesied that after we had carried out certain little plans which he outlined, the whole atmosphere would be completely changed.

However, I had my doubts.

§ 5

It would be tedious to narrate our many efforts to relieve Mrs Wrench. How we carried out the tea-things, manfully declined to have coffee after dinner, fetched wood for the fire. As I said good night to her, I looked for some sign of the change which John had so confidently prophesied. However, she only seemed to look a little blacker than usual. I sighed and decided that it was probably too early to judge.

The preparations we made, before finally retiring for the night, were exhaustive. We carefully scooped out the ash-trays, tiptoed with them up to the bathroom, washed and dried them, and tiptoed downstairs again, to place them on their appointed tables, retreating a few steps to see how clean and sparkling they looked. We shook out the cushions and dug our fingers into the chintz seats of the sofa to smooth out the creases. We both made a vow not to sit on the sofa again in case we should disturb its marble serenity. We put every chair in its appointed place, and I swept the mud off the staircase carpet, using John's clothes-brush for the purpose. We polished the tumblers from which we had drunk our whiskies and sodas, and carefully deposited a saucer under the syphon, whose nose was dribbling. We poured water on the fire to put it out—a rather unfortunate manoeuvre this, because it deluged the room with ash, which all had to be swept up again. Finally, we drew back the curtains, in order that Mrs Wrench might come down in the morning to a room of sunshine.

The moonlight flooded into a room as clean as a Dutch interior.

'We can't possibly do any more,' whispered John.

'Unless we go up and undress Mrs Wrench.'

'I'm quite tired, aren't you?'

'Exhausted.'

'I think I'll have a final whisky.'

'You can't. It'll spoil the tumbler.'

'I'll wash it out again,' said John, somewhat shortly. He then retired to bed.

In the morning I was the first to rise. We had decided overnight that we would make our own beds and clean out our own things on the washstand. I did this with a certain reluctance because, as we were returning to London that same night, I really could not see how Mrs Wrench would occupy her time during the forthcoming week. However John had so impressed upon me the necessity of treating her as a 'comrade' that I felt I really ought to be making Mrs Wrench's bed as well.

I went along to see John. He looked so highly decorative in his pale blue pyjamas that it was a shame to wake him up. As I did so I observed that the room was still littered with the tissue paper from his suitcases.

'You're going to make your own bed?' were the first words I said to him.

He yawned. 'What?' Then he blinked himself awake. 'Of course.'

'And you might empty things, too. I did.'

'All *right*.' He spoke somewhat gruffly, so I left him and went downstairs.

Mrs Wrench was in the hall, putting two glasses of orange juice on the table. When she saw me her face fell.

'Oh!' she exclaimed, 'will it be earlier than usual?'

'It' meant a pot of coffee and four pieces of toast, which was all the breakfast we ever had.

'Oh, no, Mrs Wrench.' I was bitterly disappointed that she had not made any reference to our beautiful clean room.

She breathed a sigh of relief. Then she pointed to the orange juice. 'I've got the orange juice done.' She spoke as though she had picked and pressed the entire contents of a large grove. 'I did it as soon as I got down. And then . . . Well, I mustn't waste any more time talking.' And she bustled out.

Somehow this conversation did not seem to augur very well for the future. However, the morning was too delight-ful to worry overmuch. There had been a ground-frost overnight, and the brilliant gold of the wallflowers was flanked with silver. It was one of those mornings when the air is so sweet and keen that you curse yourself for smoking, and throw away your cigarette on to the path, where it lies, sending up tiny mauve coils into the still air.

After about half an hour I returned to see how my Socialist friend was getting on. I knocked at the door.

'Come in.'

He was still not dressed. But the room was 'done'. That is to say, the bed looked as though a large body were con-cealed beneath the blankets, and little bits of sheet stuck out at odd corners. I made a mental note to come up and do it again after breakfast.

'Pretty quick work that, what?'

I agreed.

'There's nothing in it.'

'Inside the bed?'

'In doing one's own room, you ass. I wouldn't mind doing it every day of my life.'

'Then why don't you?'

'What?'

'And why do you say Mrs Wrench has got too much to do if . . .'

A wild concatenation interrupted these inconvenient questions. John jumped.

'My God! . . . what's that?'

'Only the bell for breakfast.'

'*Must* she spring it on us like that?'

'It saves her coming upstairs.'

He gave me a sour look. 'Oh, yes. Of course.'

We went down. 'It' was reposing before the fire. I observed with interest that instead of four pieces of toast there were six. That must have been a great strain on Mrs Wrench.

John rubbed his hands. 'You know,' he said. 'I could have done with a couple of eggs this morning.'

'I dare say that if you were to ask Mrs Wrench she might make a superhuman effort, and boil one. But I think two would be a little much to ask, don't you?'

And I will say that John, although a Socialist, was decent enough to allow himself a reluctant grin. However, he did *not* go and ask for those eggs!

We will now leave Mrs Wrench, for it is high time that we 'had five minutes' ourselves. But I warn you that we shall meet her again.

*Chapter 16*

## EXIT MRS WRENCH

The only minor complaint I could possibly have brought against Mrs Wrench was in her voracious consumption of Vim. But then, that complaint applies to nearly all domestics. I am convinced that they eat Vim. Or else they roll in it, or sniff it up like cocaine or do something extremely peculiar with it, because no legitimate use of Vim could possibly account for the amount of it which is used in even the best-run households.

Apart from the customary consumption of Vim, Mrs Wrench had all the virtues except the vital virtue of 'willingness'. You felt that her life was one long martyrdom of overwork. So strongly was she impressed by this idea herself, that you caught it, and worried for her.

The one benefit of all this was that she formed an in-exhaustible topic of conversation. In those days I was moving about in a great many varieties of social circles, high, low, stupid, and intelligent, and I always found that if Mrs Wrench were mentioned, she held the stage. The eyes of Cabinet Ministers lit up at the catalogue of her vices, and large, important women left conservatories, or wherever they happened to be putting spokes in the Wheel of State, and hung eagerly upon every detail.

'Of course, you should sack her *at once*,' they said in trembling voices.

'I suppose I should.'

'But *at once*. Too ridiculous—in these days. Why, there are thousands . . . thousands . . . she ought to consider herself an entremely lucky woman. How many bedrooms did you say?'

'Three.'

'And only two occupied . . . for week-ends?'

The large important women knew the answer to this, only too well, because we had it all out at dinner the night before. But they longed to be told it all again. They usually were.

Which made me think that Mrs Wrench must be a universal figure. That she must loom, in the shape of a trusted lady's-maid, behind many toilet tables, that she must blacken many a domestic hearth, in nice middle-class families, and be extremely prevalent, as a dark 'daily', in the houses of the poor.

However, in spite of her value as a topic of conversation, she was rapidly becoming so impossible that a crisis could not be far off.

§ 2

It began with a telegram.

I had arranged to go up to the cottage on Saturday as usual, with John. However, Friday morning dawned so exquisitely, so gaily, that even the roofs of Westminster looked as though they had been laid with gold-leaf over-night. 'It is a sin to stay in London on a day like this,' I said to myself, and I got on the telephone to John. Could he come up today instead of tomorrow? Yes—he would be delighted. I sighed with relief and arranged to call for him immediately after lunch.

When we arrived at the cottage, the little country gate

that leads into the garage was closed. Normally, it was always open, so that one could drive straight in. But today, the strain of opening the gate would obviously have been too much for Mrs Wrench, who had only had three hours in which to open it.

The next portent was when I walked along the path towards the kitchen, opened the kitchen door, and called out: 'Mrs Wrench.'

There was no answer.

'Mrs Wrench!' Still no answer.

Leaving John to look after himself, I went through to the front of the house. She was nowhere to be found. I ran up the stairs. And there she was, in my bedroom, surrounded by sheets, pillows, and blankets.

'Good afternoon, Mrs Wrench.'

'Good afternoon, sir.'

She lifted a pillow as though it weighed a ton, and heavily put it on the bed.

'It's a lovely afternoon.'

She turned round and looked out of the window. 'Is it, sir?'

'But haven't you been out, Mrs Wrench?'

'No, sir, I have not.' She looked at me as a tortured mulatto might look at a particularly sadistic slave-driver. 'I *was* going to take five minutes, and go up the lane, but then your telegram came. . . .'

Something began to boil in me. In a voice that cannot have been quite steady, I said:

'But why don't you take a whole day off, Mrs Wrench, if you want to? Or two or three days?'

She continued to stare.

'I'd take from Tuesday to Friday, if I were you,' I went on, madly. 'And just go out, or stay in bed, whichever you prefer. I think that'd be a good idea.' With a frantic effort I smiled at her. 'We'll have dinner at seven-thirty, I think.'

I then went down, tense with rage, knocked my head against several beams, and poured out my troubles to John.

§ 3

Now John, in the previous chapter, was a Socialist with only five thousand a year. But since then a great many things had happened. An obscure cousin, of whose exist-ence he had previously been unaware, had been bitten by a snake in Bolivia, had expired, clutching John's photo-graph to his breast, and had left him *another* five thousand a year. And though one can be a Socialist with a mere five thousand (provided one spends enough time in the South of France, and has a valet with whom one can lunch in the Blue Train without anybody thinking it odd), it is a little more difficult to do it on ten.

So John had changed, and had become a Fascist. Fascism, in those days, was mercifully confined to Italy. The youth of England had not yet begun to prance about the streets in black shirts, like perverted Morris dancers, pushing the palms of their hands in the faces of a startled bourgeoisie, and selling them sheets of bloodthirsty gossip at twopence a time. No—the Black Shirt in the time of which we are writing, was still a distant menace. It flashed across the screens when Mussolini was in evidence, and housemaids giggled at the funny way in which the foreign troops stuck out their knees. But the idea of black shirts in England. . . .

However, John was always in the vanguard. Besides, a black shirt emphasized the pale gold of his hair. That was really the chief reason he became a Fascist, I believe, although he had certainly mastered the Fascist 'philosophy' very prettily. Especially in its application to women.

'Woman,' he said, bending down to pick a grape-hyacinth, which he carelessly pushed into his buttonhole, 'should be man's Helpmeet.'

John had a way of talking about Woman, in those days, as if she were a large marble animal, with no relations. He somehow managed to make the capital 'W' seem an essential part of her anatomy.

'I know,' I said irritably, 'but Mrs Wrench isn't Woman. I mean she isn't a bit abstract, like that. She's got red hair and a hooked nose. And really the idea of being a Helpmeet . . .'

'I'll talk to her,' said John, tugging at the collar of his black shirt, and turning towards the house.

'Now, John . . . we can't go *entirely* without dinner.'

'Why should we?'

'Because she's got a grievance, and if you went butting in, she'd go.'

John snorted, pushed out his chest, and proceeded to pour scorn on me for my weakness. I, in turn, tried to point out to him, that Mrs Wrench was *not* Woman, but a woman, and that she was not in the least like the sort of creature one sees on the wrapper of patriotic magazines, covered with corn-sheaves, and surrounded by Australia, Canada and South Africa (personified by bloated infants, playing about her feet). And that the word Helpmeet, to her, was not at all pleasing . . . it did *not* suggest stirring the pot for the returning warrior (while she suckled Australia, Canada and South Africa in the pantry) . . . but it *did* suggest making an extra bed and opening an extra tin of sardines.

'You're impossible,' said John. 'You go entirely the wrong way about it. Look at me and Forsythe. I've only got to lift my finger . . .'

'And he comes and lunches at the same table when you're going to Paris.'

John stared at me coldly, and resumed, '. . . to lift my finger, and he knows his place.'

'That sounds agony for both of you.'

'I beg your pardon?'

'Lifting your finger and knowing your place. Like a frightful parlour game. Somebody says, "Peekaboo", then you all have to rush out of the room and stand in a draughty corridor breathing in each others' faces, while some woman in pink giggles round the house with an old thimble. Really! What odd things you do with your servants!'

It would be unprofitable to continue this argument. After a time John calmed down, became a little less Fascist, and a little more human. Instead of making a raid on the kitchen, and delivering an oration on Womanhood, he agreed to wait till dinner-time and take part in a little scheme which I outlined to him, as we walked up and down, under the curdling, twilit skies of spring.

§ 4

By the time that dinner arrived I was in a state bordering on hysteria. Mrs Wrench had informed us that we should have to dine off cold tongue—a depressing prospect in any case, rendered even more depressing by the acid remarks which had accompanied this information . . . such as 'the country isn't London, sir, you can't just run out round the corner'. Lord—if only Mrs Wrench *would* just run out round the corner, whatever that meant, and never come back!

When Mrs Wrench dumped the cold tongue in front of me, and lumbered to the sideboard to fetch the wine, I turned to John, and in trembling but crystalline tones observed:

'I think it so wonderful how your mother, with only one servant, manages to give all those marvellous dinners.'

John gulped. He had not been quite prepared for this. 'Er . . . yes,' was all he could manage.

'She bakes the bread too, doesn't she?'

'Who?'

'Your servant . . . Ada, isn't that her name?'

'Ada?' Another kick. Then he pulled himself together. Mrs Wrench was now just behind me, pouring out the wine, and I was able to give him a wink.

'Oh *Ada*!' He nodded gravely. 'Yes . . . of course, she bakes deliciously.'

'And helps in the garden?'

'A great deal. And then, of course, the massage takes up a good deal of time.'

'The massage?' This was a stroke of genius. I cast a furtive look at Mrs Wrench's face. It was as black as the blackest thundercloud that ever loured over the Black Mountains.

'From ten to eleven,' said John, warming to his task, 'my mother is always massaged by Ada. From eleven to twelve she bakes. From twelve to one . . .'

A raven-like croak interrupted us. It was Mrs Wrench. She said:

'Will there by anything else, sir?'

'Anything else?' With hideous brightness I smiled at

Mrs Wrench. 'Well, have you made anything, Mrs Wrench?'

I waited for the reply as one waits who has cast a stone into a deep well. And after a pause, *de profundis*, the reply came:

'No sir, I have *not*.'

The hideous brightness continued. 'In that case, we'll just have coffee.'

She turned to go. She was half-way through the door when I called out:

'And, Mrs Wrench—as it's such a lovely night, I think we'll have coffee in the garden.'

There was no reply. All I remember is that the black cloud in the doorway swelled, deepened, prepared to burst, thought better of it, and vanished. The echoes of the slamming door rang through the house.

'Well,' said John, 'that's done it.'

## § 5

However, so weak is man, so subtle and clinging is woman, that by the time the morning came, I was full of regrets for my harsh treatment of Mrs Wrench . . . anxious to make amends, and eager to conciliate her. For I could not believe that she was wholly malevolent.

The whole problem was discussed with John, after breakfast. 'You should sack her,' he said.

'Listen!'

There was a muffled thud upstairs.

'That's Mrs Wrench, making my bed.'

A quarter of an hour passes. The noises still continue.

'But what is she *doing*?'

There came the sound of heavy furniture being dragged across the room. Stamp, stamp, stamp; rattle, rattle, rattle. A pause.

'But seriously what *is* she doing?'

'Is it spring-cleaning?'

I shook my head. 'That was finished three weeks ago. Don't you remember? I went to Paris . . . "to give her a chance".'

'Perhaps she's burying something?'

Crash, bang!

'Perhaps. But she doesn't seem to have quite killed it yet.'

More draggings. The stampede continues, grows in fury. Suddenly there is a lull. We look at the clock. Since the first onslaught began Mrs Wrench has been in my room room nearly forty minutes.

'I think I shall go mad, don't you?'

'Raving. Couldn't we go and see what she's doing?'

'I wouldn't. Think what happens when you wake mediums up.'

'What happens?'

'They die. In an orgy of ectoplasm.'

'Do you think she's in a trance, then?'

'Well, can you think of any other explanation?'

'None. Oh hell . . . what *is* she doing?'

And thus and thus. Finally we gave it up. We went out. As we passed through the hall we met Mrs Wrench coming down the stairs. She looked as if she had just cleaned out the Vatican, single-handed. Very timidly I said to her:

'Oh, Mrs Wrench, do you think we might possibly have lunch at one, instead of half-past today?' (Lunch is some more cold tongue, some salad and some cheese. Mrs

Wrench never learned to cook an omelette.)

She passed her hand wearily over her forehead.

'I'll see what I can do.'

'Oh thank you, Mrs Wrench.'

'But if it's *five* minutes past . . .'

'Oh that'll be quite all right.'

'After all,' she intoned, as a parting shot, 'I've only one pair of hands.'

She slammed the door. I paused and reflected that this statement, after all, was true. Though anybody who listened to the noise upstairs would say that she had ten pairs of hands, and twenty pairs of very large feet.

I went upstairs to see if, by any chance, she had pulled down a few beams or torn up any boards. No. Everything was as it should be. The small bed stood in the corner. The one table and the one chair were in their appointed places. I could have turned everything in that room upside down, emptied a sack of soot on the floor and had it all cleaned up again in half an hour. Mrs Wrench, with none of these disadvantages, took twice that time.

What did Mrs Wrench *do*?

§ 6

The time has come when we must invoke that imaginary veil which the novelist so often draws out of his inkpot when the situation of his characters becomes too painful to record, or when, as I suspect, his inspiration begins to flag.

The veil, in this case, was provided by the arrival of a telegram which I received, not long afterwards, from the odd man. It read:

*Mrs Wrench left this morning shall I sleep in Parsons*

219

My first feeling on opening this was one of the utmost relief. I thought of the cottage, relieved of that terrible brooding presence, and never had it seemed more precious to me. Now it really *is* mine! I thought, and almost made up my mind to have nobody in it at all, to let it get beautifully dusty, and to dine off endless tins of delicious sardines. But then, I began to wonder what had happened.

I learnt, as soon as I arrived at the cottage. Mrs Wrench had come into a fortune! It was variously estimated at sums ranging between five thousand pounds and a quarter of a million. The people who hated her most, strangely enough, were those who were most positive that her fortune was immense.

This news was not quite such a shock to me as it might have been. I had often wondered if there was some mystery about Mrs Wrench. For instance, from time to time she would receive bulky envelopes by registered post, and on more than one occasion she had asked me to witness her signature to a legal document. I never read the documents, and had not the remotest idea of their nature. It was now very evident that they had been transfers of stocks and shares.

It was only gradually that I was able to piece together the full story of her departure, and it is too long to give here. But the main facts are as follow:

On the morning when the odd man sent me the telegram Mrs Wrench suddenly appeared in the kitchen door, dressed, as the old man described it, 'Like nobody.' She wore a fur coat, silk stockings, shoes with very high heels, and she carried a silver-mesh bag. In a hoarse and lofty voice, without a trace of a Scottish accent, she commanded the odd man to take her suit-case to the village Ford, which at that moment arrived outside the door. He was so thunderstruck that he obeyed, gazing at his late companion in awe.

As they walked down the path Mrs Wrench briefly informed him that she was leaving for good, as she had come into money, that she did not propose to give any address, as she was going to Canada, and was sick of the sight of England, and that she would 'waive' the question of any wages I might owe her. As she had been paid in advance, 'waive' seems the right word.

That was absolutely all. She was off, in the Ford, before any more could be said. And from that instant, a darkness as deep as the grave descends on Mrs Wrench. There is one brief flash of light, at the station where, for a moment, the astonished porters saw her entering a first-class carriage. But after that . . . there is darkness. Let her rest in it.

A few days later, the S's arrived, and from their arrival dates the Age of Peace. I no longer felt like an intruder in my own cottage. And I no longer had to wonder if it would be a terrible strain if anybody were asked in to have a glass of port after dinner.

*Chapter 17*

RAIN ON THE ROOF

Soon after the S's arrived, the Great Drought began. Although it was only the beginning of May, the skies remained, day after day, like a sheet of blue enamel, without a single flaw. This Great Drought was the direct cause of many exciting developments at Allways which we shall narrate in due course. I think that some of these developments were due to the state of emotional tension which a drought always seems to induce.

It is terrible to walk through a garden in a drought— almost as terrible as walking down the Thames Embankment during a bad spell of unemployment. You want to water all the poor flowers and you want to give all the poor devils money. There are only a few buckets left in the water butt, and only a few shillings in your pocket. What are you to do?

It is at times like this that one wishes one were a cow, or some other nice ruminant animal, that didn't worry.

Therefore, we stay indoors, waiting for the rain.

Now in case you are getting impatient, I would remind you that there was once a great man called Pascal, who delivered himself of the wisest generalization about Mankind which has ever echoed through this dusty world. Do you remember it? Pascal said: '*All the misfortunes of man arise from one thing only, that they are unable to stay quietly in one room.*' Well, you stay quietly here with me, during that

second June at the cottage, towards the end of the Great
Drought.

For really, the rain is coming, very soon, and when it has
come, and when a million scents of saved souls are drifting
through the window, we can get on with the story. You
won't care, by then, because the savour of flowers and leaves
after rain will have drugged you into a merciful oblivion.

We are still waiting for the rain, in our quiet room. The
barometer, of course, is haughtily unaware of the fact that
the skies are clouding and that a tiny breeze is blowing
through the hedges.

If your barometer is in the least like mine, it may be
likened to a guest who arrives extremely late at a party with
news which we have all been discussing for the last three
hours. My barometer registers 'Very Dry', with unfailing
fidelity, until the thunderstorm is over. Like those tiresomely amiable women who say '*Such* a success' about all
marriages, even when the parties concerned are bouncing
about on the wrong sofas with the wrong people under their
very noses. And then, when the hedges are dripping, and a
muddy torrent swirls down the garden stream, and one is in
a fearful state about the Canterbury bells, whose pale pink
faces are spattered with mud, the barometer very cautiously
and tremulously takes a step back. Just as the amiable
women, when it was all over, breathe a faint 'I told you so'.

Barometers and politicians, one might say, at random,
have much in common. They are always wise after the
event. I feel that Mr Asquith must have first said those
melodious words, 'Wait and see'—while he was tapping a
barometer at The Wharf, to see if the rain outside was real
rain, or just an illusion, like the German bombardment.

§ 2

At last the rain came. It came like a long-drawn sigh—a faint patter on the leaves, that at first I thought was the wind. And there was a ghostly, hesitant tapping on the roof of the tool-shed, as the big drops fell, one at a time. I liked the rain to come like that in big drops, sulkily, because it heightened the exquisite suspense of wondering whether these drops were only stray visitors, on their own, or whether they were the vanguard of a host that was following from above.

When the rain came in those big, solemn drops, there were a thousand excitements to be noted while I sat quietly by the open window, like a good little student of Pascal. For instance, the first drop of rain fell straight on to a volume of Keats's poems which had been left open on the little garden table outside. I hurried to fetch the poems, and as I put my hand out for the book, another drop fell, almost in the same place. These two drops had fallen, like tears lately shed, on to the loveliest lament Keats ever wrote—

> *O Sorrow!*
> *Why dost borrow*
> *The natural hue of health, from vermeil lips?*
> *To give maiden blushes*
> *To the white rose bushes?*
> *Or is it thy dewy hand the daisy tips?*

There, on the poem, the raindrops glittered, as though they were Keats's own tears. The rain fell, the print dimmed . . . the lovely words were dissolved in Sorrow's dew. It was as though a cloud had drifted over the open book and, growing heavy with sadness, had shed itself in the poet's memory.

Still I stayed indoors, drugged by the rain. The books had
been taken in, and the cushions, and the deck-chair was
folded under the eaves. The rain was coming down, fairly
heavily. And I sat by the window, as though hypnotized,
as though the rain were falling for me alone.

Any good gardener will know what I mean. For when
the rain comes, after a drought, he is *himself* the thirsty soil
and it is his own agony that is being relieved . . . his
own soul which is being saved. In spirit he bares his breast
and sighs with delight, as the trees sigh when the water
trickles down their trunks . . . in spirit he closes his eyes,
as the lids of the flowers are closed by the merciful rain . . .
'More, more!' he cries . . . and always there is the sense of
life returning, as it returns to the fainting leaves.

And how busy and anxious and tiresome he is if the
rain seems likely to stop!

'Will this have done good? Is this enough . . . surely
this *has* done some good?'

The gardener always says 'It ought to go on for another
three hours before it'll do much good, sir.'

But in the sky there is a dreadful patch of bright blue
appearing! And that lovely angry-looking cloud, that
seemed about to come down in a great deluge, has turned
out to be a sheep in wolf's clothing, for it is producing nasty
little fleecy edges, and is starting to caper away, over the
hills!

'Oh, come down . . . come down . . . go on . . .
please don't stop!'

The amount of energy I put into these invocations was
tremendous. It was, of course, as useless as the energy we
expend by pressing the feet violently on an imaginary

brake while being driven by a snorting sportsman on a slippery road. Still, it was a form of energy that I could not control. I felt that if I stopped looking out of the window for one moment the rain would cease.

'Surely this *must* have done some good . . . don't you think this will be enough?'

But I never waited for a reply because I knew that it was not nearly enough. The soil under the hedges was still dry and caked. It must grow dark before the rain can be said to have really soaked through. And indeed, if it weren't for the fact that I had been watching the rain against a dark background, it would hardly have been possible to tell that it was raining at all.

§ 4

But at last it really came down 'cats and dogs'. The anxiety was over. And the itch of exploration was upon me.

For now was the time to put on an old mackintosh, and fetch an umbrella, and trot off to see what had happened. The first place to visit, of course, was the greenhouse. Here there was a glorious gurgle going on in the tank, and all the panes were clear and glistening. Then there was the pond. It was rising visibly, and the goldfish looked happier than they had been looking for weeks, darting about . . . peppered with rain drops. Then the stream at the bottom of the orchard . . . it had swollen to a torrent which chuckled and hiccuped and tumbled, like the dirty little ragamuffin that it was. And then there were all the flowers . . . but that would take us far too long. Besides there was a sudden urgent summons from the house . . . a bell ringing violently . . . what was it?

Well, 'it' was the something which I have promised so
often in the past few pages . . . the resumption of the
story. We must therefore return to the narrative, summoned
by that tinkling bell, which sounded one stormy day in
June, not many years past.

I ran back to the house, folding my umbrella.

'What is it? What is it?'

'It's the thatch, sir. Simply *pouring* through.'

'Oh Lord.'

'I always told you, sir, we ought to have it done.'

'I know. Have you put anything underneath?'

'All we could lay hands on.'

'All right. I'll go up and see.'

I ran upstairs. Into the blue bedroom. There in the
doorway, I paused.

It was indeed a dismal sight. Large patches of the ceiling
were grey. Through several cracks ominous little streams
were running, streams of water rendered milky by the
whitewash. Pieces of damp plaster were scattered about the
carpet. All that could be done to meet the onslaught had
been done. The little room echoed with the shrill trickle of
water falling into basins.

Dismal . . . yes. Dismal . . . y-y-yes? Dismal . . .
*no*! There was something gloriously exciting about this
disaster. It was a challenge of the elements. All about me
was the smell of old wood and clean linen. Outside the rain
was shooting a million swift arrows of silver, again and
again, into the quivering bosom of the earth, on to the
proud leaves of the trees, against the frail roof of my cottage.
At such a moment I and the cottage were one. We accepted
the challenge, gladly. We declared war, together, on the
rain . . . the rain that so lately had been our friend.

I ran downstairs and sought out my housekeeper.

'Tomorrow,' I cried, 'we shall send for Mr Penthrift!' And even as I said it, there seemed to be a slight lull in the rain, as though it had heard, and taken fright.

For Mr Penthrift was the best thatcher in the whole county of Huntingdon.

## Chapter 18

## REEDS IN THE WIND

Mr Penthrift looked exactly like the Duke of Wellington. He was not so tall, it is true, and there was a twinkle in his eye which I have never associated with the Gentleman of Iron. But when I first saw him, standing outside the front door, on a summer evening, the resemblance was uncanny. The same chin, the same mouth, and most important of all, the same nose.

But the resemblance, happily, was only profilic. Mr Penthrift could not have had a gentler, kindlier nature. He gave me the impression that he loved thatching so much that if he could have afforded it, he would have done my roof for nothing.

The price was the first thing we discussed.

'Well, it all depends on whether you have reeds or straw,' said Mr Penthrift. 'And then again, whether you'll be wanting any diamonds.'

'Diamonds?' I looked at Mr Penthrift sharply. Was he suggesting that the roof was to be encrusted with precious stones?

'That's what they call the little pattern we make, sir, on the ridge.'

'Oh, I see.' In some ways I was rather sorry to hear this. It would have been nice to toy with the idea of a cottage with jewels glistening from the roof . . . with bands of emeralds round the windows and the front door thick with

229

rubies. On moonlight nights it would have looked like an immense toy, carelessly dropped by a giant in the quiet lane.

'Will it be reed or straw, sir?'

'Which do you think?'

'Well, of course, the reed'll last much longer. A good three hundred years, the reed'll last. But the straw . . .' and here Mr Penthrift wrinkled his nose a little contemptuously. 'The straw'd have to be done all over again after fifty years.'

A mere fifty years, in the life of my cottage, seems nothing at all. So the idea of thatching it with straw was obviously out of the question. Hardly would the straw be in place before it would have to come off again. It would be like putting on a hat to go to the pillar box at the end of the road.

So though Mr Penthrift told me that the reed thatch would cost a hundred and sixty-five pounds, I decided to have it.

§ 2

I asked him where, and when, he found his reeds. He took a pull at his pipe and said:

'In Fallow Water, sir . . . that's where the fen ends, over Ramsey way. We fetch the reeds in December and January . . . that's the best time. They grow six foot high in the ponds round there. A flat-bottomed boat's the best to fetch 'em in. And you have to take 'em off below the water, with a sharp scythe. It needs a knack.'

Since then I have been reeding, on winter mornings, in Fallow Water, and I can bear out the truth of Mr Penthrift's statement that it needs a 'knack'. When you first grip the scythe, and plunge in your arm, nothing happens. You only bruise the poor stems of the reeds. And even if you cut them, you only cut a few, which fall in the wrong direction, away from the boat. It needs skill and practice to bring them down in a proud sweep, with their plumes towards you.

This is what happens when I go reeding:

It is a dark, cheerless morning, with an icy wind coming over the fens. Though it is nearly nine o'clock the sky is still night-stained, and only a pool of watery yellow in the east shows where the sun is hiding. But I have had a good breakfast, and am wearing the thickest coat I could find so that I am not cold. Besides there is something so exciting about this little adventure that the blood runs more quickly through one's veins.

The little boat is waiting, half hidden behind the reeds. We enter it and push off.

'A cold morning,' says Mr Penthrift. His nose is now bright blue, making him look more like the Duke of Wellington than ever.

'Very cold,' I reply. And that is all our conversation, for the work is beginning.

We paddle the little boat towards a cluster of reeds that rises, like some fantastic city, over the black water. A gust of wind blows up, and there is a sudden wild whispering among the leaves of the reeds and in their brown feathery crests, as though they knew that their day was ended, that they were about to fall, cut down cruelly by the enemy that is coming from under the water. Sometimes, when we have come to a particularly beautiful cluster, whose stems thrust themselves proudly, six foot above the surface, whose leaves are very green, whose plumes are very gallant, I have hesitated before cutting them. They seem so happy out here, in the lonely fen, with the secrets of the water about them, and the cry of the wild fowl.

However, one has no time for sentimental musings when Mr Penthrift is about. The boat is brought to a standstill. You lean forward, grasping your curved scythe. You bare your arm, take a deep breath, and plunge it into the icy water. Oh . . . it is agony! The water is ice-cold and you feel that a sword is running down your arm. But you don't let yourself cry out . . . you brace yourself up, and with a sudden movement that is half a lunge and half a swoop you draw the scythe across. And if you are lucky, and cut clean, the reeds tremble for a moment and then fall, with their plumes stretching over the side of the boat.

Whereupon, you draw out your arm, which is stinging with cold, and pull the reeds towards you, arranging them in a pile on the floor of the boat.

§ 3

There is something very sad about the fall of the reeds. But something beautiful too. For all the time, while you are reeding, you experience that strange exhilaration of the craftsman who is in *direct* contact with his work. Here are the reeds lying before you. They are the actual substance which is to provide you with a roof . . . and the provision of roofs is, after all, one of the major preoccupa-tions of mankind. You, yourself, have found these reeds, which have been born of wind and water. And from wind and water they will protect you, till you are old, and die, and care neither for the wind nor for the rain.

Compare that occupation with the task of the average manual labourer, sitting in his factory, and then ask your-self if the Industrial Revolution was not, perhaps, the greatest affliction that ever visited this earth. For the factory worker has no joy, nor pride, nor interest, even, in his work. He may be one of a thousand men who, between them, are turning out some exquisite fabric—but what is that to him? He doesn't even see the fabric, he plays no part in its design, he does not even handle a needle. All he does is to stand day in and day out before a great machine, which roars at him incessantly, while he feeds it with oil and wearily watches its whirring steel arms.

It is as though the modern worker were some hypnotized acolyte in the service of a bloody goddess, called Capital, who never sleeps, who never smiles, who roars incessantly with an iron throat, who will starve those who do not obey, and send to destruction, impartially, those who love her or hate her.

## § 4

For weeks, the side of the lane outside my cottage was piled high with reeds, and the garden was awhirl with little pieces of feathery leaf and plume. There was a terrible amount of mess, inside and out, but I didn't care, for some of the happiest hours of my life were spent with the thatchers.

I don't know whether it was most fun indoors or out. To stand in a bedroom and hear mysterious tappings on the ceiling, to see the plaster crack by an old beam, bulge, and fall heavily on to the waiting dust-sheet . . . to wait for the iron spike that slowly threaded its way through, to catch a glimpse of light as the blue sky filtered into the dark room . . . that was delightful enough.

But it was even more fascinating, I think, outside. You scrambled up the ladder, up and up, to the dizzy height of nearly thirty feet. And then you lay with your tummy on the warm reeds, athwart the ridge, marvelling at the strange way in which the cottage appeared to you from this altitude. Why, you never realized it was so enormous. Your bedroom is miles away. And these chimneys, from which a faint blue haze of heat is rising, are gigantic. The bathroom, you see for the first time, is a little crooked . . . the eaves project at an odd angle, which explains why you can never get a proper view of the laburnum tree while you are lying in your bath.

The whole quiet pageant of Huntingdonshire is visible from this roof. It is like a lovely scroll unfolded. There, far away, is the bluebell wood, with the chequered fields beyond. There, to the east, is the white spire of Conington Church . . . and the Great North Road is just visible, with its silly procession of cars, some hurrying north and some hurrying south. (I often wonder what would happen if all the people who were hurrying north were suddenly switched round and compelled to hurry south, with angry expressions. And vice versa. Would the world be very different? Would they, themselves, be very different, even?)

However, that is getting us back to Pascal and his quiet room, and we must not look back, but forward.

§ 5

It was not till the thatch was done that I began to take any serious interest in the accommodation upstairs. And the first thing I worried about was the bathroom.

Now, although I wanted to improve my bathroom, I did *not* want a 'super-bathroom,' especially at Allways. I have never understood the recent passion for rich, repressed women to pour their superfluous emotions into their bathrooms. I remember being shown over the house of such a one, not long ago. The house was a delicious square Georgian house in Hampstead . . . down a cul-de-sac, with enormous chestnut trees round the court, hanging the spring airs with their white candles, which the London winds blew to a sweeter flame.

We walked through this poor tortured house, with dreadful little squinting modern statues glaring at us from Sheraton alcoves. We walked up a staircase with glass banisters . . . '*So* amusing . . .' panted my hostess. (Lord, how I hate that word 'amusing'!) And after a number of doors had been opened, and we had observed white rooms, with cactuses, and yellow rooms, without cactuses, and green rooms, that looked like an immense cactus, with a prickly bed in the middle, we were privileged to witness the hostess's bathroom. It was done entirely in yellow glass. Yellow glass on the ceiling, yellow glass on the walls, yellow glass on the floor. And she said, with a roguish smile:

'I can see myself in sixteen different places, when I'm sitting in this bath.'

'I didn't know women *had* so many places,' I replied, remembering the exquisite wit of another lady.

And I am not asked to that house any more.


§ 6


Though I did not want a super-bathroom, I wanted an efficient one. I thought, until the Great Drought, that I had it. The water all had to be pumped up from the well into a little cistern under the roof, but the well had never failed. One only had to be a little careful of the water.

THE GIFT OF A GARDEN

It was lovely brown water, as soft as silk, that plashed out of an ancient tap into a tiny white bath that lay in a corner under the eaves. I always had very small but efficient baths, in which one did a lot of soaping and wriggling to get the best effect. But my guests were not quite so considerate, which accounts for the following sort of conversation which has frequently echoed under the roof of Allways.

We are retiring for the night, having settled who wants what, and when, for breakfast. (It makes no difference by the way, what they say. The result is always eggs and bacon, at nine, in dressing gowns.)

Myself: *Do* have a bath in the morning, won't you?

Guest (somewhat startled): Why . . . yes. (And then adds coldly, as though suspecting an accusation of uncleanliness). Thank you very much.

Myself: I should hate you not to have a bath.

Guest (emphatically): So should I.

Myself: It's just that all the water has to be pumped up So if you wouldn't mind *very* much not filling it *quite* to the top?

At this the guest usually enters into the spirit of the thing. Some guests even say that they will go so far as only to wash 'bits' . . . a statement that causes us to look away from each other, hastily. I urge them to wash every bit, but only, if they don't mind, not to lie in the bath with the water running indefinitely.

In the morning they usually forget, and I hear them lying in the bath with the water roaring out in torrents. This means that I have to go outside the door and clear my throat very loudly and bang suitcases about. Whereupon the tap is quickly turned off, and a dead silence intervenes. The guest comes down to breakfast looking very clean but very guilty.

236

*Chapter 19*

# LEAVES AT THE WINDOW

We have now arrived at the second autumn. Every time the front door is opened the little calendar in the hallway flutters madly in a breeze that is sharpened with a hint of frost. The calendar marks:

OCTOBER 1ST

And then adds, in a sinister *sotto voce*:

'Pheasant shooting begins.'

What strange minds calendar-makers must have, I think, whenever I pass it. For them, something is always 'beginning', and it usually begins with a bang. Or if it does not begin with a bang, it informs us that some distinguished person is having a birthday. It is almost impossible to open one's calendar without being reminded, either that some bloodthirsty man is loading his gun, or that some weary creature is dictating polite replies to ambassadors who have felicitated her on an event which she would infinitely prefer to forget.

I would like a calendar that drops subtler hints. I would like one that told me not to forget to go and look for spindle-berries in the wood, because already they will be stained pink, bringing the days of apple-blossom to the heart of winter. I would like to be reminded that there may still be a few mushrooms in the sheltered valleys—mush-rooms that never grow very big but are excitingly black

237

underneath, and taste all the sweeter because you are only just in time to rescue them from the ground-frost. I would like to be told to order paper bags for the chrysanthemums, because if you put a nice big paper bag over the flowery crowns of your tall chrysanthemums you will never suffer the agony of seeing their golden petals tarnished at the edges. If you think it must be a bore to do this, I assure you that you are mistaken. Nothing is greater fun than going out in the morning, lifting off the paper bags, which are frozen stiff, and finding the brilliant, glowing flowers underneath. You can stand up the paper bags all the way down the path, and when they are all off you can squash them in your hands, with a delicious crinkling noise as you breathe the acrid sweetness of the grateful blossoms.

During that second autumn I was greatly exercised about this problem of sheltering the flowers outside. Some of them had to suffer, I knew. Nature must take her toll, and all that. But the little creepers by the house . . . the flowers that were nestling under the eaves so near and yet so far. Could one not do something about *them*?

I was particularly worried by a grape-vine which I planted in the previous November. This was not the vine to which I referred in my previous chronicle of Allways. No—this was a new comer. It had been planted in a rose-bed in the Secret Garden, and was trained against the wall outside the Garden Room. The rose-bed was about three feet from the wall, and there was a path in between, so the vine had to take a flying leap over the path, and land on the wall, which it did extremely gracefully. As the path was a tiny cul-de-sac people did not walk up it, or they would have tripped over the stem.

All through the summer this vine produced grapes galore. However, very few of them had ripened before the first frost came and turned them brown. This is so bitter a memory to me that I hate to think of it.

'Why, oh *why* did the frost have to come just then?' I sighed; on the morning that it happened. 'And why, oh *why* didn't I know it was coming? I could have got an oil stove, or something, or a blanket.' It made me feel terrible to think that I had been sleeping, like a loathsome profiteer, wrapped in quantities of blankets, with the radiators filling my room with warmth, while the wretched vine had been stabbed to the heart by the cold arrows of the frost—the sweet bloom of its grapes rudely destroyed.

I stared at the vine, and as my regret grew more intense, so my brain began to work out little plans for next year. (It is always 'next year' when you have a garden.) And suddenly I realized that I had the germ of an idea. It developed from a wild thought that if one had only known, the stem could have been loosened from the wall, and the whole vine could have been trailed into the Garden Room for the night, if the window were left an inch open to allow the stem to pass through. I should have had to leave a note for the housekeeper, so that she would not stagger back in the morning under the impression that the vine had come to life, and was stalking through the house, seeking what it might devour. But that would have been a detail.

Seriously, was it so impossible? Here on the other side of the wall was warmth and comfort. Only a few inches away. Was it beyond the ingenuity of man to bring some of that warmth and comfort to the vine?

It was not.

This was what we did. (It is terribly difficult to explain without a plan, but all the plans I have drawn look like soda-water syphons standing on a map of the battle of Waterloo, so it is better to stick to words.)

The Kitchen

I summoned Mr Joy and got him to build a long, coffin-shaped box. (He makes coffins, by the way, and complains bitterly that his nephews always spend his coffin-money on riotous living before he has time to put anything by for his old age.)

We bored two holes through this box, one at the side and one at the top, and then we took the box to the vine, threaded the stem through—(the box had to be cut in half, and put together again, but that is an unnecessary complica-tion)—and set it against the wall.

The situation was then as follows: The end of the vine stem, where it plunged into the earth, was exposed, as it should be. But six inches up it entered the box, remained in the box for about two feet, and then emerged at the top of the box and proceeded to clamber up the wall.

The box was then painted white, so that it looked like a long garden seat, set against the wall, under the window.

And after that, I had grooves made along the edges of the box, got four large pieces of fabulously expensive glass, set the glass in the grooves and set another piece of glass on top. Then one had a little sort of greenhouse, which looked like an extra bay window, completely covering the vine.

I rushed into the house to see what it looked like from inside.

As soon as I opened the door I breathed a sigh of relief. You would not have know the glass was there. You just saw the original window, and the Secret Garden beyond.

I walked across to the window and opened it. Stretched out my hand. Tapped the glass. Stroked a leaf of the vine. Said to the vine: 'I'm terribly sorry I didn't think of this before. But next year. . . .'

## § 2

Next year, we were amply rewarded. The glass remained in place all through the winter, except during a very mild week when we removed it. (It only took about a minute and a half to slide the glass out of the grooves and prop it up against the wall.) And though you would never know that it was there, except when it was snowing, or raining, there was always the delightful consciousness that the vine was being protected, that it had become, as it were, a member of the family. On bitter grey days, in March, when the wind had the sting of a lash, I would open the window in the Garden Room and gloat over the tiny green buds that were already swelling on the vine. 'I wonder if you realize how spoilt you are,' I would say indulgently. The vine did not answer. 'I suppose you know' I went on, 'that even the Scotch firs are looking down in the mouth? That the *Berberis bealii* is nipped to the bone? And that the *Lonicera fragrantissima* is a positive wreck?'

But though this vine did not answer, in words, it answered, most lavishly, in deeds. For on the following summer, it had a good two months' start over the rest of the creepers. By the end of June its plentiful clusters had already begun to form. The glass had long been removed, of course, though the box-seat remained.

In the last week of July, when the grapes were black, I took great pleasure in leading people out to this seat, and asking them, carelessly, if they would not like to sit down for a moment.

'But grapes . . .' they exclaim.

'Grapes?' I say vaguely, looking in the wrong direction.

'But *masses* of grapes—out of doors—in July!'

'Oh *those*,' I say, unmoved. 'Yes. They really ought to be thinned out.'

'But how do you do it?'

Whereupon I sit down, blocking out the view of the tell-tale glass, which is only half concealed under a cascade of clematis.

'There is something very remarkable', I say, 'about the climate of Huntingdonshire.'

§ 3

However, one could not build little glass-houses outside every window in the cottage. The vine happened to be ideally situated for such treatment. If one had tried it on other creepers, it would have looked ridiculous. And so, as far as that was concerned, I had to be content with protecting a few of the rarer winter flowers with sacking.

And every night, when I went to bed, I opened my window, and gently lifted in a spray of wistaria, which had clambered up to the glass and was beating its frozen fingers on the pane.

There were, however, many other ways in which I succeeded in bringing the garden indoors.

One of them, of course, was with great baskets of ever-lasting flowers.

I do not think most people take enough trouble with their baskets of everlasting flowers. They stuff them in untidily, and half the flowers rot, and the whole affair is soon covered with dust, so that it reminds one of those gruesome collections of pampas grass and honesty and sea thistles which are arranged on the mantelpieces of seaside boarding houses, with the Black Prince, in bronze, on the left, and a view of Mont Blanc, with real frosting, on the right.

For the basis of my everlasting bunches I found, after the first year, that it was best to form a groundwork of statice rather than of the popular helichrysum. (That sounds very pompous, but statice, as you probably know, is sea-lavender, and helichrysum is the Sunday name for the ordinary 'everlasting' flower.) There are three sorts of statice which are absurdly easy to grow from seed—pink, yellow and mauve. You should pick them, the instant they are in flower, and dry them in the sun, because if you leave them too long on the plant the stalks will grow mouldy.

Nothing could be prettier than a basket which has a groundwork of these three shades of statice. (By the way, you want to sow about twice as much pink and yellow as mauve, if you wish to obtain an equal quantity.)

When you have your groundwork you can add the everlasting flowers, to taste, and also a few sprays of that very delightful flower, which is not nearly well enough known, called xeranthemum. I never hear that word without thinking of a limerick which runs:

> We've got a new maid called Xeranthemum
> Who said 'I've been living at Grantham, mum:
>   But my mistress took fright
>   For I snored in the night,
> To the tune of the National Anthem, mum.'

The xeranthemum is a most versatile flower with as many varieties of colour as the nemesia. You can sow it out of doors in April, and cut it in August, again remembering to cut it the moment it flowers.

There are only two other things I put in my everlasting bunches. One is obvious and the other is An Invention.

The obvious one is maidenhair fern. I do not know if it is very Philistine of me, but after cutting the sprigs of maidenhair, and after drying and pressing them, I dip them in green ink. Ordinary green ink at a penny a bottle gives them a beautiful grass green colour which lasts all through the winter.

The Invention—which *sounds* vulgar and hideous, but *is* gay and delightful—is feathers. Ordinary white hen's feathers, about four inches long, pushed in between the dry, rustling petals. They give just that touch of white which you cannot get in everlasting flowers. And they look like flowers themselves . . . you would not know they were feathers until you went close up to the basket.

Reading this over I seem to have given a detailed and touching description of How To Make A Hat That An Eccentric Female Could Wear In Church On Palm Sunday In The Year 1901. The sort of hat in which one could feel *really* thankful that King Edward had made such a speedy recovery from his operation for appendicitis.

Well, let us leave it at that. If you could see my little bowls and baskets, glowing in dark corners throughout the winter, by the side of a bed, on a window-ledge, in an empty space on a bookshelf, you would not laugh at them. Rather would you praise the gallantry with which they keep their sweet complexions even in the face of flaunting cinerarias and elegant cyclamens; that are like débutantes, dancing for their few days of life, while the well-preserved wallflowers watch them from the shadows. But no . . . the everlasting bunches do *not* remind me of wallflowers. They have an eternal youth. And if you take them to your heart, something of that youth will flow through their strange, dry petals into your own heart.

§4

This is a book about a house, as we have said before, and
it is not fitting, therefore, that we should deal here with the
lore of bulbs, nor peer into the attics and cupboards to see
if the Cynthella hyacinths are sprouting, nor inquire,
querulously, why nearly all the winter irises send up such
deceptive fountains of green leaves without a single flower,
like heralds that blow their trumpets flamboyantly for kings
that never come.

Yet, as we are talking about bringing the garden indoors,
I would like to tell you of one funny little experiment I
made during this second winter at the cottage.

Flowers, I had, through the everlasting bouquets. And
bouquets. And creepers, through the vine. And quantities
of gloriously bronzed beech branches. (It seems almost
impertinence on my part to remind you that if you wish to
keep branches of bronze beech leaves all through the winter,
you must plunge their stems in a mixture of half water and
half crude glycerine. But there may be some small, depraved
person, living in a damp cave somewhere, who does not
know this vital fact. If so, I would ask the small depraved
one not to forget to ask for *crude* glycerine. Why is it called
*crude*, I do not know, because its results are most elegant,
and will keep your beech leaves in perfect condition till
spring is well on the way.)

My experiment was due to a sudden aching realization
that though the flowers had been induced to walk, as it
were, into the house, and the leaves too, and the vine, the
*wood* had shown no signs of coming in. And I did so
bitterly want an indoor wood. For weeks I toyed with the
idea of a model Japanese garden, but the more I saw of
model Japanese gardens the less I liked them. There was

something a little uncanny about them . . . those stunted trees, whose roots must surely be tortured against the arty china in which they had usually been repressed. And those sinister little cactuses, and the even more sinister tin coolies, wandering over a bridge into a whirl of moss. What happened to those strange figures, when they crossed the bridge? Would they sink into the moss, or would they walk on and on, until they came to the edge? And having come to the edge would they have the decency to remember that they were only tin, or would they suddenly take on a hideous mimic life, and jump over, and crawl up the dinner table, and present themselves against one's wine-glass at awkward moments? That stork, too—that inevitable stork that is always to be found in Japanese gardens, glaring with an imbecilic expression at some dreary little water plant—I felt that that stork should not be encouraged. It had probably been produced by the hundred thousand in unhygienic factories in Yokohama, by men who burn widows with the utmost alacrity, and say *yam-yam*, and eat rice with a barge-pole, and then go out and burn some more widows. (That is all that Balliol ever taught me about Japan.)

No—I wanted something simpler. A *real* wood, indoors, with the tang of wet earth about it, and a sense of blowing branches. A wood over which the desolation of winter would brood, and the mists of spring would hover—a wood which in summer would cast its shade and in autumn its leaves.

It sounds an impossible ideal, when you remember that all these emotions had to be concentrated in a couple of square feet of pottery, which could be placed on a side table. Yet . . . it succeeded. The secret was beech-nuts.

§5

There are but few beech trees in Huntingdonshire. They do not take kindly to our particular brand of clay. But here and there, in a valley, or alone in a far-flung field, you will find this lovely tree—this tree whose trunk, in winter, is gay with emerald moss, while the winds play their sweetest tunes in and out of its bleak choirs. Such a tree I found, and loved, that stood in solitude on the edge of the bluebell wood as if it had been sent to Coventry by the other trees, or as if it were too proud to join them. Often I would go and lie beneath this beech. I know it so well that the shadows must surely have thrown their pattern across my heart.

On this second autumn I was lying under the beech one day when I suddenly saw a tiny beech by my elbow. I sat up and saw another. And another. The whole ground was dotted with tiny beech trees. They never seemed to be more than a year old . . . something happened, apparently, after the first year. But at least they *did* seed themselves, and push their stems through the earth, and produce their little silky leaves, that were as green as the eyes of very small, very timid kittens.

Why not collect some beech-nuts, find the choicest possible soil, place them in a big earthenware bowl and see what happened? If the worst came to the worst they would only go to sleep. And meanwhile, one could recite poems over them, imploring them to make an effort, telling them that the world was waiting for them, that there was a very white ceiling hovering over them, and a golden-forked fire, leaping with excitement about them.

I filled my pockets with beech-nuts. When I returned, I chose twelve of the brownest, glossiest nuts I could find. Then I placed them, very gently, in an earthenware bowl

248

filled with the softest earth. I did not water them. I put them in a dark cupboard. And waited. And waited. And waited.

November came, with a canter of wild winds, and a scurry of sleet. December was silent, and awe-struck . . . one had a sense of a giant, hooded figure, brooding beneath a canopy of frozen stars. January was gay and absurdly spring-like. Birds sang. There were sheets of golden aconites under the elm. The snowdrops laughed all day long. Some-body had told them that life was hard and difficult, whereas they found it bland and easy and delightful. February stamped an iron foot on the snowdrops—stamped so sul-lenly and so long that the earth was like a sheet of iron, stiff with sorrow, and hardened against all adversity. March was tempestuous: there were days of snow and days of sun— black days and white days, flashing past in a fierce kaleido-scope.

April came.

I opened the door of the cupboard.

Twelve little beech trees got up and bowed.

You must forgive the dramatic licence. Needless to say I had opened the door of the cupboard a great many times before—so often, in fact, that the hinges were almost worn off. But it happened that I had to be away from the cottage for a whole month during the time that the little beech-nuts were making their last effort. And when I *did* open the door . . . there they were. All twelve of them. With leaves so tiny that it hurt. Of a green that baffles description. A green that is almost yellow, but with a magic that no yellow has ever attained in this world.

The beech trees flourished all through the year. They are now three years old. They are about a foot high. They do all the right things. They respond most exquisitely to the seasons whose vagaries they only know by instinct. Yet, by the manner in which they burgeon in spring, and swell in summer, and flush in autumn, and despair in winter, you would say that they were outside the house, instead of in. It is as though they heard the call of the Seasons, as they marched by, as though the Seasons entered, and caressed them or ravished them, as the case may be. I hope it is like that. For they are brave and beautiful, and I love them.

## Chapter 20

## WOMEN ABOUT THE HOUSE

And now, a man might say, the tale is told. There is nothing more to be said. For we have seen, stage by stage, how the cottage was made clean and white; how the new windows let in the air of heaven, how the spirit of the garden flowed through it, how it was warmed and lit. What more can there be to write about?

The average woman will agree that with me there can be a great deal more to write about. For these things which we have recorded are only the foundations of the story. They are merely the background against which the principal drama moves—the drama of 'managing the house'. It is very much easier, if you can afford it, to make structural alterations, even if they are extremely elaborate, than to achieve domestic peace and happiness, to manage to have good food, to avoid 'rows', to obtain cleanliness without feeling that you dare not flick any ash on the carpet.

You may say that all these things are only the result of being lucky enough to have a clever housekeeper. But really it isn't quite as simple as that. There are many women who have excellent housekeepers, whose lives, none the less, are a desolation of muddle and worry.

In order not to be unjust, let me take, as an object of criticism, Mrs M., for she is really a very efficient woman. And yet . . .

We will let her speak for herself. We will go to lunch with her, as I did, not long since.

§2

The lunch was on Palm Sunday.

Mrs M. always goes to church on festival days. She goes in order to count the flowers she has given, so that she may be sure the vicar has not kept any of them back for his own drawing-room, instead of grouping them round the pulpit. Why she should do this, I cannot imagine, because the vicar has never shown any inclination towards this nefarious practice—indeed, his own garden is as bare as a desert on the Saturday evenings before such events. Nevertheless, Mrs M. always goes to church early when she has given flowers.

You can see her sitting in her pew, her eyes darting from pot to pot. 'I gave seven cinerarias,' she is muttering. 'I only see six.'

I have observed her, on certain occasions, leave her pew, before the service begins, and pretend to go over to borrow a Prayer Book from Mrs Joy, who sits on the other side of the church, in order that she may see if she can trace the seventh cineraria. It is usually lurking at the steps of the pulpit. Mrs M. smiles at it, nods, forgets to borrow the Prayer Book from Mrs Joy, and returns to her pew leaving us all, I fear, a little distracted.

The object of my lunch with Mrs M. was to help her choose things for a jumble sale, because she was having her annual tidy-up. However, there was also an ulterior motive behind the invitation.

'It will do you good to see how a *woman* keeps her house in order, for a change,' she observed.

I humbly agreed that it would do me a lot of good, and accepted, I also went to church, because the sermon would obviously be an excellent topic of conversation if there were any awkward silences at lunch.

Mrs M. sits just behind me. She has quite a pretty con-tralto and she is not unmusical. But unfortunately, she invariably scorns the tune and insists upon singing 'parts'.

The result is highly disturbing to the humble person, who, like myself, tries to sing the tune without feeling too self-conscious about it. The little organ begins the *Te Deum*. We stand up. I prepare a timid A natural, on which the chant opens. But Mrs M., a second before I have given out my A, sings a ferocious D. I descend in sympathy, but she promptly rises. I come down again, trying to meet her half-way, because when anybody is singing a very loud second behind you, your voice wobbles and eventually falls to her pitch. But no sooner have I got to Mrs M.'s D than she has leaped to my A natural. However pleasing the harmonics may, or may not, be, this practice is not conducive to a state of religious fervour.

## §3

We had roast beef for lunch, and Yorkshire pudding, and lovely baked potatoes which were *all* brown, all over, like a biscuit. Usually there is only one really brown, hard potato in the dish, so that one doesn't know whether to be greedy, and take it—pretending airily that one thinks it is just like all the other potatoes—or whether to be polite and pass it by. But at Mrs M.'s, all the potatoes were brown, so this problem did not arise.

There was also some beautiful cooked celery, covered with a white sauce.

'Out of the garden,' said Mrs M., with a bright smile, as I took some of the celery.

I smiled back. But as I lifted the celery on to my plate, the smile faded, for I noticed that the celery looked slightly darker than ordinary fresh celery. It looked indeed, exactly like a certain tinned variety which I used myself. I do not like many things out of tins, but there is an English firm which sells wonderful tinned celery, green peas and rasp‐ berries. And there are some tinned American soups which are delicious.

Well—I should soon know. I dug my fork into the celery. Before eating it I would give Mrs M. one more chance.

'Out of the garden?' I repeated innocently.

But Mrs M. flushed slightly. She did not repeat the assertion in so many words, but she said, sharply, 'I always wonder why you find it so difficult to grow celery.'

That settled it. I devoured a piece of celery.

Tinned!

There was absolutely no question about it. The celery mind you, was grand—much better than the average fresh celery. But it happened to have come out of a tin. I felt very angry with Mrs M. for telling such fibs. I said acidly:

'Your cook always does these things so well.'

'My cook has gone, if you're referring to Daisy.'

'Gone? But you had her only about six months.'

Mrs M. snorted. 'She was impossible!'

'But how?'

Mrs M. paused a moment, as though wondering whether she could take me into her confidence. 'It was a question of the hours she used to come in at night. Ten‐thirty . . . eleven . . . sometimes nearly midnight!'

I nodded sympathetically. 'I suppose she used to make a fiendish noise, and wake you up.'

'On the contrary, she was so quiet that I had to sit up for her, or I should have never known when she came in.'

'But, in that case what did it matter?'

'What did it *matter*? Really! I can't have my girls staying out all night.'

'But she didn't stay out all night.'

'Well, till midnight, then. It's the same thing in the country.'

'But why not, Mrs M.?'

I was not trying to embarrass poor Mrs M. And it was a full minute before I realized what she meant. 'Certain' things, it appeared, might be happening to Daisy in her nocturnal prowls. That was the trouble.

I protested against this suggestion. 'She was *hideous*, Mrs M. Very fat, and shortsighted, and a revolting complex, ion.'

'What has that got to do with it?' inquired Mrs M., coldly.

Now that she asked the question, I supposed that it really had very little to do with it, judging from the ghoulish girls who apparently rouse passion in some men's hearts. Yet, I was still unsatisfied as to Mrs M.'s explanation.

'But surely, Mrs M., if Daisy wanted to be led astray, she could be led astray just as well between the hours of eight and ten, as between the hours of ten and midnight.'

'That's beside the point.'

'On the contrary, it *is* the point, the whole point, and nothing but the point. You can't keep servants because. . . .'

'Ssh!'

The door opened and the housemaid appeared with the apple tart. For two minutes we both made feverish remarks about the cream and crust and how things were still going up. As soon as the door closed, I resumed:

'Because you don't allow them any liberty. You *say* it's because you have to look after their morals. . . .'

'It is.'

'But if you paused to think for one minute you'd realize that you're not affecting their morals one way or the other.'

'I may be old-fashioned, but. . . .'

'Well, Mrs M.,' I said, somewhat hotly, 'I think that in this matter it *is* a little old-fashioned to . . .'

'In that case we won't discuss the matter.'

We finished our apple tart in silence. I was burning with the wrongs of the dismissed Daisy. It seems a small matter, but I happen to feel deeply about it. Domestic servants, as a general rule, lead lives of unspeakable drudgery. They only get one night off—or possibly two—a week. What conceivable difference can it make to their employer if they come in at ten, or twelve, or six o'clock in the morning, provided that they do their work? If they are of the sort that 'goes wrong', they most assuredly *will* 'go wrong', at whatever hour they come in.

That is one of the charges I would bring against many women who run houses. That is why I am writing about this lunch with Mrs M., because she is about to give us another very flagrant example of feminine sin.

§ 4

But first . . . the celery.

In order to reach the hay-loft, where the objects for the jumble sale were accumulated we had to pass along a little brick pathway that led past the kitchen door, into a yard.

When we had finished our coffee, we went through the french windows, across the lawn, and made for this path. As we neared the kitchen door there were loud sounds of washing up, accompanied by hymns. I saw Mrs M. frown. She intensely dislikes these domestic noises. She has an amazingly keen ear for them, and can hear remarks which

WOMEN ABOUT THE HOUSE

no ordinary woman could possibly hear, provided that these remarks are made in the kitchen.

There was a feeling of thunder in the air, although it was early spring. Our footsteps echoed hollowly over the pavement. And just as we came past the kitchen door, out bustled the new cook, a pleasant, robust-looking creature of about fifty. She was walking so quickly that she collided with Mrs M., and dropped something which she was carrying in her hand.

'Oh!' said the cook, in one tone of voice.

'Oh!' said Mrs M. in another tone.

'Oh!' said I, in yet another.

And the 'something' rolled over and over the pavement with a loud, clattering noise, eventually coming to rest at the foot of the dustbin to which the cook had been bearing it.

The 'something' was an empty tin of Blank's celery. It lay there, glistening in the sunlight, with the title shining out in terrible and accusing clarity: *'Blank's Superfine Hearts of Celery.'*

Time stopped.

How it ever started again, I do not know. But eventually our legs moved forward once more, our lips formed aimless sentences, the attic stairs were climbed, and we found ourselves in the jumble saleroom. But it was a long time before we could really get down to business. We were both too shattered.

It says much for the sterling character of Mrs M. that she was able in the next half-hour to give a positively firework-like display of the other feminine vice to which I previously alluded—the vice of hoarding.

§ 5

It began with a photograph, which was lying partly hidden under a piece of old mink. I picked it up, and looked at it.

The photograph portrayed a heavily-moustached gentle-man staring with a look of grave suspicion at a Grecian urn.

'Who is this?'

'That? Oh—that is my Uncle Frederick.'

I looked at Uncle Frederick. It seemed terrible that he had been forced to stare for all these years at that urn. Could he not have a little excitement, and go to the jumble sale?

'I think somebody might buy it for the frame,' I sug-gested tentatively.

Mrs M. spoke very sharply. 'You don't imagine I'm going to send *that* to the sale?'

'Well . . . I suppose it is a bit . . .'

'Really!' She rose from her knees and snatched the photograph from me. 'With all its associations!'

'What associations?' I asked this question because I knew that Uncle Frederick had died of apoplexy at the funeral of Queen Victoria. We had often been told this, by Mrs M. It seemed, somehow, to reflect a certain grandeur upon her. I thought that Mrs M. might be able to give me a few historical details.

'Associations,' Mrs M. repeated loftily.

'But you were only a little girl . . .'

'And I was taught to *respect* my relations.'

'Well, I don't think Uncle Frederick would be par-ticularly honoured to be lying in the attic under a piece of old mink, if it comes to that.'

It was lucky I mentioned the mink, because the conversa-tion was again becoming a little heated.

Mrs M. took up the mink and shook it violently in her

258

irritation. A cloud of dust came out of it. We both squeezed the outside of our noses to stop ourselves from sneezing.

'I must have this cleaned,' said Mrs M.

'Is there time, before the sale?'

'And why should I send *this* to the sale?'

'But it's quite good enough, Mrs M.'

'Good *enough*?' she shook out the mink once more. And this time she could not squeeze her nose quickly enough to stop herself from sneezing. When she had finished, she said, 'It's far *too* good.' She sneezed again. 'It's bound to "come in", some day.'

I had been waiting for her to say that. All over England there are dusty hoards in cupboards which ought long ago to have been destroyed—old pieces of material; odd shoes, worn-out tennis racquets, balls that have long ceased to bounce, ornament boxes, keys that fit nothing—all kept because they may 'come in'.

That phrase gives me terrible visions. I cannot help interpreting it literally. I see myself sitting in an empty room. There is a dull scratching on the door. Slowly the door opens, and the mink 'comes in'. It stalks across the room, sending out clouds of dust. And just before it springs upon me, I sneeze and wake up.

Often these objects are kept for sentimental reasons. But usually the sentiment has long faded.

Mrs. M. pointed to a little cluster of ebony elephants in a corner. They were one of those frightful 'families' of elephants, the biggest about five inches high, and the baby being the size of a pea. You are supposed to think it is terribly amusing to have a baby elephant the size of a pea. Housemaids, who have to dust it, do not always see the joke.

'Those elephants,' said Mrs. M.

'Yes,' I could not decide whether she wanted me to say

how loathsome they were, or whether I ought to suggest that they would 'come in'.

'My cousin in India sent them to me—Colonel Waters-Thompson—you remember?'

I not only remembered him, but I also recalled that Mrs M. heartily detested him.

'Then let's send them to the sale at once,' I suggested brightly.

'But supposing he comes home on leave, and comes up here, and asks to see them?'

'You could say they'd all gone out for the day.'

Mrs M. projected her rabbit's teeth at a certain angle which warned me that she was not amused.

'I happen to be related to him,' she said.

I was growing hot and tired and impatient.

'But you're not related to the elephants, Mrs M.'

Which finished it. We descended from the attic, in silence, having chosen nothing at all for the jumble sale. I tried to make up for my abominable rudeness by sending Mrs M. a huge sack of gladioli bulbs. But it was a long time before we were really friends again.

In the end, she sent the mink to the sale. It was bought by Mrs Joy for five shillings. She wears it round her neck, on cold Sundays, in church. It becomes her very well. And often I have looked out of the corner of my eye, during the Psalms, and seen Mrs M. glaring with a very unchristian expression at Mrs Joy and her mink, saying to herself, 'It *would* have come in, after all.'

§ 6

If I did not know better, and had read the foregoing pages, I should have formed a very unfavourable opinion of myself. It seems that I am always grousing about the follies of 'women about the house'. I can't think why. I probably realize their problems, as sympathetically as most men.

Oh yes—there are a hundred and one little irritations in running a house, and perhaps it is because women have to face them, day in and day out, that they occasionally lose their sense of proportion—grow angry with young servants who are full of life and want to stay out till all hours of the morning. Poor dears: *they* can't stay out till all hours of the morning, themselves. Their families have too many insistent claims on them.

One day I want to write a book which shall show some-thing of the heroism of the average ordinary woman. A heroism that most men do not even suspect, or, if they sense it vaguely, take it for granted.

One very small example will suffice to show you the sort of book I want to write. And then this sentimental homily can be finished. The example is the 'family meal'.

Family meals are not, in themselves, inspiring things. But have you ever thought that they might be rather terrible, rather frightening, if it weren't that the women make them otherwise? There might come moments when sons and fathers and daughters and wives suddenly paused, and set down their glasses, and stared about them, in a sort of horror, saying, 'Who are these people? These men, and women, and children? Why are they sitting here? What have they to do with *me*? What is it all about?'

Those moments do come, even in the best regulated families. But somehow, by some miracle, the quiet woman who is sitting at the end of the table saves the situation. She herself is an entity—don't forget that—she herself has her dreams and her moods, her frets and her aches. But she sets them aside.

She says:

'I saw Miss Thompson this afternoon. Her sister is going to get a caravan.'

One son—the clever one—sniffs contemptuously. What does he care about Miss Thompson, or her caravan? However, the subject has been introduced, and he is led subtly away from his brooding on a more dangerous subject—a subject which *she* noticed, and understood, and feared.

The other son—the dull, elder one—also sniffs contemptuously. Really, mother and her old Miss Thompson, what the devil is there in that? All the same, a caravan would be fun. It might be grand in a caravan. Before he knows what he is about, his mind is off, over the hills, and the smoke of gipsy meals is assailing his nostrils.

'What *can* she see in that old Miss Thompson?' thinks the father, wearily. Yet for him, too, there is a momentary respite from the thoughts that were torturing him. If only he had sold, instead of buying! If only he had bought instead of selling! Well, if things go on like this, they'll be lucky if they have even a caravan between them.

They don't answer the quiet woman who is sitting at the head of the table. They say 'Oh' or 'really', or other words that cost nothing. But somehow the atmosphere is changed.

And she? Does she care about Miss Thompson and her caravan? Does she? You know that she cares not at all. That this little sentence is only one tiny symbol of the constant, tireless effort she makes, all her life, to keep the family a going concern, to keep its members happy, holding up their heads, each fulfilling his separate purpose—a purpose, generally, far higher in her imagination than it will ever be in reality.

No. She does not care about Miss Thompson and her caravan. And as she sits there, in the fading light, looking at the faces of her family, the man she loved, the children she bore him, she wonders if it is all worth while. For a brief terrible moment the longings which for years she had been suppressing descend upon her, tearing her with eager talons.

'If only . . .' she cries to herself. 'If only . . .'

But she never finishes the sentence. It might be dangerous for her.

It would certainly be dangerous for me.

*Chapter 21*

## SWEETS TO THE SWEET

Adventures were always happening at Allways. And the last adventure of all was, in some ways, the most exciting.

You remember the little alcove we found in the Garden Room, with the White Lady walled up in it? Well, that was a thrill, if you like. But the last thrill was greater.

It happened one day when Undine Wilkins came for sherry. Undine never drinks cocktails. There is nothing olde worlde about them, you see. But she drinks quantities of sherry, and is fortunately quite unaware of the difference between Amontillado 1900 and Smith's Best Cooking, 1933. Whichever she gets, she quivers her nostrils, and half closes her eyes and savours the sherry, murmuring 'Ah!' A quite sincere 'Ah!' I may say, even if it is a quite sour sherry.

While we were drinking our sherry, we talked about ghosts. Undine, I need hardly mention, was 'psychic'. She saw auras. At least she told us she did, and nobody except Mrs M. ever contradicted her. She also heard strange sounds at night—hissing sounds in the lane outside her cottage. Mrs M. said the sounds came from Mrs Joy's stray geese, but Undine knew better.

Anyway, after talking about ghosts for some time, Undine said that she should like to go upstairs and 'sense the atmosphere'. At first I wondered if this was a Tudor way of saying that she would like to wash her hands. But no . . . she really did wish to sense the atmosphere. And so we prowled about upstairs, in and out of the little bed/rooms, while she walked in front, breathing very heavily.

Nothing happened, and we were both a little dis/appointed.

It was just as we were about to come downstairs again that Undine suddenly stopped, like a pointer.

'What is in that cupboard?' she hissed.

'Which cupboard?'

'There! In that corner!' She darted out an accusing finger at the corner of the room.

'Good Lord!' I stepped up to it. 'I didn't even know there was a cupboard there.'

I knelt down. It was a very tiny cupboard, which had been so often whitewashed over that it was almost indis/tinguishable from the wall. The handle had long ago been torn off, or worn away. The woodwork had been painted many times, and the paint had mingled with the whitewash, so that it would need a knife to prise it open.

'It's pretty well glued up.'

'There is something in it,' breathed Undine.

I looked round and stared at her. She spoke with such conviction that for a moment I almost believed her.

'What sort of thing?'

'I don't know. I can only . . . I can only . . . sense it.'

I paused. It would be a great bore to make an ugly patch on the wall by tearing open the door and breaking the paint. On the other hand, there *might* be something in it. The spirit of adventure seized me. I felt in my pocket for a knife. Good! Here it was. I took out the knife, ran it down the edges of the cupboard, inserted the blade, prised it very gently. There was a sudden creak, and the door flew open.

Before I knew what had happened, Undine had rushed

over like a whirlwind, and thrust her arm into the cup⁄
board. She drew it out quickly again, bearing with it a
white object which I could not see clearly, because she
instantly hugged it in her arms.

'Oh!' she screamed . . . 'Oh! Oh! *Oh*!'

'What's happened? What is it? Have you been bitten?'

'*Oh*!' cried Undine again, a little less shrilly.

'But what is it? What *is* it?'

'A Booke,' she breathed. I swear she made it sound like
that. It *was* a book, a very old book, bound in yellow
parchment. But only Undine could have given it such an
ultra⁄Tudor intonation.

'Where? How? Let me *see* . . .'

'It was in there,' she gasped, pointing to the hole in the
wall, but keeping a tight hold of the book, which I was
longing to seize from her.

I lit a match and flashed it into the cupboard. It revealed
nothing but a tiny alcove, about three feet deep. I put in my
hand and tapped the walls. They were quite solid. It was
obvious that the Booke which Undine was clasping was
the only discovery we were going to make.   So I turned to
her.

'What . . .' I began.

'Listen!' She raised a long, tapering finger on which an
immense moonstone glistened, commanding silence. With
her other hand she smoothed out the dusty parchment that
was lying on her lap, and read in a voice that trembled, but
was clear; the following receipt:

> *To make Sugar plate to print.* In mouls or to make any
> Artificial Frutes or Muscardine comfits.
> Take a small quantity of gum dragaunt, and lay it in
> steep in rosewater till it is desolved into a gelly, then

strain it through a Cloth and beat it in a morter, till it looks very white, then put some searced sugar into it, and beat together, & when you have beaten it wi$^{th}$ so much searced sugar, y$^t$ it is so stif, y$^t$ you may take it out of yoe Morter, take it forth and work it into a stif paste w$^{th}$ searsed sugar, so you may print it in yo$^e$ mouls or use it otherwise, as you pleased.


§ 2


This is a true story. And because it is true, it will probably sound false. Oscar Wilde once said, 'Nothing looks so like innocence as an indiscretion.' In the same way, nothing sounds so like a lie as the truth.

Yet we *did* discover that book in that cupboard. And if anybody doubts it, I will show it to him, in its faded parchment, with the title-page half eaten away by rats:


A
RECEIPT BOOK
OF
COOCKERY.
1698


Some of the recipes are a good deal older than 1698, as Undine and I discovered.

Eagerly we leant over that book, in the fading light—a golden October sunset that flooded in on the yellow parch-ment—yellow to yellow, with the grave black letters dancing before our eyes, as though they were overjoyed to be read again, after two hundred and fifty years of neglect. And as we turned the pages it seemed that there was a scent in the old room of ghostly sweetmeats; there drifted back to us the perfume of curious country wines, the aroma of forgotten preserves, the bitter-sweet flavour of kitchens which have long crumbled into dust.

Why—the very titles were dripping with poetry, like jars of country wine that cannot contain their sweetness. Listen!

To Preserve Quinces Red or White.

To Make Paste or Apricocks Very Goode.

To Make Red Muscardine Comfits.

To Make Slipcoat Chees. The Lady Bray's Recipe.

To Dry All Manner of Green Ploms.

To Boile Sugar to a Thine Sirrup.

To Know When Sugar is Boiled to a Manus Christie Heighte.

To Make Quodeny of any Kind of Plumes.

And then, there were other recipes—secret recipes—a page of very faded print headed Aqua Mirabilis, which made me feel like an alchemist who at last has discovered the philtre of immortality.

I will skip these ecstasies, and draw a veil over the unfortunate 'difference' which arose between Undine and myself over this book. She said that as she had 'sensed' it, the book belonged, by rights, to her. I differed. The result, in the long run, was eminently satisfactory to both parties. I spread the fame of Undine's psychic powers all over Allways, and sent her a copy of the book, beautifully typed, and accompanied by a dozen really good Amontil-lado. I also asked her, on many occasions, to come and taste the recipes at dinner. She came, bless her heart. And whether they were good or bad, she adored them.

Here are a few of the recipes for which I can vouch by personal experience.

§ 3

There are three recipes for cowslip wine. Each time the word cowslip is spelt in a different way. Thus:

Cowslep
Couslepe
Couslip

Of these, the first recipe is the best. I copy it below, and will add that when we gave it to the men who were digging out the new pond last spring, two of them fell into the pond, and all of their wives complained to me, 'which pleased me mightily', as Pepys might say. Here it is:

> *To Make Cowslep Wine. Martha Benthall.* Take 7 gallons of water put in as much sugar as w<sup>ll</sup> make it so strong as it w<sup>ll</sup> bear an Egg, set it on y<sup>e</sup> fire till it w<sup>ll</sup> be clear that no Scum w<sup>ll</sup> arise, so let it stand untel it be but blood warm, so poure it on 2 Pecks of couslep pips, then put in 4 Lemons cut peell and all in, then let it stand w<sup>th</sup> a quarter or half of a pint of good lite yest fo<sup>r</sup> to work, then let it stand a day and a night, then strain out the Cowleps, then put y<sup>e</sup> Lemons into y<sup>e</sup> barrell, then let it stand about 2 weeks before you bottle it.

§ 4

Here is a recipe for making snuff. If you have never taken snuff there is obviously something lacking in your life. The first time I ever had it was at Trinity College, Cambridge, where I once dined at the High Table with the dons, for some obscure reason which neither I nor the dons appeared to have grasped. At this college they hand round a large and most exquisite early Georgian snuff-box, while you are having your port in the Combination Room. The silver is so brightly polished that you can see all the windows latticed in silver, and your own face reflected, like a lovely pink balloon, as you bend over to take your snuff. There are five sorts . . . or is it six? I forget. But I remember that they are graded very delicately, in varying degrees of fineness.

I always forget if a gentleman sneezes or doesn't sneeze when he takes snuff. There is a very definite rule about it. As I always sneeze, I assume that gentlemen do not.

Here is the recipe for Snuffe:

> *To Make Snuffe.* Take 2 Ounces of bestt Tobacco 2 Nutmegs of Sweett marjorum Rosemary Germandor Bittony & Bassilli thimes one handfulle pound all these welle together & pouder them very fine & youse it for snuffe.

§ 5

However, these recipes are a little esoteric for the average housewife. She would be more interested in a recipe dated 1752, 'To Make Blummonge' . . . A lovely word, Blummonge, which makes one think of a baby, bubbling out its lips rather angrily, as it bangs a petulant spoon against its sillabub. But an even lovelier word is 'Marchpane,' for which I will certainly give you the recipe.

Why do we insist upon calling Marchpane 'Marzipan'? Marzipan is a bastard Teutonic innovation. It is the sort of word that a fanatic spits out at his troops, when urging them on to further follies. Cakes of marzipan, I feel, have

evil omens printed on their bottoms. But Marchpane . . .
ah! that is cool and delicious. A fragrant word, pastoral
and English, in the best sense of the word 'English', recalling the days when England was tiny, and young and
infinitely lovable. Here is the recipe:

> *To Make Marchpane Paste.* Take a pound of Almonds
> & blanch them, and beat them to mash in a Morter,
> then put half a pound of sugar to them, and beat them
> together an houre, and it w$^{ll}$ be in a paste, and if you
> see your paste beat Oylie put into it a little Rose water,
> and beat it together and that w$^{ll}$ take away the Oylinefs
> from it, and so you may print it in your moulds, make
> a Machpane w$^{th}$ it, or use it otherwise a s you please.

I can vouch for that recipe. It makes the best marchpane
you ever tasted. I gave a supply of it to a very charming
American girl only six months ago, to use on her wedding
cake. She is not yet divorced. So you see that it must have
magic qualities.

$\S$ 6

As I wander through this Receipt book it becomes more
and more evident that I shall have to publish it, one day, in
its entirety, with a preface of enchanting prose, that will
drift as lightly and as savourously as the scent of roast meats
from the kitchen when the door is open on winter nights,
and hunger is gripping you. Yes, that will be a happy
task! But it would be wicked to make you wait so long for
some of the other recipes. I will choose them quickly, before
I relent.

What about *Mifs Leblanc's Receit to Hew Carp?* Would
you like that? Not very much, I imagine. Apart from the

fact that neither you nor I have the faintest idea how, or why, you should 'hew' carp, apart from the fact that it suggests a deadly female poised, at twilight, with a hatchet, over an enormous and rather bloody fish; apart from the fact that we know, by instinct, that carp is uneatable; apart from all these facts, there is that dreadful feeling about Mifs Leblanc. Whenever I read F's for S's, in old books, whenever I read, in fact, about misses who are spelt Mifses, I always feel that these ladies are fizzing, protruding their rather prominent teeth and . . . well . . . fizzing. And I do not want anybody to fizz over my carp. So we will leave this recipe, and give you three other recipes—two of which I can recommend, and another which I can't. Here are the two which I can recommend.

*To Stew a Rabit or a Hear—from Ann Bruton.* Quarter him and wash him and of nutmeg Clover Mace Cinaman and pepper of each a small quantity & mix it w^th salt y^n take a small quantity of pot time and marjorum & strip & shed y^n mix y^e spice and herbs together and so season y^e rabit w^th it. There must be a small quantity of water in y^e stewing as mich as will cover y^e botom of y^e pot or something more it must stew gently for an hour and a half & before you take it off y^e fire you must put in a good peice of buttor and shake it about if you stew a Hear 2 or 3 hours it w^ll be little enough.

If you cook a rabbit in this way, it tastes more delicious than chicken.

Here is the other recommended recipe.

*Scotch Collops.* Take Veal and cut it thine pieces then take some sweet herbs minse them very small w^th Clove Mace & Nutmegs pounded w^th a little Salt

then put it on Your Veale Fry it in Butter, make some
strong broath, put in Mushromes, Anchovie & Clarrit
& pickled Oysters & butter make Veal bales & Frey
them broune, take yᵉ Yolke of 2 or 3 Eges then dip ye
Clary in it, then Frye it Broune then Slise some Baken
thin & Fry it, then Lay it on Your Meat.

I might have chosen more sensational recipes, but I
wanted you to feel that this book had *some* utilitarian value,
and was not merely a wild egotistical meandering, shot
through with occasional flashes of poetry and laughter. For
the sensation-monger I append the final recipe, which is
written across two pages, and emblazoned with such a fury
of whirling capitals that even the centuries cannot dim the
shock it gives you. Thus:

*Mad Dog.* Doctʳ Mead's Remedy for the Bite of a mad
Dog.

Let the Patient be blooded at the Arm 9 or 10
Ounces. Take of the Herb called in Latin Lichen
Cinerieus Terrestris, in English, Ash-colour'd
Ground Liverwort, clean'd dry'd and powder'd,
half an Ounce.

Of black Pepper powder'd, two Drachms.

Mix these well together, and divide the Powder into
four Doses, one of which must be taken every Morning, fasting for four mornings succefsively, in half a
Pint of Cow's Milk warm: after these four Doses are
taken, the Patient must go into the Cold Bath, or a
cold Spring or River, every morning fasting, for a
month; he must be dipt all over, but not stay in (with
his Head above water) longer than half a Minute, if
the Water be very cold: After this he must go in three
times a Week for a Fortnight longer.

273

The Lichan is a very comon Herb and grows generally in sandy and barren Soils all over England. The
right time to gather it is in the Months of October or
November.

The Doct^r says in the Experience of above thirty
Years, upon more than 500 Patients he has never
known the above Remedy to fail of succeſs: He says
That the sooner the Medicine is taken after the Bite,
the better, though he had often found it to answer,
though not taken 'till a Fortnight, or even a longer
time after it.'

'The sooner the medicine is taken after the bite,' you
see, 'the better.'

And the sooner I say good-bye, the better. For we have
lingered long enough.

## Chapter 22

## ANCIENT LIGHTS

The drama was only just beginning.

It was a drama that could have been played only in England. For only in England does there exist this white-hot passion for keeping oneself to oneself.

Only in England, do women stand at windows, and stare with frightened eyes at a distant hill, on which they can just see the outlines of a building, rising up to mar their hitherto inviolate horizon. 'The enemy is here,' they seem to mutter, 'he is at our gates!' They clutch the curtains, and stare into the distance. So, one feels, their ancestors must have stared out on to the hills, for the sight of alien lances piercing the skyline. The civil wars are over now, and neighbours are at peace, provided they speak the same language. But the war of property continues. And it is as fierce in the gardens of the suburbs as in the widespread acres of the great estates.

'Ancient lights!'

That is a strange archaic phrase, that one sees on dusty plaques against many little English walls. I never see that phrase without a quickening of the heart. It might well be taken as the ringing motto of the liberties of England. 'This light we had, this light we will keep. This window was ours, for dreaming, for receiving the blessing of the sun, for opening wide to the winds of the world, that they might blow in upon us, freely. This window we will guard, as we guard the freedom of our own hearts.'

'Ancient Lights!' That might also be the title of this chapter. And with marked approval on glancing at the top of the page, I observe that it is.

§ 2

I called this a drama. But it is a drama of the spirit, rather than a drama of the body. And therefore, thank heavens, we are not compelled to rush out and witness a lot of harrowing sights, nor make things go off with a bang. We can sit back and give ourselves up to the exquisite luxury of intelligent reflection.

'Ancient lights.'

In America, that phrase would be meaningless.

Nothing surprised me so much, in the United States, as the endless rows of gardens, open to the road, which one passed in the suburbs of all the great cities. There was not even a hedge to protect them. It was, in fact, difficult to know where one garden began and the other ended. They might as well have been public property.

'But . . . why . . . why?' I used to ask, for the hundredth time, gazing round in distressed astonishment when I saw these parodies of gardens.

'We don't like shutting ourselves in,' was the usual burden of the answer. 'We don't think it would be neighbourly.'

'But do you like people only a few yards away, with nothing but a brick path to separate you, seeing everything you *do*?'

'We've nothing to be ashamed of,' they observed brightly.

It was all a deep, deep mystery to me. I would rather have ten square yards of sour soil, surrounded by a hedge

so high that it blocked the sun out, than a hundred acres
of land without a hedge. No—perhaps that is an exaggeration, but it is not a really very gross exaggeration, and most
English gardeners will share it with me.

Oh, how we hate being 'overlooked'! The eagerness
with which we watch the vine creeping up the trellis!
'That will prevent Mrs Smith from seeing us,' we mutter,
with dark glee. From the way we go on we might be about
to set up a coining establishment—we might be attempting
to bury a large and important body in the seakale bed. We
might be going to take off all our clothes and wave scarves
round our heads, like the young ladies in Nature camps,
whose photographs always surprise me. For they look as if
they were shooing away birds from the newly-sown grass
lawn. But why, with such protuberant figures, do they
want the scarves? Any modern bird would take one look,
bury its head under its wings, and fly off to the village
pump for a drink.

However, we continue to shut ourselves in. Oh, the
horror when there is a gap in the laurel hedge that separates
us from the kitchen garden.

'We can see the gardener walking through to the greenhouse!' we gasp.

'See him?' the puzzled foreigner demands, wondering
what monstrous things he can be up to.

'See him!' we repeat. Surely that is enough explanation?
The expression on the foreigner's face tells us that it isn't,
so we add, to clinch it, 'And he can see us!'

'See you?' repeats the foreigner blankly.

We give it up. We cannot explain to foreigners that we
have a horror of being seen when we do not wish to be
seen. It is not because we want to take off all our clothes.
It is not because we wish to talk to ourselves, nor make

faces like idiots, nor scratch our heads, nor blow out our cheeks, all by ourselves. It is just . . .

Well, I suppose it is just because we are English. I can think of no explanation.

It is a pity that some other nations cannot catch a little of our curious psychology.

§ 3

I called this a drama of the spirit. But it very soon became a drama of the body.

After Mrs M.'s vain endeavour to persuade me to buy her field, I hoped that I might be left in peace. But no.

It happened like this. I was going for a walk with Whoops, who had not been for a walk for two days, and had been driving me to distraction with his dramatic yawns and highly affected stretchings. It is impossible to deny Whoops on these occasions. The power of canine suggestion is too great. He meets you at every corner of the garden, and stares fixedly at the gate. He stands over you, while you are watering, with an expression of martyrdom and casts his eyes longingly to the hedges. And if you definitely tell him that a walk is impossible, the measured tragedy of his slow return to the house, and the weary droop of his limbs as he sags beneath the dining-room table, are such that for your own peace of mind you have to take him.

So we set out for a walk together.

As we were passing Undine's cottage, a faint voice breathed over the hedge.

'Can I see you?'

I looked up and saw Undine. She was drooping, in an attitude of picturesque despair, over her garden gate. So

278

startling was her appearance, that I stopped dead, to the
intense disgust of Whoops, who stayed about fifty yards
up the lane, with his body facing towards a walk, and his
head sharply turned, in interrogation.

Undine was in pitch black. She looked like those
French widows who are blacker than anything known in
nature. Her dress was of crepe, and with it she wore a heavy
black necklace and jet ear-rings. Her powder (which was
usually of the shade known as Naturel, and which is about
as *naturel* as a dyed peacock), had been changed to dead
white, which looked a little strange on her sunburnt face.
Small drifts of powder remained at the sides of her nostrils,
and under her ears, like snow which had refused to melt.

'You startled me,' I said.

'I am sorry.' Her voice seemed to come from a great
distance.

'I'm just going a walk. But I'd love to come in for a
moment.'

She achieved a smile and opened the gate. And then,
very slowly and gracefully, she proceeded to walk up the
path, backwards, in order to avoid seeing the Galloways'
bungalow.

'Of course,' she murmured, 'it's all too terrible. I simply
can't see it . . . I daren't.'

At this point she tripped slightly over the root of a
clematis, and nearly fell, so that her smooth glide of grief
was slightly interrupted.

'But you can't see the bungalow from here at all,' I said.

'It is *there*,' she replied vaguely, continuing her promen-
ade.

'But you can't *see* it,' I repeated.

'*I* can see it,' she said.

How Undine could see the Galloways' bungalow

through a thick hedge of may and privet, to say nothing of a ten-foot mound of earth, heavily planted with Portuguese laurel, I did not inquire. I gathered that I was intended to understand that she could see it with the eyes of the spirit.

This strange progress continued all round the house, till we found ourselves in the kitchen garden, Undine walking backwards all the way. As soon as her feet touched the gravel path opposite the raspberry bed she turned round, sighed heavily, and said . . . 'There! Safe!'

I commiserated with her. What was she going to do?

What *could* she do? she wailed. She could not leave All-ways. It was an impossible situation, didn't I think? And certainly, I did, if her hatred of the Galloways was going to force her to walk backwards all her life. It would be an admirable training for anybody who wanted to obtain a post as lady-in-waiting to the Queen of Roumania, but as she had no such ambitions, it was just a bore.

§ 4

Meanwhile I wondered why Undine had taken me into the kitchen garden. And why she was delivering such a fierce tirade against kitchen gardens in general. There must be *some* significance in this, I felt. One does not rush people out into kitchen gardens merely to deliver lamentations against the vegetable kingdom.

'I really think,' said Undine, 'that I shall give the kitchen garden *up*.'

'But what will you do about vegetables?'

'I shall buy them. In the ordinary way.' (Which made me think, how would one buy vegetables in an extraordinary way? Would one put on a bathing suit and go down to the market and pick up beans with one's toes?) 'That's what

I shall do,' continued Undine. 'I've gone into it very carefully, and I've come to the conclusion that for practical purposes a vegetable garden is a *little* overrated.'

I had long come to the same conclusion myself, but had not dared to say so in public.

'I've reckoned it all out,' she sighed, 'and I find that with labour, and fertilizers, and everything, each lettuce costs me exactly five shillings. It really is a little *much*, isn't it? I mean, I simply *can't* eat them, not at that price. They'd choke me. Don't you think?'

I did. It was frightful to think of Undine being choked by a lettuce, however expensive.

'And these gooseberries,' she said, 'I *cannot* eat gooseberries. There are enough gooseberries to feed an army, but personally I hate them. To me there's something very *definitely* hateful about them. That frightful *hair* that they grow . . . and those *uncompromising* pips . . . it's sheer agony.'

'Won't you miss the asparagus bed?'

'I suppose I may. But don't you think it's rather a bore if one has a whole bed entirely to oneself, for a whole *month*?'

My unpolished mind detected a sinister significance in Undine's innocent remark. And apparently, she detected it too, for she suddenly blushed violently, and burbled on at great speed:

'I mean, one *can* get bored, even with asparagus, don't you think? And beans? It's having everything at *once*. And then when one really wants anything, it's never there. And the gardener *insists* on growing *acres* of potatoes, and I never *touch* a potato, they're rank poison to me.'

While Undine was talking, I thought how right she was! I love a kitchen garden. I love going out and seeing cabbages, wild and untamed, and naked brussels sprouts,

furiously sprouting. Nothing is more agreeable than picking a pod of peas that has been warmed by the sun, splitting
it open, and running one's finger down the glistening row,
gathering the peas into one's palm, and crunching them up.
Broad beans too, are quite delightful. The beans, when you
open the pod, look so startled and innocent, that it seems
almost a sin to devour them. I love taking off the lids of
rhubarb pots and seeing the pale shoots groping upwards
in the dark. And pulling young spring onions out of the
earth, wiping the dirt off on one's sleeve, and having an
orgy of onion-eating before dinner. And persuading the
week-end guest to eat onions too, in self-defence. And
carving my initials on a very small vegetable marrow, and
seeing the letters swell out as the sweltering weeks go by,
till an enormous B.N. proudly proclaims itself under the
cool shade of the leaves.

I love tomatoes, hot from the sun, and the crisp feel of
lettuces with the dew on them, and the little patch of herb
garden, when mint and sage and camomile and tarragon
and thyme send their alluring fragrance far and wide, so
that one is constantly being summoned, by their scents,
from the flower garden, merely to kneel down, and sniff
and sniff.

All the same, from a practical point of view, it is cheaper
to buy. Infinitely cheaper, safer and less troublesome. For
unless you have dozens of under-gardeners, scurrying about
all over the place with determined expressions, your
vegetable garden will destroy you, in the end.

'And so,' said Undine, interrupting these meditations,
'I really think I shall sell it. And of course, the *one* person
I should like to sell it to would be *you*!'

§ 5

How I persuaded Undine that I did not require her vegetable garden, either for vegetables or for meditation, and that even if she offered it to me as a gift, I should still refuse it, and that I was already a landowner on a scale which made me feel a little guilty (seven acres is far too much for any self-respecting person)—all this must be told at some other time.

The whole idea was grotesque. Undine had much more money than I had. If she didn't want vegetables, why not turn it into a lawn? Why persuade herself that she ought to sell, and then terrify herself with the idea that if she sold, somebody would build another nasty little bungalow on top of her?

But by now the ladies of Allways were beyond reason. In their dreams they saw bungalows springing up every-where. And they all seemed to imagine that it was my duty to prevent it.

Even Miss Bott joined in.

We were leaning over the little gate at the end of my wood, one day, looking out on to the broad field beyond. There is something very exciting about looking at an open field, naked to the sunshine, and glittering with buttercups, from the quiet shade of a wood. The wood is like a window —it protects you,—it offers a little frame for your tiny human personality. And while your body is in the shelter of the wood your spirit can rove out over the great meadows, free as the wind, and as swift.

'You're mad,' she said, 'not to buy that field.'

I sighed. Oh dear . . . she was beginning it now.

'Why?' I asked wearily.

'Supposing somebody built on it?'

WINTER

I looked at her. Yes . . . she appeared to be quite sane. 'Nobody,' I said, with infinite patience, 'is going to build on that field except . . .'

'Except?'

'Well . . . the reincarnation of Walt Whitman, or the ghost of Thoreau, or some other charming lunatic, who doesn't mind about there being no water, no road, no shelter, and no anything. And if anybody like that wanted to build, I should be only too happy.'

She tried another tack. 'It would be a marvellous investment.'

'But it's forty acres,' I said. 'And do you know how much I had to pay for a single acre, last year, to round off the wood?'

'Fifteen?'

'On the contrary, seventy.'

'Then you were robbed.'

'Perhaps I was,' I said, in grating tones. 'But then I always *am* robbed, and always shall be. I'm not proud of the fact. It just happens. It's a law of nature. I am made to be robbed, just as certain spiders are made to be destroyed when they make love.' I was quite hot by the time I got to the bit about the spiders.

'Forty times seventy is only . . .'

'Two thousand eight hundred pounds. Thank you very much.'

'It would be a marvellous investment,' she repeated. 'Now that flying's coming in. Think what a landing-ground it would make.'

I thought, regarding Miss Bott with what is called *hauteur* while I did so.

I thought of that quiet field, which was so spangled with cowslips in spring that it looked like a sequin cloth, and so buttoned with mushrooms in September that it looked like a coster's jacket . . . that field which was tunnelled with mysterious rabbity caverns, down which my dog had thrust his nose a thousand times . . . that field over which I had wandered so often, with the grasses brushing my ankles, while the slow and languid brush of twilight lazily traced a purple rim on the distant hills.

I thought of that field. If you stood in the middle of it, towards November, when the evenings were drawing in, there would pass, constantly, over your head, a swift and lofty flight of starlings, from elm to scattered elm. That is one of the loveliest sounds that echoes over the winter world, the high flight of starlings, in their urgent troops, at dusk. And see, over there, that great elm looks as though there were leaves upon it. A puff of wind and the tree is bare, the leaves are gone, for they are not leaves, but wings, and they are above you now, clouding the dusky sky. And as they pass, hundreds of them, you hear a long-drawn fluttering sigh . . . like the swish of a silken garment in a high corridor of heaven. It has gone. You look up. The corridor is empty, its gathering shadows lit only by a white and lonely star. But over there, in the next elm, the branches have suddenly blossomed once again into a thousand leaves . . . the leaves that are wings . . . warm wings, that trembled there for a moment on the naked boughs, before the wind blows them once more to destinies unknown.

I thought of that field.

'Forty acres,' I thought. 'Enough for a nice little, smart, dinky snorting puss-moth with revolting smells coming out of its perky tail to lay a smear of grease all over the bank where the white violets grow. Lovely. And young men with snub noses and bright Empire-building eyes will tramp over the fence where the clematis is trained and will demand a spot of water. Why do young men like that always want spots of things? Spots of whisky? Spots of sleep? Spots, spots, spots.'

I turned to Miss Bott.

'You are making me see spots before my eyes,' I said, with restrained passion.

And she nodded. I think she must have been thinking of the field too. 'I know,' she said, gruffly. 'It *would* rather put a damper on our mushrooming, wouldn't it?'

§ 6

However, nothing could stop Miss Bott, in her determination that Allways should be rendered safe from the intruder. If I wouldn't buy that field somebody equally 'desirable' must be obtained. And if *they* wouldn't buy the field, they would be made to buy something else. Allways was full of her machinations, and we expected to hear, at any moment, that she had arranged that the National Society for Preserving Ancient Monuments should buy the entire village.

'If she does,' said Mrs M. acidly, 'I suppose we shall have to ring up the Prime Minister before we can put in a new pantry sink.'

However, Miss Bott was not aiming at anything so nebulous as a National Society. She was aiming at a very real person . . . a distant cousin, by name Victor Shelley. And she eventually hooked him.

She came round to see me one morning to tell me all about it. It was a glorious morning, when the whole earth seems to smell like a chrysanthemum, and the rosebuds are very sturdy and glossy, and will open up into miracles of beauty in water, even though the outer petals are a little puckered by the frost.

'You remember Victor?'

'Of course.'

I had seen him several times in London. He was a very thin, ascetic man of about fifty—dainty in his ways, but not exactly effeminate—a man with silvery hair, who loved cats, collected miniatures, treated his few books with reverence, always lived on the right side of his income, and took three days to pack for a week-end in Paris.

'Well, he's coming up here for the week-end. And I've decided to get him to buy the Manse.'

'You've . . . *what?*'

'To buy the Manse,' she repeated airily.

'But it's the most hideous house ever built.'

'Victor can alter all that. He's got exquisite taste.'

'And it's enormous.'

'Well—he can shut some of it off.'

'But does he want to live in the country?'

'Not very much. But he will.'

Miss Bott's optimism baffled me. Only an insane millionaire, who wished to be constantly reminded of the asylum from which he had just escaped, would think of purchasing the Manse. It was a long low building that glared at you like an angry and dangerous animal. Its cavernous door gaped wide as though it were snarling. The date of the main building was about 1845, and as if that were not bad enough, dreadful wings and turrets had sprouted out, in the 'sixties and the 'eighties, making it look more like a dragon *couchant* than ever.

Moreover, it was in an impossible situation. It lay next to an unsavoury farm, which always passed rapidly from owner to owner, at a decreasing price. This farm at the moment was inhabited by three brothers who looked as if they had stepped straight out of the pages of *Wuthering Heights*—so thundery were their faces, so immense their capacity for liquor, and so staggering were their oaths.

And these were to be Mr Shelley's neighbours—Mr Shelley who was so set in his ways that he pined for a whole week when the elevator man, at his block of service flats, changed his uniform from blue to brown!

It was with misgiving that I accepted Miss Bott's invitation to lunch, to help persuade her cousin to become one of us. I am not a good liar, and even if I had been, Ananias himself could not have lied away the Manse.

But Miss Bott was more than a match for Ananias.

§ 7

'Oh—we are driving?' said Mr Shelley, when he saw the car. 'I thought it was in the village?'

'No—about a mile out.'

'Isn't that a little . . . thank you, the rug *would* be more comfortable like that . . . isn't that a little . . . if we *might* have the window, just a fraction? So kind . . . a little remote?

'Just what you want, after London,' said Miss Bott cheerfully.

Mr Shelley seemed about to reply, but closed his thin lips, and sighed through his nose.

As we drove on, I marvelled at the miracle which Miss Bott had wrought in inducing him to consider this fantastic project at all, for he was perfectly happy where he was, in London. However, perhaps he was a little touched—I think he was—by the thought that any of his relations should so eagerly desire his presence. For he was a lonely man.

Just as we were turning the last corner before you arrive at the gates of the Manse, a strange person staggered out of the hedge, carrying a very bloody rabbit in his hand. He was so drunk that I had to jam on the brakes, so that we skidded round the corner. As we passed him I had a vision of blood-shot eyes, and a hairy fist uplifted against us, while the air was thick with curses.

It was one of the brothers of the farm, Mr Shelley's future neighbours.

'What a *frightful*-looking creature?' said Mr Shelley, in a trembling voice, as we got out. 'Did you see?'

Nobody answered. It was an embarrassing moment.

'But didn't you see?' quavered Mr Shelley. 'The most monstrous man. Covered in blood?'

'Local colour!' observed Miss Bott, brightly. And marched us in, through the creaking gate, whistling hymns.

§ 8

In some ways I was glad that we had met the drunken gentleman, because Mr Shelley was so shattered that he did not fully appreciate the uncanny hideousness of the Manse as it first burst upon our view. True, he took one look at it, and shuddered, but then he glanced over his shoulder again, to make sure that he was not being followed.

It was not till we had passed through the front door, that he had begun to take notice. He took one glance at that door, and one glance was quite enough, for it was decorated by an arch of sea-shells in concrete.

Mr Shelley stared round him into the shadows. That was all the impression you got of the house at first—shadows. Only when your eyes had become accustomed to the gloom did you see the monstrous things that lurked in them.

'Well, plenty of room, what?'

Mr Shelley gave a sickly smile.

'It's a little larger than I thought,' he said, weakly.

'Good! More value for money, what?'

Mr Shelley looked at me with despair in his eye, as though to ask what arguments he could possibly employ against such logic. He said:

'I was thinking of servants.'

So was I. And a lot of other things besides. But it was not my place to say so. Therefore, I averted my eye, and stared with assumed interest at a stained glass window, about 1890, which showed a young man rising from the grave, with an angel hovering over him with a forbidding expression, as though it were saying: 'If you come out of there, young man, I'll give you what for!'

'*What* about servants?' said Miss Bott, beginning to climb the staircase.

'I only have *one* maid. Maud, you know. She's been with me thirty years.'

'Well—what of it?' Miss Bott paused, half-way up the gaunt staircase.

Mr Shelley blinked and peered around him. On all sides one had vistas of rooms, rooms which could easily have been used as hospital wards to accommodate thirty beds.

'Isn't it . . . just a *little* much—for one maid?'

'Much? Rubbish!' Miss Bott waved away the suggestion.

'Her feet . . . are not what they were.'

'Well, I don't know what Maud's feet were, so I can't say whether that's a tragedy or not. But she'll be doing step-dancing before she's been here long. Exercise, that's all she wants, exercise. Come on.'

Mr Shelley still paused. 'But my furniture,' he quavered. 'I really didn't want to buy very much.'

Miss Bott drummed on the banisters. 'Why should you? You've got tons.'

Mr Shelley gaped at Miss Bott, wondering, presumably, how any woman could tell so frantic a lie. And as I saw his thin ascetic face, with the kindly lips, parted and puzzled, I felt pity for him, but I also felt a very urgent desire to burst into hoots of ribald laughter. For I had seen Mr Shelley's tiny flat. A pocket drawing-room, a pocket dining-room, two bedrooms, a maid's room, and a minute hall. And even this modest apartment was furnished with an old-maidenish sparcity—a single period piece against an almost blank wall—that was the general idea.

I tried to visualize what would happen when he came to arrange his little pieces here. He would have to put the spider-legged Queen Anne bureau in the archway between the vast double drawing-room, to give a faint illusion of furniture to that room. The little Marie Antoinette sofa could be placed in the middle of the other double drawing-room. If one sat on it one would look like a symbol of Man's futility in a setting of *The Dynasts* designed by Gordon Craig. The little Empire clock, resting on a gilt swan, could go in the hall, with as much effect as a sparrow in the Albert Hall. As for the small Bokhara rugs—he had only rugs because the flat had parquet flooring—they could be stuck about the place like postage stamps, over the worst holes in the floor.

'Furniture?' Miss Bott repeated scornfully. 'Your

things'll look all the better for having a little space round 'em. Now come on, and don't make difficulties.' She put her foot on the next step, and then suddenly shouted:

'Hell!'

There was a sound of cracking wood and falling plaster. I ran forward, fearing that the whole staircase was about to collapse. But a cheerful laugh reassured me. 'Only my clumsy old feet,' she observed brightly. 'But you'd better tread carefully there. One or two steps are loose.'

'D'you think it's safe?' pleaded Mr Shelley.

Miss Bott was already nearly at the top of the stairs. 'Come on!' she cried out. 'I'm the heaviest of you all, and I've got up, so why can't you?'

A pale and acutely depressed Mr Shelley tiptoed up the stairs, hugging the wall. I brought up the rear.

We went into the first room on the right. It was as large as a concert hall, and it smelt like a fungus.

'Isn't it a little musty?' asked Mr Shelley.

'Musty?' echoed Miss Bott. 'Musty? Of course it's musty. You'd be musty if you hadn't had any fresh air inside you for donkey's years. Come on, let's open a window.'

This simple suggestion was not, however, easy to carry out. The window was warped with damp and only after a violent struggle, which Miss Bott tried to disguise by singing out 'Heave ho! Heave ho!' in a breathless voice, did we succeed in opening it a few inches.

However, those few inches were enough to let in a sharp and acrid perfume. I sniffed. Sniffed again. I glanced at Mr Shelley. He too was sniffing.

'Pretty, isn't it?' said Miss Bott heartily, gazing on to a mouldering slate roof, under which a few starved lauresti-nus were sheltering. 'You could sleep here.'

'Could I?' breathed Mr Shelley.

'Of course, it could make a very nice spare room.'

Mr Shelley sniffed again.

'Got a cold?' boomed Miss Bott.

'No . . . oh no . . . it was merely . . .' he sniffed, 'is that *pigs*?'

'Is what pigs?' Miss Bott's voice was very sharp.

Mr Shelley turned to me. 'Can't *you* smell something?'

I could. I could smell the most aggressively perfumed pigs that I had ever smelt. It was a smell that hit you be- tween the eyebrows. But how could I say so? Fortunately Miss Bott snapped:

'Nonsense! I can't smell anything at all.' (I noticed how- ever that she was surreptitiously shutting the window, by sitting on it. It went down with a bang which made us all jump.) 'I can smell nothing, and I haven't got a cold. You must have a cold or you wouldn't be sniffing so much.'

Mr Shelley had no reply to this assertion. And when Miss Bott snorted, 'It's all imagination', and led us through the door, he assented that perhaps it was. For the odour of pigs, though still intense, was so mixed up with the odour of damp and decay, that it was a little difficult to tell which was which.

And so the tour continued. On and on we went, through room after room, each more depressing than the last. Miss Bott's spirits never flagged. I marvelled at her genius for salesmanship. As each horror presented itself, she deftly turned it into a thing of beauty—or, at least, a thing of con- venience.

She was such a wonderful saleswoman that I believe she would have sold the Albert Memorial to a collector of Louis Seize miniatures.

But she did not sell the Manse to Mr Shelley. There was

something unexpectedly determined in the spirit which lurked beneath his frail body.

As we came out, wearily, and paused in the front door, breathing the odour of pigs, he summed up the whole situ, ation by glancing at the horrific pile behind him, smiling timidly, and saying to Miss Bott:

'For *me*, I think it would be a little . . .' he paused.

'Well?'

'A little *much*.'

Miss Bott shrugged her shoulders. She was a sensible woman, and she knew when she was beaten.

'Perhaps you're right,' she said, cheerfully.

## § 9

The tour of the Manse very definitely unsettled me.

Up till then, I had regarded the Great Land Panic as a joke. But now, I began to be affected by the prevailing un, rest.

I began to prowl round my few little acres, glaring over hedges to see who might come to molest me.

I took to tiptoeing round the house, staring through every window, to spy out the land, to search for distant fields where buildings might arise, and gaps in the trees through which I might one day catch sight of unwelcome roofs.

But, I must admit, that as soon as I entered the room and went to the window, I forgot why I had come up. The whole process of opening a window in a country cottage, is so exciting, especially if it is a lattice window and has a little perforated bar to fasten it, a bar which you have to move gently for fear of tearing one of the tender shoots of the vine.

You lift the latch, and push the window out. The cool air blows in, and there floats with it the eternal sigh of rest-less, blowing branches—a sigh of happiness, that is ever about you, in the country, though you do not notice it, till you open a window. You lean your elbows on the sill, pushing aside the curtains, and you notice that the pattern on the curtain is very faded at the edges. The painted roses are pale and wan, where the sun has caught them, and the green leaves drift like ghosts across the fabric. But on the other side, where they are in shadow, against the big black beam, the roses are still a gay crimson, and the leaves are as bright as on the day you bought them. You ought to change the curtains you suppose, and buy new ones. But you won't. You like them as they are, and you do not grudge the hues that the sun has stolen back to himself, for the sun has given you plenty of colour, in your time.

You look out again. What are you here for? Oh yes . . . to see whether anybody can spoil the view. For a moment or two you try to be methodical, to make a note of that field over there, where the cattle are grazing, to map out, in your mind, the gaps in the coppice, and to remember the parts of the road they overlook, so that you can take some sort of action about it. But even as you form these fine, business-like ideals you begin to smile. Because you can't help noticing that the chestnuts, over the way, are just spreading their fans, and that reminds you of the time when you were walking in the wood this morning and discovered a chest-nut breaking bud, and were unable to resist the temptation to take one of the sticky, silky things between your fingers and open it out, spreading its fan for it. And then you were seized with remorse, in case the night should be cold or the wind unduly harsh, and you tried to stick the baby leaves together again.

Land—acreage—frontage—desirable sites—options. You frown. You *must* try to decide something about all this. But even as you make this firm resolution, old Miss Grant passes in the road below, on her bicycle. She has one of those bicycles which go so slowly that any normal pedestrian has to slow down in order not to pass her too quickly. And she always seems to be bicycling against the wind. Her big black hat, of immense age, unmistakably Queen Anne, is blown up behind her head until it stands like a sort of arrogant crest. Her very thin and faintly disgusting dog slinks behind her.

What a long time she takes to pass! Pedal, pedal, pedal, pedal . . . against the wind, her hat standing more and more erect, and her dog assuming Russian Ballet attitudes every few yards. At last she is gone. She has gone to her field for which she pays three pounds a year, for grazing her cows. And that brings you back to finance. For three pounds a year represents a capital of a hundred pounds. And they could probably get at least two hundred for Miss Grant's field. And if they invested that two hundred in some new pill which made women thinner, or fatter, or kept them the same, or did something radical to their insides, they would probably make a fortune.

You shake your head. It is all most perplexing. Why can't people leave things as they are? Why can't they let beauty sleep?

Why?

You look out of the window. The light is fading. The drama of the day is almost done. Slowly, slowly the dusky curtain falls. The giant elms are lit with a last gleam, a theatrical flare from the dying sun, and then, they are but shadows in the wings. Only faintly now can the stage be seen, in lingering fragments—a few panes still glimmer in the church windows, there is a ripple of gold on the quiet pond, and the lawn beneath you still glows with a radiant green. But it is a green of the night rather than a green of the day, silvered over by a rising moon, whose pale face, high-lifted, casts a polite scorn on the last efforts of the honest sun. The curtain falls, falls—it has almost reached the earth now —the church windows are dimmed, the great stage manager has given his signal. As though it were an anthem, the birds sing their final song, and cease. And the world is in dust sheets, till the morning, with only the white owl as caretaker, hooting mournfully round empty corridors, and the scornful moon, like an artificial lamp, illuminating the deserted arena.

That is what happens when one goes up to a room at twilight in order to be severely practical about protecting one's estate.

§ 10

I think that the other inhabitants of Allways must have been opening their windows, too, and forgetting their troubles.

For gradually, quiet descended once more upon All-ways. Nobody bought any more land. Nobody built any more bungalows. And as far as one can see, there is no reason why anybody ever should.

Even the Galloway bungalow has lost something of its original repulsiveness. The ivy, and the Gloire de Dijon roses, and the wistaria and honeysuckle, have seen to that.

At any rate, Undine no longer finds it necessary to walk backwards into her cottage. Unless, of course, somebody happens to be watching.

Chapter 23

## A SYMPHONY OF SILENCE

The reader will, by now, have realized that this book is a very quiet book. So quiet, that, I fear, a lot of people will go raving mad if they attempt to continue to read it.

'Oh dear—how can you *stand* it—this silence?'

Quite charming people have asked me that, often enough, after a few hours at the cottage.

'But it *isn't* silent,' I tell them!

'Well—I can hear that awful cuckoo, doing its stuff over and over again. And a little boy passed in the lane, about an hour ago, whistling. But that's all.'

When people like that arrive, the only thing to do is to put them in the garden, as far away as possible, with a gramophone and a packet of loud needles, and let them drug themselves with the sounds of 'civilization'.

'Civilization' is the death of the finer senses of man. If a cigarette is always between your lips, you can't ever smell the sweetness of the bean fields, on a summer evening. If you begin to drink cocktails at twelve, you forget, for ever, the keen, silvery taste of cold water in a clear goblet. Which sounds like one of the most embarrassing moralizations of *Eric or Little by Little*, but it happens to be true.

It is particularly true in the matter of sound. For the people who go crazy because there isn't a gramophone playing, or a telephone ringing, or a bus roaring by—these people are, quite literally, deaf. Otherwise they could not possibly talk such nonsense about Allways being 'silent'.

A cuckoo . . . a whistling boy . . . that was all they heard! While even as they were speaking, I heard the following sounds:

1. A high wind in the elms. They were a long way from us, it is true, but all the morning there had been a song in their branches—a song of the sea. As the wind surged through them there was a sound akin to the sweep of surf over shingle—the wide, thundering advance, the sighing mournful retreat, as the truant surf is drawn back by the long arms of the sea.

2. A clock ticking. It was not a loud clock, but it had a cheerful, busy tick, that made you think the passage of Time was a grand joke, and that every minute you were dancing on to better things.

3. Birds innumerable. Starlings under the eaves, thrushes in the may, sparrows on the path—and not only the song of birds, but the many other sounds that birds make—the scurries in the bushes, the flutter of wings from branch to branch—even the *tread* of birds—for many birds make distinct sounds as they hop down a brick path.

4. The bleat of lambs, carried down from the hill by the vagrant wind.

5. But why bother about 5? Or 500? Either you know what I mean, or you don't. And if you are one of the few who do, I think it will be fun if we listen to the sounds of Allways together, and leave the rest of the people to play their gramophones.

§ 2

I called this chapter a symphony of silence, for that is what it really is. The symphony is always the same, and always different. For our conductor is the Weather, and he has as many moods as there are hours. Sometimes he stresses the wood wind, till you would say that there was no sound about you but the high clamour of the elms—sometimes he can bear nothing but strings, and when you go to bed at night you can remember only the way the wind hissed through the rushes on the bank of the stream.

Sometimes, when the sky is a brazen gong, vast and still, he taps very gently on it, so that there is a roll of distant thunder. You start, and wonder if he is working up to a wild finale, an *allegro tempestuoso*. But no—not yet! He puts his fingers to his lips, waves his hand, and the long grass in the meadow sways in time, at the hint of a freshening breeze. Tap, tap . . . tap, tap, tap, tap . . . What is that staccato sound? Only a big thrush, knocking a snail on the stones outside your window. It has been dry for so long, the earth is parched, the insects are in hiding—happy thrush to have discovered so rare a morsel at this season!

But the conductor has signalled to the drummer once more, and he taps again, a little louder this time, for the thunder is coming closer. And with the sound of the drums comes another sound which is exactly like pizzicato strings, the sound of the first drops of rain falling on the glass of the greenhouse. You hurry indoors, for you must not be late for the Symphony, the weather would punish you severely for that. Even as you run you note that the orchestration is getting fuller and fuller, the wind higher and higher, till it has the echo of shrill clarinets, and deep in the wood, over yonder, there is a sound of stormy 'cello music, as the boughs of the big ash trees grate together.

You are just in time. Breathless you take your seat by the window, and listen.

And now, the drums have it! Roll upon roll, till you

would say the straining surface of the skies would split—louder, louder! This is intolerable, you mutter. No composer can possibly keep it up, even with so amazing a subtlety of rhythm. Suddenly, the conductor makes a lightning gesture from bronze roof to green floor. There is a second's pause, and then the whole vast orchestra of Nature bursts out in a throbbing melody of rain and wind, of blowing branch and straining leaf. The thunderstorm has begun.

§ 3

I cannot think why I began with a thunderstorm, because anything less typical of Allways cannot be imagined. I intended to begin with a sound which must be common to all dwellers in old cottages, though I like to think that it is peculiar to Allways. The sound of beams cracking at night.

It is a queer, brittle noise, as though somebody were tapping on the door. I suppose the beams crack by day, too, but you do not hear them then, because the birds are singing, or the fire is burning, or some other sound is distracting your attention. But in the stillness of the night, as you lie in bed, with a candle by your side, as you play games with the shadows cast by your hands on the ceiling . . . fluttering those long, grey, ghostly fingers, bringing to birth phantom ducks and grotesque rabbits—as you lie there, then the beams begin their strange jerky conversation. You start. Your hands drop on to the sheets. Crack again! The house, you see, is sinking, sinking, little by little, through the centuries. These are its tiny sighs of protest, the proof that its limbs, though strong, are growing weary.

'Well, it will last my time,' you say to yourself. And as

you fall asleep, the beams crack again, as though in re-
proach. 'It was not very kind of you to say that.' No, you
agree, it was not very kind.

Although this slow sinking of all our houses is picturesque, although it gives an amusing twist to a gable, and
cocks a window to one side, as though it were winking at
you, it has its disadvantages. For example, every year we all
begin to find that our doors are sticking, because the ceiling
is pressing upon them. And we have to send for Mr Beard,
the village carpenter, to shave off a fraction of the lower part
of the door for us. While he is performing this office,
we hover round him, and the following dialogue takes .
place:

Tenant: I suppose it's the damp?

Mr Beard: No, sir, it's not the damp, it's the subsidence.
(He pronounces this with an air of authority. The tenant
heaves a sigh of relief. Mr Beard has said it's the subsidence,
once more. One knew it already, but it's good to hear it
again.)

Tenant: Do you think it's . . . subsiding . . . more
quickly than it ought to?

Mr Beard: No, sir.

Tenant: That cupboard in the spare room, though. You
really can't stand in it any more. The floor's so sloping . . .
you just slide down.

Mr Beard: You always did, sir.

Tenant: How much do you think it sinks every year?

Mr Beard: Well, sir, I reckon the left wing of this house
has sunk two feet since it was built. That's pretty well 400
years. That's one foot in 200 years. That's one inch in
roughly seventeen years. So that makes about a seventeenth
of an inch every year. Which is quite enough, sir, to account
for the way this door is sticking.

But the main disadvantage of our cracking beams is ex-
perienced by those who have new and timorous maids from
London. These poor creatures are scared stiff.

'But, mum, I swear, there was somebody tappin' on the
stairs.'

'Nonsense, it's only the beams.'

'I'm sorry, mum.' A pause. 'But even if it were the
beams, supposin' they cracked in 'alf, and come down on
my 'ead?'

'There's no possible chance of that.'

'A big piece of plaster fell in the 'all only yesterday.'

And so on. I dare not think how often that dialogue has
echoed, at Allways, between mistress and maid. Nor how
often the village Ford has borne a tremulous maiden back
to the railway station, back to the sounds of 'Civilization',
where there are no barbaric beams to mar her rest, only the
sounds of creaking radiators, of angry lifts, of passionate
trams, and other comforts.

§ 4

Some of these sounds I have mentioned are shared by the
whole village. Others are my own—heard only by me—and
these I guard most jealously.

I would not willingly share with anybody the strange
excitement which I gain from the dripping of water into the
well. But you, who are reading this, aren't 'anybody', because, for the moment, we are living together. So I will
share it with you. This is what happens.

You walk out on to the little brick pavement in front of
the kitchen. You look round, like a conspirator. There is
no one about. In the distance, through an open window,

you hear snatches of the 119th Psalm, punctuated by dull thuds, proving that your bed is being made, the pillows beaten. (Why do so many servants always sing the 119th Psalm when they are making beds?)

Nobody about! You get down on your knees. You seize the cool iron ring of the well-cover. You heave, and heave again . . . the moss has grown thickly round it. Now, once more . . . it pulls open. You lay it back, you fall on your stomach, a cold air blows up, and you stare into the depths of the well.

You wait.

Drip!

The dark mirror of the water is troubled—its dreams shattered. A moment ago, life was reflected placidly on its surface, such life as the well may see—the vagrant bough of the cherry tree, a darting bird, a smiling sky. But the ceaseless march of the little underground river disturbed all that. True, it has shrunk to a mere drip—it is only a ghost of its wintry, turbulent self, but it still has a spirit of its own.

Drip . . . drip . . . drip!

No instrument ever made by man has a sweetness akin to this. It is a high, fluting sound—never quite on the same note. If you wrote it musically it would be something like this. . . .

Drip! C

Drip! C♯

Drip! E

And then, after a pause, a very heavy, pompous. . . .

Drip. A♭

And all the time the mirror of the well is being shattered, its dark depths disturbed, its pattern marred. But it does not care, for in this shattering of the mirror many strange and lovely patterns are formed, as though a kaleidoscope were shifting before us. The reflected branch of laburnum blossom which, a moment ago, made a single gesture, a delicate, arrogant sweep of gold, is suddenly shattered into a thousand stars, which spin to the edge of the well for a moment, quiver, and then hurry back again till they are hung once more on the mirrored stem. The cloud that hovered, as though frozen, is suddenly puffed to atoms by the water-drop—it looks as though a shell were bursting—and for a time the ripples seem to be painted with puffs of white, in violent agitation, till the storm passes, and the mirror is clear again, and the cloud, once more, has gained its repose.

'What's all this?' mutters the avenging imp, who is always peering over the shoulders of conscientious writers. 'Hundreds of words about a drip of water into a well?'

'Hundreds of words,' I reply, 'have been written about subjects that have left no deeper trace on the world.'

'Yes, but by fools.'

'Did I ever claim to be anything else, in the face of Beauty?'

And for once in a way, the avenging imp has no adequate retort.

§ 5

Have you ever heard a mole? It is one of the sounds of Allways that you must certainly hear, during your stay.

It was the mole-catcher who first made me hear it. The mole-catcher looks as if he had stepped straight out of some novel by D. H. Lawrence, some novel which had been very heavily banned, barred and bolted, in case the British public might suddenly develop a morbid passion for mole-catchers. For he is very virile, and has a look in his eyes which makes young maidens catch their breath when they meet him at the corner of a lane, when the may is in blossom. And he wears corduroy trousers and has an enormous Adam's apple and a voice like old sherry and is twenty-one and unmarried. All of which interests me less than the fact that he catches moles exceedingly well.

'How much shall I pay you?' I asked him, one evening in December, when he looked so D. H. Lawrence that he really ought to have been taken at once to the Café Royal.

'Eh?'

'How much?' I repeated, adding, diffidently . . . 'per mole?'

As soon as I had said 'per mole' I felt strangely uneasy. It sounded as though one were a beauty specialist, holding a nickel-plated mole-catcher in one hand, confronting a spotty-faced dowager, and coming to terms. 'The fee is twenty guineas per mole, moddom, although the mole in the chin is *reely* a thirty guinea proposition—that is to say —should you wish it to be permanently eradicated.'

I wished my moles to be permanently eradicated. They were doing unholy things to the roots of my new silver birches, which were far more important to me than any-body's chin. So I muttered 'per mole' again, feeling pecu-liarly idiotic.

'Tuppence.'

'Right.'

'I'll bring 'em to you every morning.'

'Oh!' I blinked, and looked at the mole-catcher. If D. H. Lawrence had observed him at that moment he would have burst into a Lawrence prose poem about the dark earth and the loins of the moles panting through the dark earth and the dark earth being very cool and soothing and bee-autiful to the loins of the moles. And all that sort of

THE GIFT OF A GARDEN

thing. And I thought that breakfast would really be rather an ordeal if one had to go out every morning, in a dressing-gown, and inspect battalions of mole-corpses, just before eating eggs and bacon. So I said:

'I don't think you need bring them to me. Just tell me how many you have caught. At twopence . . .' I gulped 'per mole.'

'You'll trust me?'

Trust him? Lord . . . what a question. I hate trusting people. It's a coward's game. I like people I can't trust. People with knives up their sleeves . . . people with a life of which I know nothing . . . people who have dark alleys in their souls, down which they skulk when they think I'm not looking. That's the fun of friendship, the double personality of those we love.

The avenging imp is at it again.

'You were talking, I believe, of a mole-catcher?'

'So I was.'

'Or rather of a mole?'

'Good Lord I'd forgotten.'

'And the noise that a mole makes?'

'Of course.'

'Perhaps, if it is not troubling you too much, you would make a noise like a mole?'

## § 6

A noise like a mole.

I must write very softly. I must smooth out the paper. The ink must be very clear, and flowing freely. We must all put our fingers to our lips, hold our breath.

'Crunch . . . crunch . . . crunch. . . .'

No. That is not it. That is not the sound that the mole makes, at dusk, when the blackbirds have gone to bed, and the air is dizzy with the scents of the earth. It is subtler than that. For the mole's snout is very tiny and delicate. It is sensitive to a degree. It is, in fact, incapable of making a sound so vulgar that it could be described by any man's pen.

For it is not a 'crunch', nor a 'munch' nor even a 'swish'. It is the sort of sound that a goblin gravedigger would make. Not that the mole is digging a grave . . . far from it . . . he is digging what is, to him, 'a desirable residence'. And so we may as well leave him at peace.

There are many of these tiny sounds, made by animals and insects, which play important parts in the Symphony of Silence at Allways. Some of them are so commonplace that I blush to mention them. There is the sound of the moth as it taps impatiently against the lampshade at night, and the quite different sound of the daddy-long-legs doing the same thing, but doing it far more clumsily, and making much more fuss about it. I have a sneaking fondness for daddy-long-legs. They look as if they had been designed by Mr Walt Disney and might at any moment do a gavotte across the ceiling and sit down at the piano and bang the keys with those absurdly comic limbs.

I have also a great affection for a bluebottle, especially on a summer afternoon, when it is being more than usually idiotic about getting out of the open window. I go over and watch it, and become almost as distracted as it is itself. 'You fool . . . you damned fool . . . there is the open window . . . and the wide air and the flowers waiting for you. You have been up and down that piece of glass at least seven hundred times. Why don't you go outside?

And I gave it a gentle prod. But this only arouses the

violent indignation, and the bluebottle booms away at the glass with redoubled energy, until at last I catch him in a handkerchief and put him outside. And as I watch him fly away I think how like bluebottles we are ourselves, wearily beating against the glass, when the window is open all the time.

I am writing far from Allways, and the traffic roars by in the street outside, so fiercely that you would say that the street was full of wild animals, bellowing and screaming after their prey. But above the din I hear, clear and sweet, the tiny sounds of Allways, which are so far clearer to me because I hear them with my heart, and not only with my ears . . . the soft patter of petals on to the parched earth when a rose in summer passes, the hard knock of a chestnut in the road when the November winds are full, the hiss of apple logs when the fitful rain spits down the chimney. These sounds I hear, high above the clamour of the city. Maybe I walk with dreams. But the dream is clearer than the reality.

§ 7

Dreams!

At Allways . . . even when the human voice is heard it has a dreamlike quality and the phrases that drift to you when you meet the labourers in the lane seem, somehow, as though they came from a land of make-belief.

'Fine day!'

'Ay—but a drop of rain'd be welcome.'

The greeting has been given. You pass on. The heavy boots crunch away into the distance. Did you say those words, or hear them? You do not know. They have gone. They were part of the Symphony of Silence.

It is the same with the sounds of 'civilization'. There is a lane outside my cottage, and venturesome vehicles, occasionally charge down it, on their way to villages even more remote than Allways. But as soon as they have turned off the Great North Road they are caught in the same magic their wheels are captured in the same silken web. All right —tell me I am romancing, and laugh at me to your heart's content. You will not alter the facts. For I swear that even Miss Grant's bicycle bell, as she ploughs slowly along, with her disgusting dog behind her, has a silvery tinkle that is not quite of this world. I should never be surprised if I saw a Poltergeist, with a peaked cap, sitting on her handle bars, ringing away, just for fun. Which makes me think that Miss Grant must ring for fun, too, for there is never any obstacle in her path, except the wind. Perhaps she *is* ringing her bell at the wind? I hope she is. It is a nice idea, which the wind . . . (the only element who has a sense of humour) . . . would appreciate.

As this chapter has to stop, some time, I suppose I must draw a line. I have not told you a thousandth of the sounds of Allways. I have not told you of the 'plop' the goldfish make, when you step on to the path by the pond, and a hundred glistening bodies dive down into the depths. Nor of the church bells, that play C D E F G F E D C and so on, ad infinitum. The G always gets the biggest bang, and I always wonder, on Sundays, if it objects, or if it is pleased by this attention? Anyway, it is a very sweet note, and seems somehow truer and more vibrant than the others.

I climbed the church tower once, to see if the G bell was any different from the others. I stood among the bells, with the wind lashing the tower, and the great bells hanging still and silent before me.

'Which is the G bell?' I asked the sexton.

'Eh?'

'The G bell . . . the highest?'

'The highest?'

'Yes.'

'Eh? They be all the same height. And a pretty job it wor, gitting of 'em up.'

Which was another way of looking at it.

Oh—this music—this eternal music of the English country! It is too quiet to be echoed by any human hands, too subtle to be set between staves or disciplined to the rhythms of art, too delicately coloured to be mirrored in any orchestral score. Eternally it sighs, through field and lane, and every hour a new masterpiece is born—a masterpiece in which each echo has its appointed place, and even the pauses—the hushes when the birds are still and the wind has dropped—seem deliberate, ordained and commanded by the baton of the Conductor of All Things.

## Chapter 24

## SMOKE BEFORE FIRE

The problems of life, at Allways, never seem quite so harsh or so crude as in the world outside. A dilemma presents itself, worries us for a little while, and then it seems to drift away, like the smoke of an autumn fire in the kitchen garden, when all the weeds, the docks and dandelions and dead roots are smouldering in a black, savoury mass. The fire goes on, but for days, sometimes for weeks, it is forgotten. And then, a chance wind will set it glowing again, and over the clumps of battered cabbages and ragged broccoli the acrid smoke will blow, in drifts of blue and grey.

So it was with Miss Hazlitt's problem. It was there. It would have to be faced, one day. But meanwhile, all I could do was to work quietly in the background, trying to find a way out. It would have been a restless task had I not realized that she, more than any woman I have ever met, was happy, with a happiness that could not be pierced by any slings and arrows of outrageous fortune.

It is strange that the simile of the fire in the kitchen garden should have flashed across the page, for these were the days of log-gathering, the days when, after tea, in the sallow twilights, when the wind had a savour of frost and the spindle-bushes glowed like warming torches, you set out, over the fields, in search of the treasure of the trees. You breathed deeply, and hummed a tune under your breath . . . a good tune, it must be, a wide and lofty tune, like the main theme of the Dvořák 'New World' Symphony . . . for this was exciting business you were on. You were out to draw fire from the cold earth. That was what it really amounted to. Yes . . . as you bent down, and heaved a branch from the grass, and clasped it to you, and smelt the damp lichen that clung to it, already it seemed that it was warming you, already you saw it glowing on your hearth, in the wild dark winds that were cantering down from the north.

§ 2

During the first few days your task was easy. There was a rich haul under the lonely elm that stands in the centre of the field at the end of the wood, and all along the banks of the stream there were stray fragments of willow (an extravagant wood), of oak and of coarse-grained ash. Sometimes, as a special tit-bit, you were rewarded by a branch of crab-apple, which had been beaten down by the storms of summer, and dried by the winds, an enticing branch that snapped easily when you trod on it, and emitted fragrant essences when you consigned it to the flames.

But after you had scoured the neighbouring fields and lanes you had to go further afield. That made it a strenuous job. Of course, you could have taken the car, but that you felt, would be 'cheating'. It would have been akin to using blotting-paper when you were doing a water-colour in the nursery. No nice child uses blotting-paper when it is painting a pink cow and the pink is trying to run down in driblets under the cow's stomach. That is 'cheating'. Any-body can paint if he uses blotting-paper. But it is not ethical to do so. Nor is it ethical to use a car when collecting logs. You must use only your two legs and your two arms. The fire, I swear, will burn more brightly if you abide by these unwritten rules.

And if you are a real countryman, you soon become cunning in the ways of logs. You know that there is a coppice on the hill where the wind is cruel, and where the elms are old and brittle, and you will set out after a night of storm and gather many branches. You will know that there was an ash that was struck by lightning, down by the pond near the farm, and you will hover about it, like an amiable vulture, till the last armful has been taken.

You will learn, too, the logs that deceive by their beauty, but give no heat, and the logs that look so dull in the field but glow so magnificently in the fire. In the first class is the silver birch. Many is the bright bundle of silver birch that I have carried home, and many the basket of pale-barked wood that I have proudly arranged by the fire. And many the time that I have sadly shovelled away a bucketful of half-digested ashes, asking myself when I will realize that the silver birch refuses to be burned? Its sap is cold and virginal, it will not yield to the hot caresses of the flames. It shrivels and turns grey . . . there is no passion in it.

But the apple wood! Ah . . . there is a wood of intoxicating fragrance. If you can find a derelict orchard, and rid yourself of the haunting melancholy that must come to any man who sees these boughs bereft and broken, that were once so brilliantly laden, then there is a treat in store for you, if you have a fireplace, and box of matches, and a few evenings to spare, when the darkening airs are damp and chill.

All right. Tell me that these are tiresome rhapsodies. That it would be much easier to order a sack of coal, and to leave it at that. Tell me that the energy expended in making my little log-pile could have been more profitably employed in writing articles on 'Should short women marry tall men?' I am sure that it would have been much more profitable. But if I had not been allowed to go log-gathering something would have died within me, and the brightest and most expensive fire of the latest and most hygienic asbestos would have given me no warmth.

For this was nature's way of 'making' money.

'This is *free*,' I said to myself, as I staggered back, over the fields, with my arms full of logs.

'Free! A fire for nothing! Warmth out of the earth!' I said it again as, with a sigh of relief, I let the logs fall in a heap on the pile. My arms were aching and my chin was covered with green moss and several peculiarly sinister woodlice had to be shaken from my trousers, but these were only minor details. The main thing was that I had been getting something for nothing.

# Chapter 25

## A GREEN HILL FAR AWAY

For most of that winter, and some of the spring, I had to be away from Allways. For nearly three months I was obliged to look at the world from the fortieth floor of an hotel in New York.

There are worse places than that from which to regard the world, I suppose, but I can't say that I liked it. I used to peer over the window-ledge and see the stream of human ants below. And although it was all very grand and impressive, and aroused the loftiest thoughts of Man's Conquest of Nature, I preferred my bedroom window at Allways, which is so close to the ground that you can easily jump from it, without hurting yourself.

It must be a sign of galloping middle-age to carry your home in your heart, like this. To scribble in your dairy these two memoranda side by side:

Thursday. January 10th. Dine with J at Ambassador's 8 o'clock not dressed, go Harlem afterwards.
Write B. to plant twelve hollies in gap between pond and road.

It is terrible to be thinking of a cottage when you are in a palatial hotel. To gaze at a radiantly beautiful fountain, all lit up in shades of puce and purple, and decorated with exquisite chastity by bunches of Moorish bananas, and to think 'what a waste . . . if I had a quarter of that water

317

in the sunk garden I could grow water-lilies which would make Mrs M.'s hair turn white overnight'. Even more terrible, when sitting in a Harlem dance palace, watching a thousand oozing couples swaying together, to be reminded by the star saxophone-player of the cow in the farm that always wakes you up in the small hours.

Such reactions, one supposed, are the signs of a narrow, provincial, and utterly unfashionable mind. In the faint hope that some of my readers may be equally weak and despicable, I will make the ultimate confession, which is that I actually carried photographs of Allways about with me, in a leather photograph case. That, we will admit, is definitely not chic. It is positively suburban.

I didn't care. I used to prop the pictures up on the window-ledge, and stare at them. The cottage looked very strange against the background of sky-scrapers. A little blurred building, with dim trees and shrubs around it. And behind, the wild towers of the great city of Today, the white, slashing lines of the sky-scrapers, the million windows, glaring at each other with arrogant distaste.

§ 2

But even if I had not had the photographs to remind me of Allways, the mail would have done so. I was kept in constant touch with everything. The new planting of trees for the wood had been carried out successfully, in spite of an error in delivery, by which they had arrived two days too soon, and had been forced to lie in the field, covered with sacking, while holes had feverishly been dug for them in the frost-bound earth. Undine was getting up a concert. The shop was progressing wonderfully, and Miss Hazlitt was very happy.

The mail arrived in two batches a week. One day, as I inquired at the titanic rabbit-hutch in the hall, where the letters were kept, I found a very large batch waiting for me. Nearly all of them were from Allways. I sped up in the lift, jangling my door-key impatiently, promising myself a happy hour.

But the hour was very far from happy. The first letter I opened was from the Professor. This is what I read:

> I am very sorry to have to tell you [he wrote] that our good friend Miss Hazlitt has been very seriously ill. I know what a shock this will be to you, but I felt it better to warn you because there is a faint danger . . . so faint that I feel sure we need not take it seriously . . . that matters may have got beyond our control by the time you return.

I stopped reading the letter. 'Beyond control' . . . what did that mean? I dreaded to read on. It was only with a great effort that I could continue.

> God forbid that I should criticize her, especially now, but if only she had behaved normally, and reported herself to the doctor when she first felt the pain, she might not be where she is now. But as you are aware, she never complains, she is always resigned, everything is God's will, everything for the best. And so . . .
> I'm sorry. I am telling you all this very badly. Here are the facts. Miss Hazlitt was taken to Peterborough hospital for a very serious operation, a week ago. The shop is shut up. Lord knows when it will open again. We have got a woman in, to look after things and to feed the kittens.
> I went to see her yesterday. She gave me the most extraordinary lesson in heroism that I have ever known.

In the past I have sometimes had harsh things to say about religion, and I still feel that the Church has often used its influence in the service of obscurantists throughout the ages. But when one sees examples of Christ's teaching like Miss Hazlitt, one hesitates to criticize a philosophy which can have such magnificent results on individuals.

I was the first visitor she was allowed to see. 'But what is she suffering from?' you are asking. I've written this letter over and over again to try to break it gently. But I can't. And you'd better know. It is a malignant growth. In the breast. I wish to God I could tell you this, instead of writing it.

They had performed the first operation a few days before, but another is due as soon as she is strong enough to stand it.

I shall never forget the extraordinary happiness—yes, happiness—of her smile as I stood by her bed. She had a little bunch of crocuses by the side of her bed, which Mrs M. had picked for her. 'My own crocuses, my very own!' she said. You remember how her voice seemed to sing when she was describing even the simplest pleasures? Well—it had that same singing quality now, though of course it was very weak.

She could only say a very little but her whole talk was a song of praise. It was the crocuses that seemed to please her most. She was afraid that Mrs M. must have been put to a great deal of trouble—it was so kind of her—everybody was so kind—and now that the flowers were here, in this little glass by her bed, she could enjoy them almost as much as if she were sitting at the window of her sitting-room, watching them dance in the cold wind, against the dark earth.

*Enjoy* . . . that was the word she used the most. And even when she spoke of the coming operation she said, 'Isn't it wonderful? You see—they would not operate again if there were not hope.'
I think there is hope. H—— is a brilliant surgeon. I had a word with him after I had left her and he said, 'Miracles do happen, sometimes. And Miss Hazlitt believes in miracles!' It was rather a cryptic remark, but he is not the sort of man who tells one lies just for the sake of saving one a *mauvais quart d'heure*. At least, he wouldn't do that to *me*. We had a rather acid correspondence about glandular therapy in the *Lancet* last year . . .

And then, to my astonishment, the letter suddenly stopped, and for nearly half a page the paper was covered with extraordinary symbols . . . partly algebraical, partly geometrical, and partly animal. For the mention of the *Lancet* had apparently started the Professor off on an entirely new train of thought. And, as usual when he was working out a problem, he drew animals. There was a large snake hissing at a giraffe, and a whale spouting, and six cats rushing across a roof after another snake. And then, as though nothing had happened, the letter resumed:

I fear that all this will make bitter reading for you, and as I said before, I would have given a lot to be spared the task of writing it. We drew lots as to who should tell you—Miss Bott, Mrs M., Undine, the vicar and I. The lot fell to me.
Mrs M. is very worried about the shop. Not for any personal reason . . . she has been grand all the way through, but because she realizes that if Miss Hazlitt comes back. . . .

And then, once more the letter stopped. This time, for good and all. A maze of figures finished it, and underneath, a big circle with a sparrow sitting on it.

I stared at the circle and the sparrow. I suddenly realized that the telephone had been ringing for five minutes. I got up and took off the receiver. I went to the window and looked out. It was just growing dark. The million arrogant eyes of the sky-scrapers stared at me with that remorseless cruelty which only New York knows.

I went back to the telephone. I called up a shipping agency. Within a week, I was sailing home.

§ 3

Although April was well advanced when I left New York, there was little sign of spring in America. The trees in Central Park were bare as ever, and though the florists in Park Avenue were full of blossoms from the south, the flowers looked pale and frightened, like poor little rich girls who didn't know what it was all about.

But in England, spring was holding high revel. Never had the grass been greener, nor the cliffs whiter, nor the birds more absurdly sweet. Even the station seemed to echo to the sound of thrushes and blackbirds. I remembered that lovely phrase which somebody once coined for Elizabethan England, when the air rang with rhyme and poets strode down every alley. 'A nest of song-birds.' That was how England seemed, that day.

But it was because of the garden that my home-coming was made so exciting. For all the joys that a garden can give you, the chief joy is the excitement which it adds to the wanderer's return. As soon as you land in England you start staring about you to see what is 'out', and as the train bears you to London you keep wiping away the moisture on the window-pane to look at the little suburban gardens which flash by, for they will give you advance tidings of what awaits you at home.

There are, of course, more important things which you ought to be doing. You ought to be making your head ache over the evening newspapers and congratulating your-self that you are at last 'up-to-date', instead of being several hours behind. You ought to be absorbing the latest details of a trunk-murder case—for after all, it is terrible not to know that the police have discovered a blood-stained handkerchief in Manchester to which 'they attach the ut-most importance'. *You* ought to attach the utmost import-ance to it, too, but somehow, you don't. Why? Because you are not a good citizen? No. Because you happen to be a good gardener. And as such you realize that all this 'news' is just silliness, just tap-room gossip for tired minds, just a sort of mental *apéritif* for people who have no flowers, to tend, poor devils. For people who are shut in four walls, with no escape, whose only blossoms are the faded blossoms on the wall-papers, which never change, but grow more pallid and more monstrous and more mocking with the passing of the years.

It must be sad to come home, if you have no garden waiting for you. For then, you have no alternative but to read the silly news-sheets instead of spending your time in the best of all ways, in looking out of the window. But we, who are gardeners together, need not occupy ourselves so drearily.

Look! Over there, a bright splash of pink against a line of washing, is a double pink cherry. That means that the little avenue you planted two years ago, will now be a blaze of colour. And the daffodils are not over yet—it must have

THE GIFT OF A GARDEN

been a very late year. That means that if you rush up to the country at once you will catch them in their last beauty, for you live much farther north and there will be a good week of daffodils ahead of you.

And of course, you *do* rush up to the country at once. You have to exercise a great deal of self-control to prevent yourself from running down the path. The dialogue that takes place with the gardener is staccato and artificial. You can't pay attention to what he is saying. There are too many things to be seen.

'Were the crocuses good?'

'Fine, sir. We had lots of people stopping and looking over the hedge. But the mice are still bad. A regular torment, the mice are.'

'What about the new trees?'

'They look pretty well, sir.'

'Had much rain?'

'Not enough.'

'Has the wind been bad? I say . . . this tree wants staking. And we must keep this grass down. And . . . my word, that cherry avenue's a success!'

'Thought you'd like it, sir.'

You drift away by yourself. You don't want anybody near you, not for this first hour. You want to gloat, or growl (as the case may be), in private. You don't even want a pencil and paper, not at first, to make notes on. Time enough for that tomorrow. You just want your little hour.

But it was only an hour that I could afford, on that homecoming. For Miss Hazlitt was calling me. And even though I hurried through the garden, and brushed down the little avenues of the wood, I felt guilty, as though I might arrive too late.

*Chapter 26*

## THE LAST MIRACLE

She was in the garden, under the apple tree. And as soon as I saw her my heart sank. For it seemed that it was a ghost that was lying there, in the wheel chair, a ghost that might drift away into the branches above.

And it was with a ghost's voice that she welcomed me, and excused herself for not getting up, for she was 'a little weak'. But she said that she was very contented, and that the little village girl who was looking after the shop, and helping her, was being so kind and efficient.

'And the garden!' For a moment the old ring of delight came back to her voice, that strange, singing quality which was the happiest sound I have ever heard in a human voice.

'Have you ever *seen* so many flowers?' she went on. 'Look! *They are all doing their best for me, in case I may never see them again.*'

'Please . . . please don't say that.'

She put her hand on my arm. It was as light as one of the leaves that fluttered overhead. 'But there is nothing to be sad about!' Her face was radiant. 'Where I am going, there will be flowers too . . . far lovelier than these.'


§ 2


It was then that the miracle happened.

325

The breeze freshened. And the flowers and the branches
swayed in it, dancing, pirouetting, twisting and turning so
eagerly, as though they were trying to show her that they
were brighter than any of those ghostly flowers which were
waiting for her, in the dim fields of the spirit. Yes, it was
as though there were a wild whispering from branch to
swaying branch, through the green channels where the
sap runs, and the gold is minted for the blossoms. 'More
speed . . . more speed!' they seemed to sigh, in the restless
wind, and with each breath of the wind one had a strange
sense that the hidden gold was drifting down, down to the
green blossom, till soon it would hang heavy on the
branches, and all the trees would rejoice in its riches and its
glory.

And among the irises, too, there was a stirring, as though
the butterfly flowers that slept there were restless to spread
their purple wings. 'Somebody is waiting for us . . .
somebody is waiting!' And the winged petals, so delicately
folded, throbbed in the sunlight that filtered through their
green casings, and the purples deepened, and their myriad
eyes of tawny gold were opened wider, wider.

I looked at Miss Hazlitt. She was lying back with half-
closed eyes. I wondered what she was seeing. The white
snows of the cherry blossom in her garden? Or the deeper,
purer snows of the trees of Paradise, whose branches are
the clouds and whose roots are laid in the stainless fields of
the sky?

'I am very happy,' she whispered. 'I am very thankful.'

Even as she said it, her face contorted with a spasm of
pain. The thin hand gripped my arm with a feverish force
which I should not have thought possible. I knew something of the agony she was enduring, for the doctor had
told me, before I had gone out to see her, that it was

almost incredible that she should be able to endure these attacks without morphia.

'I can't understand it,' he had said. 'Any other woman would be screaming half the time.' Then he had looked at me with a certain amount of suspicion in his honest eyes. 'Do you think she has any drugs of her own . . . that she takes without my knowledge?'

'Yes,' I said, 'she has.' I was very tired, and I felt the doctor was rather stupid.

'Ah!' He rubbed his hands together. 'I thought so. Her condition, altogether . . . her pulse too . . . but most of all, her extraordinary calm . . . now, d'you know what drug it is?'

'Yes. It's very simple, really.'

'Well?'

'She believes in God.'

I was sorry when I had said it. I had not meant to be rude to the doctor. He was an honest man, doing his best. But a little knowledge of the power of mind over matter would not have hurt him.

It was a pity he could not have seen Miss Hazlitt at that moment. For he would have realized that no human drug could possibly have fought for her as her faith was fighting, no earthly anodyne could possibly have brought relief so quickly, nor smoothed the furrows from her features, nor enabled her to say once more, in a voice that did not tremble: 'I am so thankful.'

The wind freshened again. It blew, sweet and cool, on to her forehead, which was damp with the agony through which she had passed.

She smiled. She said:

'Yes . . . the flowers are doing their best to hurry.'

She lifted herself in her chair. She stretched her arm out.

A
Bedroom

'*And look—they are staying up for me . . . too!*'

Staying up?

Then I understood what she meant.

## § 3

And now I felt that a cloak of magic was drawn over the little garden, that she and I were sitting in enchanted chairs, under trees laden with silver from the land of Faery. That was my Pagan reaction to her Christian conviction.

Somewhere, I felt, a wand was being waved . . . a wand that could wantonly dominate the forces of nature, swelling the pear blossom at its will, checking the daffodils, hastening the sap here, staying its departure there.

For as I looked out, through the dying light, I saw many things that made me rub my eyes . . . there was a lingering among the flowers, a tardiness, as though they were loath to leave. 'If she must go, then we would be here, to say good-bye.' It was a bitter thought, and I put it from me. Yet, it was strange how the winter honeysuckle still breathed its sweetness, over there, by the water-butt. In ordinary years, it had long ago dropped its last flower, and given itself up to greenery. And here we were, and it was nearly May.

Nearly May! Yet the winter jasmine was still spangled with flowers. They shone there, in the twilight, like late lamps burning in a secret wood. The daffodils still danced as though they could never weary, forgetting that for a whole month they had turned the fields to a dancing floor, and swirled and laughed and tossed their heads in the wind's music. As for the primroses, they bubbled on and on, yes,

329

they bubbled and they foamed over the banks, and sparkled, cold and sweet . . . they poured in endless profusion over the ditches, jostling the periwinkles, joining hands round the jonquils, and bearing their brave and delicate torches into the deepest darkness of the shrubbery.

'Nonsense!'

'Tiresome sentimentality!'

I *know* that all this is nonsense, and that it may be tiresome sentimentality. But I also know that it is true.

For there are some miracles in which a man must believe, or perish. And one of those miracles is the kinship between mankind and the green things of the earth.

There is a lovely phrase, which country people use, about a man having 'green fingers'. If you have green fingers, the flowers know it, and they let you do with them as you will, and they gain something of your spirit, and flourish, and you gain something of theirs too, and are at peace. I believe that I have green fingers myself . . . in spite of all my failures and stupidities. I believe, when I touch a plant or a tree, that there occurs some contact more subtle and intimate than the mere laying of human hands on vegetable substance, I believe that my blood and the blood of the tree are mingled . . . green to red, and red to green, as the blood of a man who has died is mingled with the earth.

Dust to dust, ashes to ashes.

That is the litany of death, the dirge that blows always through the damp church ailes.

Green to red, red to green.

That is the litany of life, the chant that blows through the forest, when a man is on his feet, under the sunlight, with the wind in his eyes.

And so, I swear, there was this queer magic brooding

about Miss Hazlitt's garden in those late April days when life seemed to be deserting her. For the flowers loved her, and were trying to help her. I make no more apologies. I just leave it at that.

For flowers know if you love them.

§ 4

The flowers *were* doing their best for Miss Hazlitt. She never saw them again.

That night she took a turn for the worse I don't like to think of the agony she must have suffered, for, towards the end, she herself asked for morphia—she who had always refused it. The doctor told me, afterwards, that she whis-pered that she would have 'just a little, because otherwise I might cry, and I would not like to . . .' She could not finish the sentence for some little time, then at last, she beckoned to him. The drug was just beginning to work. 'I did not finish my sentence,' she said. 'I meant to say, "I would not like to go home, crying".'

Those were the last words she ever spoke.

She died at dawn. For most of the night her good friends at Allways had waited. One by one I persuaded them to go away. There was nothing they could do.

It was just growing light when the doctor came down and told me. As soon as I heard his slow step on the stairs I knew that it was all over. I told him I would go up later. He nodded.

I went out into the garden.

The cool air was shrill with the first clamour of birds. Shrill . . . shrill . . . they stabbed my aching head. God, why can't you tell those damned birds to stop? Why must they go on, with this mockery of song, when she lies dead in that little room?

Shriller, shriller. Would those birds never stop? I lifted my head to the skies. They were cold and curdled. They were like a blank stage over which the bird chorus was calling . . . a deserted, rehearsal stage, with only a few cold clouds, like properties which had been left overnight.

'This is ghastly,' I thought. 'It's unworthy of *her*, to go on like this. What would she want me to do? Pray for her, I suppose. But I can't. Not yet. Later on, perhaps, but not now.'

I looked round the garden. What could I do? What would she like me to do? And then, suddenly, I knew.

I have gathered many bunches of flowers, spent many happy hours of life, searching for brighter yellows and more brilliant blues. But no bunch which I have ever gathered in the past or shall ever gather in the days to come, can be as sweet or as fragrant as that which, an hour later, I laid by her side.

*Chapter 27*

## LIGHTS OUT

And so the lights fade over Allways. And from the pages of this book. If any glow has illuminated them, we must blow it out, and sit back, and watch the ashes of these dreams, as they turn from red to grey, from grey to black.

And so, one day, I suppose, the lights will fade, in bitter reality, from Allways. It will go downhill; it has no purpose in life; it is just a little piece of England where a few people lived, and were happy. There is no reason for such places, nowadays. If there were a golf-course . . . but the fields are not fitted for that. If there were a river . . . but there is only one tiny stream, which is extremely temperamental. If there were coal . . . but there is only homely clay. If there were iron . . . but there is none. The only iron is in the hoofs of the horses, as they plod, plod through the dust of summer and the puddles of winter.

No, I fear that Allways, and the scattered villages which resemble it, will go down. Maybe it will live for fifty years more, maybe a century. What does it matter? The new world is killing it, slowly but surely.

Take one little example, the village shop. It is still there, though Miss Hazlitt has gone.

But people have no use, nowadays, for a little village shop, with a tinkling bell, and it irritates them to find that the single lattice window is so thickly overgrown with yellow roses that they have to look twice at the shelves, which

333

THE GIFT OF A GARDEN

are bathed in a green gloom, splashed with gold, so that all
the bars of soap, the bottles of sweets, and tins of polish seem
as if they were sprouting . . . as if they were magic pro-
ducts from a little shop in the woods. They do not like to
have to peer about like this. They like great stores, blazing
with electricity, and filled with a million things which they
do not really want.

You and I know, of course, that if these people were
sensible they would realize that they could get all that they
could ever need in the village shop, in a quarter of the time
and at half the expense. Instead of fighting their way to an
elevator they would only have to put out their hand from
one shelf to another. Instead of walking down miles of corridors, they would only have to peer down to look under
the counter. And instead of being called 'Moddom', by a
girl who does not care whether they fall dead before her,
they would be called by their own names, and they would
hear all the local gossip.

If something new arrives at our shop it is a real event. Not
an event like a new cold cream in a London emporium,
where they arrange ten thousand pots of the cream in a
miniature reproduction of the Taj Mahal, and play a
coloured fountain in the middle, and get quantities of bulg-
ing actresses, powdered like clowns, to sell it. Nothing
quite so ineffably dreary as that. No . . . if a new cold
cream arrives at the village shop, the total instalment is
probably four pots, which are proudly arranged on the
counter, with a little card written in ink, telling the village
maidens what marvellous things it will do to them. For
some days these four pots are regarded with wonder by all
of us. And then, one morning, there are only three, and
before lunch we all know that Mrs M. has purchased a pot.
And for weeks ahead we have the excitement of looking at

Mrs M.'s face, politely but earnestly, to see if the cream is really going to work.

This seems to me, I confess, more fun than anything which the great stores can provide. Most people will not agree with me. They cannot believe that a thing can be good unless they see ten thousand of it, in a blare of coloured lights. That is one of the many reasons why Allways is doomed.

§ 2

I will not trace the probable course of the decease of All-ways. It would hurt too much. The shop, I suppose, will be the first to go. Then the post office. The new generation will not have the patience, when they want to telephone, to walk into a charming kitchen, and if the post-mistress (who has the exquisite gentility of a long line of country ladies), should inquire after their health, they would regard her as a bore. They do not like the purchase of stamps to be a little social event . . . (the stamps are handed to you with a smile, and a kind word, as though they were some secret passport to happiness . . .) no, they will want to buy their stamps from a machine. They will want to do everything by machinery. For all I know, they will want to make love by machinery.

I don't like to think of it. Better to be vague about it. To admit it with a shrug of the shoulders. Just to say—'Time will pass'.

Time will pass. And the great trees that shadow the village green will grow weary, and fall, and the saplings will take their place, and spread their arms wider and wider, exalting in the sun that blesses them, and the rain that purifies them. And they too will grow weary, and droop at last, and die.

And there will be alien trees at Allways.

§ 3

But one day I shall come back. It would be worth centuries
of torment, of celestial boredom, of ethereal anonymity, to
come back to Allways again, for a little while. To come
back, and see what has happened to it, when one is a ghost.

It will be dark, I suppose. It is always dark for a ghost.
And there will be no calendar to tell me what year it is, only
the calendar of nature, which will be written in the coloured
leaves of the trees, the widening curves of the river, and the
slowly wheeling dial of the night sky, whose every second
is commemorated by a silver star.

And I would pray that I might approach Allways from
the wood where the bluebells grew, the wood whose
November shadows once sparkled with the fire of the wild
spindle, whose April twilights were mysterious with the
moth-winged bloom of the wild white cherry.

That is where my ghost will start, for its last journey. It
will stand there, in the shadows.

And it will be waiting, listening . . . listening for a
companion, for it would not make this journey alone.

There he is!

Again, there in the far distance, a faint bark! Very faint
indeed, as though it came from over the hills of the moon.
But once more, much nearer to the earth—oh, the Fates
have been kind indeed! I try to call out, to whistle, to tell
my dog that I am here. But there is only a faint rustle in the
leaves, however desperately I shout.

Will he find me? A ghost has no scent . . . will he find
me? Oh please . . . please. I start to meet him. And even

as I glide forward, there is a rustle in the bracken, the rabbits flee affrightened from the phantom who pursues them, and there, through the clearing he flies towards me, and we are together again, as we used to be, when the world was very young, and we were its masters.

And so we set out together. For many moons, I expect, the rabbits will whisper, with horror, of the phantom dog who suddenly and silently bore down on them with icy breath, the dog whose bark was like a distant trumpet, whose bite was so fierce and yet could do them no harm.

§ 4

In the livening breeze, and under the eternal stars, my ghost will set off, down the hill, will revive its tenuous veins with the vigour of the wind, and raise its heavy-lidded eyes to the moon. Thus, silently, my limbs will jerk themselves down the hill, while I whisper desperately:

'See! The stars are just coming out! They were mine once, they are mine still!'

On, on, jerk the creaking limbs, in the appalling silence. 'See! I can still feel the wind! Cold, so cold . . . through my bones . . . it was not so cold, once . . . when my bones were covered. No, it was not so cold, it was warm and fragrant and desirable . . . oh! it was utterly desirable on a night in June, when I had blood, and hands that could take branches, and break them, and fingers that could seize flowers, and pick them, and press them to my face. But now I have no blood, no hands, no face. What have I? What am I? Oh God . . . tell me what I have, what I am, that I may know!

§ 5

Allways!

We are in it now. Past the forge. It is still there . . .
though there are some strange buildings which I dare not
look at. Past a big clump of trees by the village green.

But what are these other trees? This immense avenue
stretching before me, cavernous and infinite in the aqueous
light of the moon? These were never here . . . I do not
know them. They are alien to me, this cannot be Allways! My dog and I stand at the entrance to the avenue,
two black dejected shadows, like beggars at the door of a
great mansion, at night.

And then, the clouds drift away from the moon. And
through the Gothic tracery of branches I see, once more the
little hill where the bluebells grew, and the valley that is
shaped like a heart, and the familiar S of the winding
stream. It is still Allways. And these trees, that I planted,
these trees, that were only as high as my shoulder, on the
last year I saw them, are welcoming me home.

Thank you, trees. When I was alive I used to say 'things
*do* grow, if you will only be patient'. But in those days I was
not patient. I never saw the trees I planted. Not with my
living eyes. But I am seeing them now, with the eyes of a
ghost. They were worth waiting for.

We start down the great avenue, my dog and I. But now
our footsteps are slow and halting, and our eyes downcast.
For we are nearing home. And we do not know what sort
of home it will be. We do not know if there will be anyone
there to welcome us. We are afraid.

On and on . . . slower and slower. Here is the bend in
the road. We shall be able to see it, when we turn the corner.

But we are not sure whether we want to turn the corner. We pause in the chequered shadows.

I look down. 'Well,' I whisper. 'What about it? Shall we go back?'

He tries to wag his tail. He is shivering a little.

'It used to be home,' I plead.

He wags his tail, very feebly.

'We have come a long way and it was cold, among the stars . . . there might be a fire, if "they" are kind . . . it would be a treat . . . we should remember it, for many years, for centuries perhaps, even for eternity.'

## § 6

Above us, a wild rushing in the trees, for the wind has risen.

Before us. . . .

A shape.

Just a shape. For what else can I call this ruin of the thing I had loved? It stands there forsaken, deserted . . . its roof has long fallen in, there are thick strands of ivy coming from *inside* the windows.

I step closer. I am shaking with impotent anger. 'How dare they . . . how *dare* they?' And my whole being is wreaked with an agony of longing, to have power once more, and strength, and the authority of this world. To have power, if only for a few hours! That must be the longing of all ghosts who revisit their old homes, who see the havoc that is wreaked by the fools who come after them, who wail disconsolately through ravaged gardens and weep in despair over the woods that their descendants are destroying. For a few hours only, to come back, to issue orders, to set men to work, to enforce obedience, to start the business of salvage, to bring beauty once more into the desert that the others have made, in the wake of one's death.

'How dare they?'

But ghosts have not much strength. When I first cried out, there was a cold breath, and an owl fluttered, startled, from the ruined walls. But now, my force has gone, and the owl is back again, and is perched, in arrogant possession, on the wreck of a window-ledge. The window-ledge of my old bedroom.

I stare at the owl. I do not attempt to cry out any more. I have been hurt too much. And with the perversity of those who are in an extremity of pain, I press closer, to more pain.

And I drift through the doorway.

I have come home.

The moonlight shines through the roof. But the centre beam is still standing. Grand old beam . . . it's still there. But the ivy is choking it, dragging it down. Feebly I lift out my hands, but they are as star-dust, they have no power. They fall to my sides.

I see in front of me a square ruin, thick with weeds and brambles. It is the Garden Room. My head bowed, for I cannot bear much more, I drift through it. There is still a gap where the window was. Here I am. The garden is before me. I dare not look.

I had better go back.

I whistle to my dog. He looks up at me.

I turn. But I do not seem to be able to move.

I *must* move. I dare not look at the garden. It couldn't be borne . . . even a ghost, with ice in its veins, couldn't stand this last humiliation. I must never see the garden again. It has gone, and I must go back through that ruined door, and up the lane, and over the hill and into eternity. Never must I look back.

But I can't move. Something is happening to me. A stirring in the blood . . . almost, a feeling of warmth. As though someone had laid his hands on my shoulders, and were turning me, against my will, were whispering 'Be of good cheer!'

It is happening. Call it what you will . . . call it a reincarnation, a fluke of astral fluid, or an odd psychic phenomenon . . . it does not matter. All I know is that the old magic is working, once again. The old call is being obeyed, the call that was always too strong to resist.

The call of the garden.

'I remember . . . I remember.'

I remember, on bitter nights in January, how I would arrive at the cottage, long after Allways had gone to bed. And in spite of the wild winds and the driving sleet and the animal hunger in me that craved for a warm drink, I would fling wide the french windows, and grip a torch, and make my way to the little patch of snowdrops under the damson tree, and feel amply rewarded if I found one pale blossom staring at me, startled, in the light of the torch, with the frost sparkling like diamonds on it. It never mattered, in the old days, what the hour was, nor the month . . . the darkest hour of the blackest week of the year could not hold me back, could not keep me indoors, when I arrived. Somewhere, on some branch, there would be a bud to be welcomed. Somewhere, in the kindly shelter of a sturdy shrub, there would be the lifted tip of an emerald spear, thrust aloft through the dark earth by an impatient herald of spring.

That is *me*. It is the strongest part of me, that will endure through death and through the cloudy wastes that we call

Afterwards, and will shine through the uttermost mists. That is my strength, that cannot ever be denied, the strength that must break down all doors that bar me from the garden.

And that is what is happening now, in this little scene from the Future, that I am foretelling.

I turn, once again. I go forward. I pause and look up. The garden is before me.

Something happens.

## § 7

And once again, over this little patch of earth which I have so dearly loved, there will be a sighing and stirring, and the scents will drift back over the centuries, for my delight. The white roses will flutter, like ghosts, from the heart of Time, and light upon their aery branches. Once again the lilies will ring their bells and the lavender will spear the night-air with sweetness. Once again I shall walk down the path saying 'you are mine, still mine, always mine'. And Antinous will be there, on the little lawn, smiling in the moonlight.

For the beauty of the garden has not died. It *could* not die. No garden can ever utterly die. Even if it only flowers, a dim memory, in the heart of a ghost.

And so this book ends on a platitude. Better that it should end so, than on an epigram. For a platitude has a glow of truth in it, that burns on through the centuries. An epigram is a firework that sparks for a moment, but is revealed as an empty case in the morning.

Beauty lives. That is the one platitude that I know. It is not guesswork. It is knowledge. And it is knowledge which bears infinite comfort.

Whatever we may find behind the dark curtain, when it falls with our falling lids, when there is silence and the bird-song is stilled, whatever we may find when we step on to the stage where all must play their part . . . we shall find flowers.

LARES
ET PENATES